THE KING'S *Beast* 麗

5

STORY & ART BY

Rei Toma

THE KING'S *Beast*

Characters and Story Thus Far

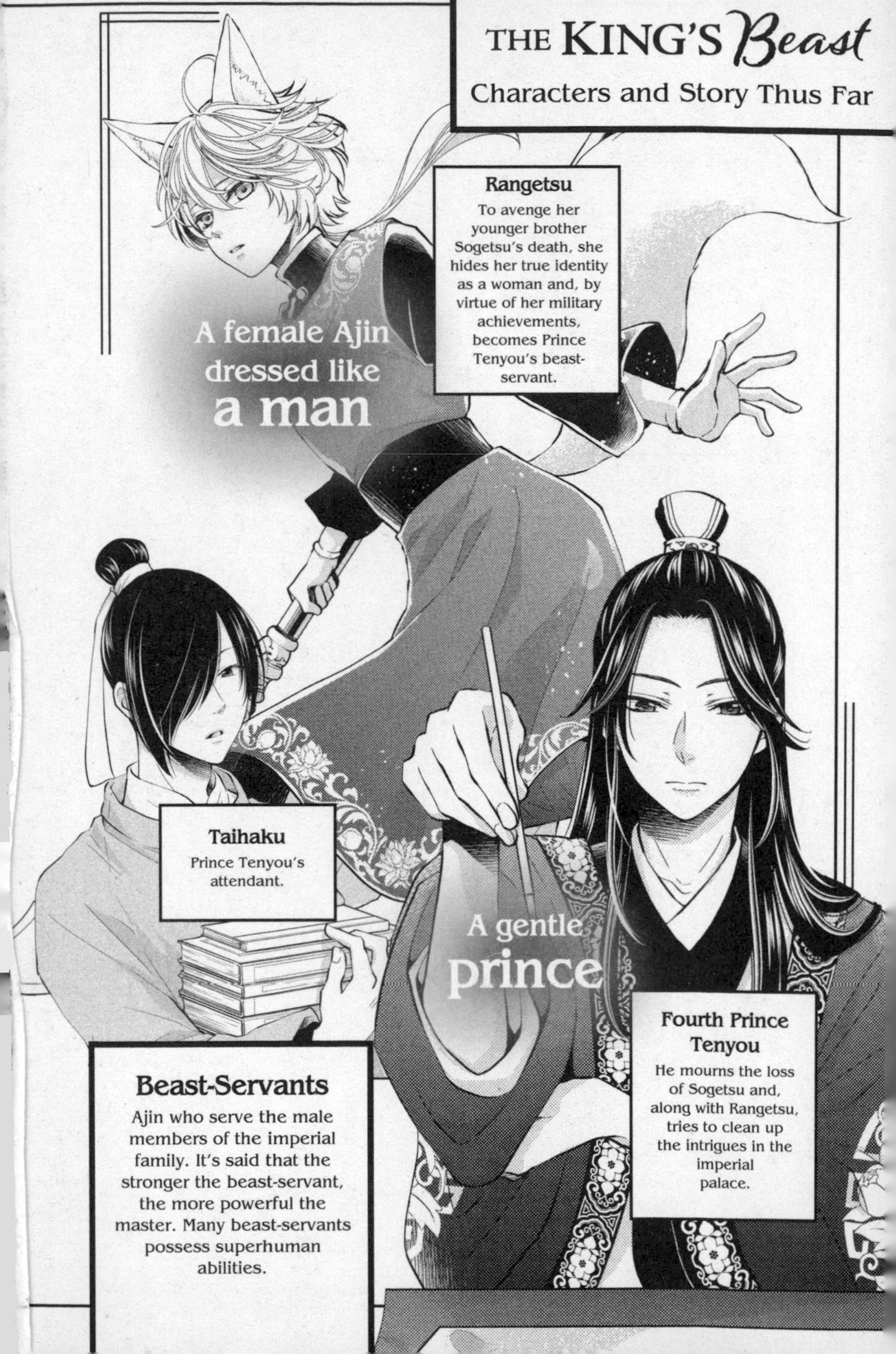
Rangetsu
To avenge her younger brother Sogetsu's death, she hides her true identity as a woman and, by virtue of her military achievements, becomes Prince Tenyou's beast-servant.
A female Ajin dressed like a man
Fourth Prince Tenyou
He mourns the loss of Sogetsu and, along with Rangetsu, tries to clean up the intrigues in the imperial palace.
A gentle prince
Taihaku
Prince Tenyou's attendant.
Beast-Servants
Ajin who serve the male members of the imperial family. It's said that the stronger the beast-servant, the more powerful the master. Many beast-servants possess superhuman abilities.

Prince Tenyou's Brothers and Their Beast-Servants

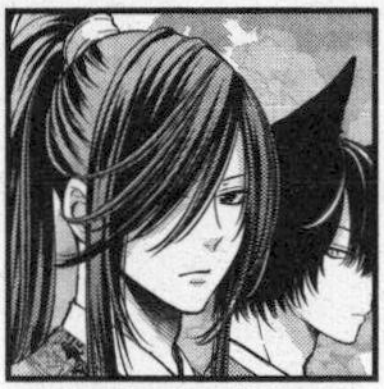

Kougai

The third prince. Two-faced and ambitious.

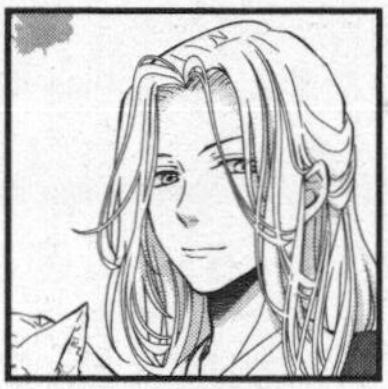

Reiun

The second prince. Intelligent and bored by his own idleness.

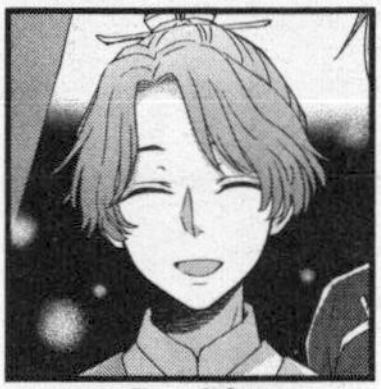

Oushin

The first prince. Sickly and passive.

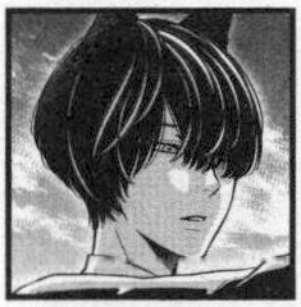

Boku

Prince Kougai's beast-servant.

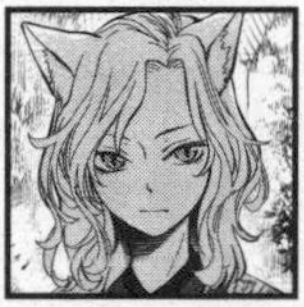

Youbi

Prince Reiun's beast-servant.

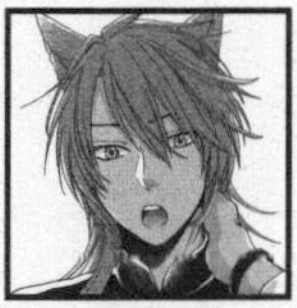

Teiga

Prince Oushin's beast-servant.

The Assassination of Sogetsu

Rangetsu's twin was brought to the imperial palace to serve Prince Tenyou as his beast-servan, but he was brutally killed soon after.

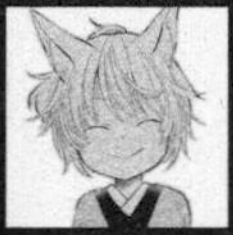

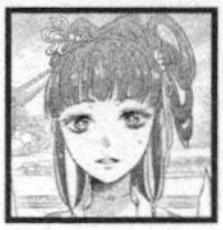

Ririn

An imperial princess.

Summary

In a world where humans rule the half-beast Ajin, Rangetsu disguises herself as a man and proves herself in battle in order to enter the imperial palace and become Fourth Prince Tenyou's beast-servant so she can avenge her brother's murder. She initially regards Prince Tenyou as an enemy but eventually comes to support him in the battle for the throne.

Rangetsu suspects that Prince Kougai is behind several suspicious incidents. But once she has a chance to spend more time with him, she is impressed by his commanding manner and sees his potential as an emperor.

Meanwhile, Prince Kougai wants Prince Tenyou to take their competition more seriously and convinces Rangetsu to be the prize in a bet between the two brothers. When Prince Tenyou wins, Rangetsu is forced to admit that her feelings for her master have grown far beyond mere respect!

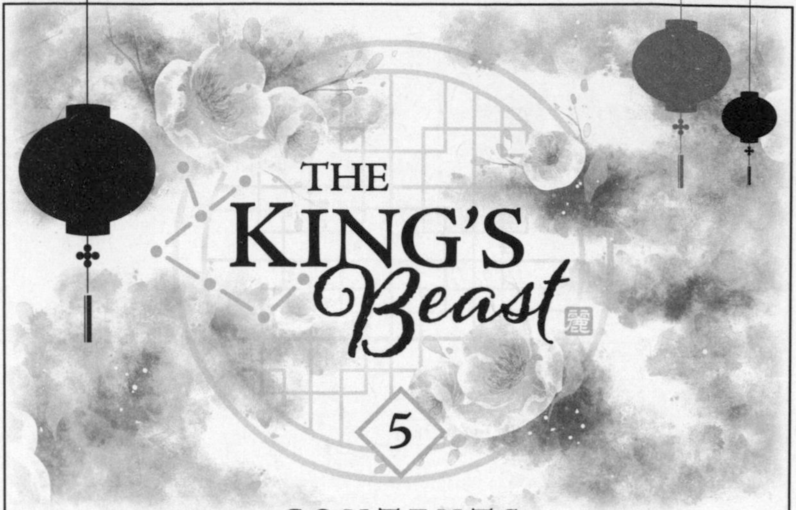
THE KING'S Beast
5

CONTENTS

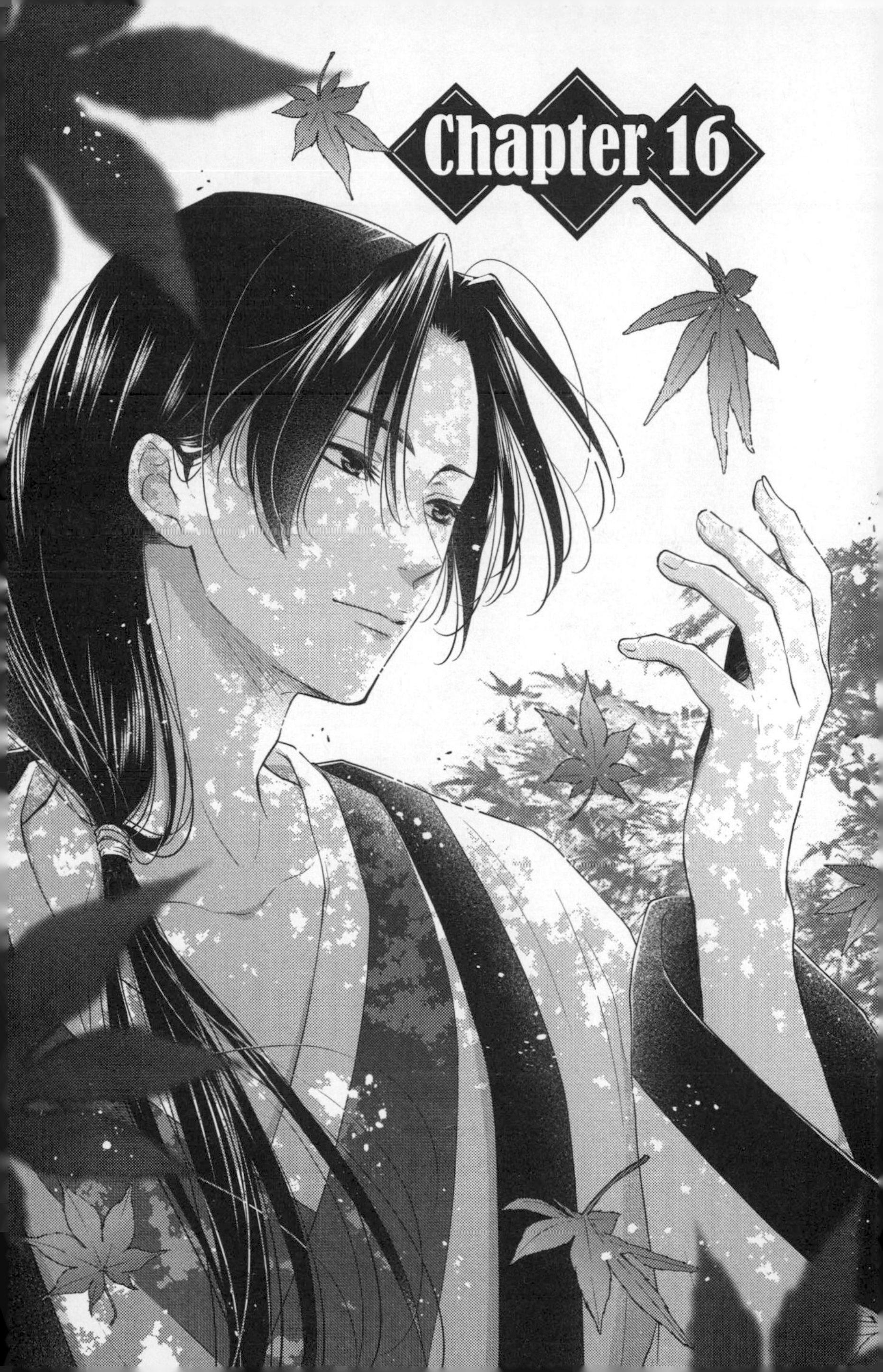
Chapter 16

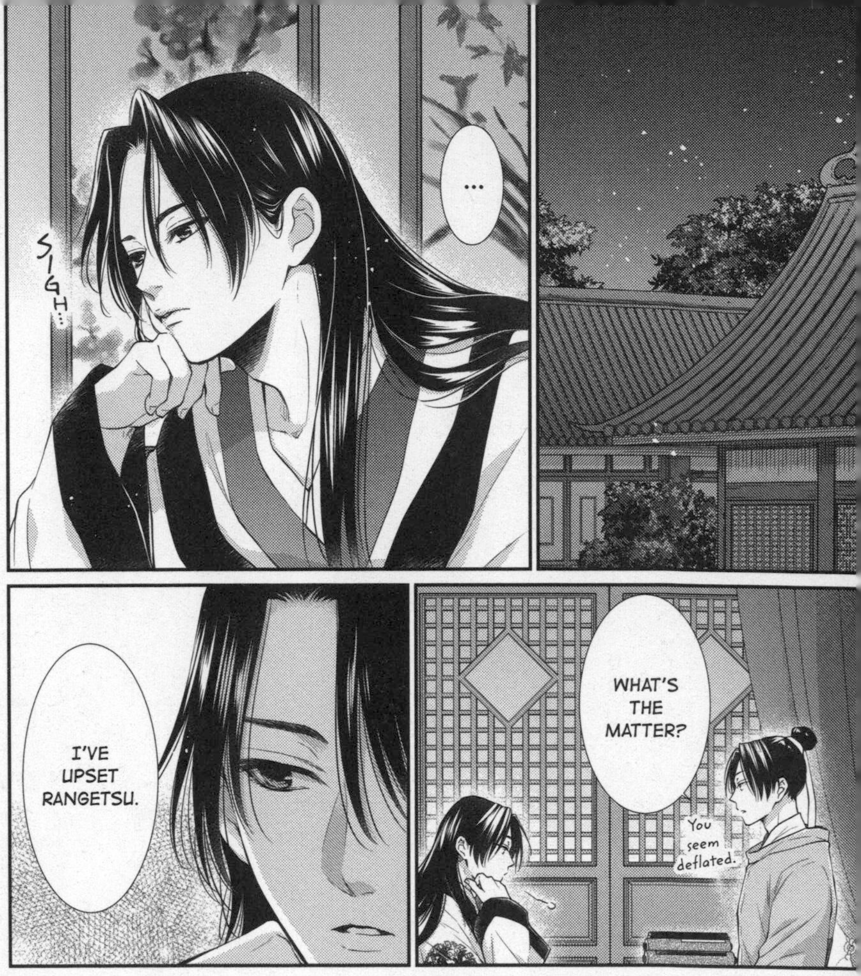
...
SIGH...
WHAT'S THE MATTER?
You seem deflated.
I'VE UPSET RANGETSU.

THE KING'S Beast

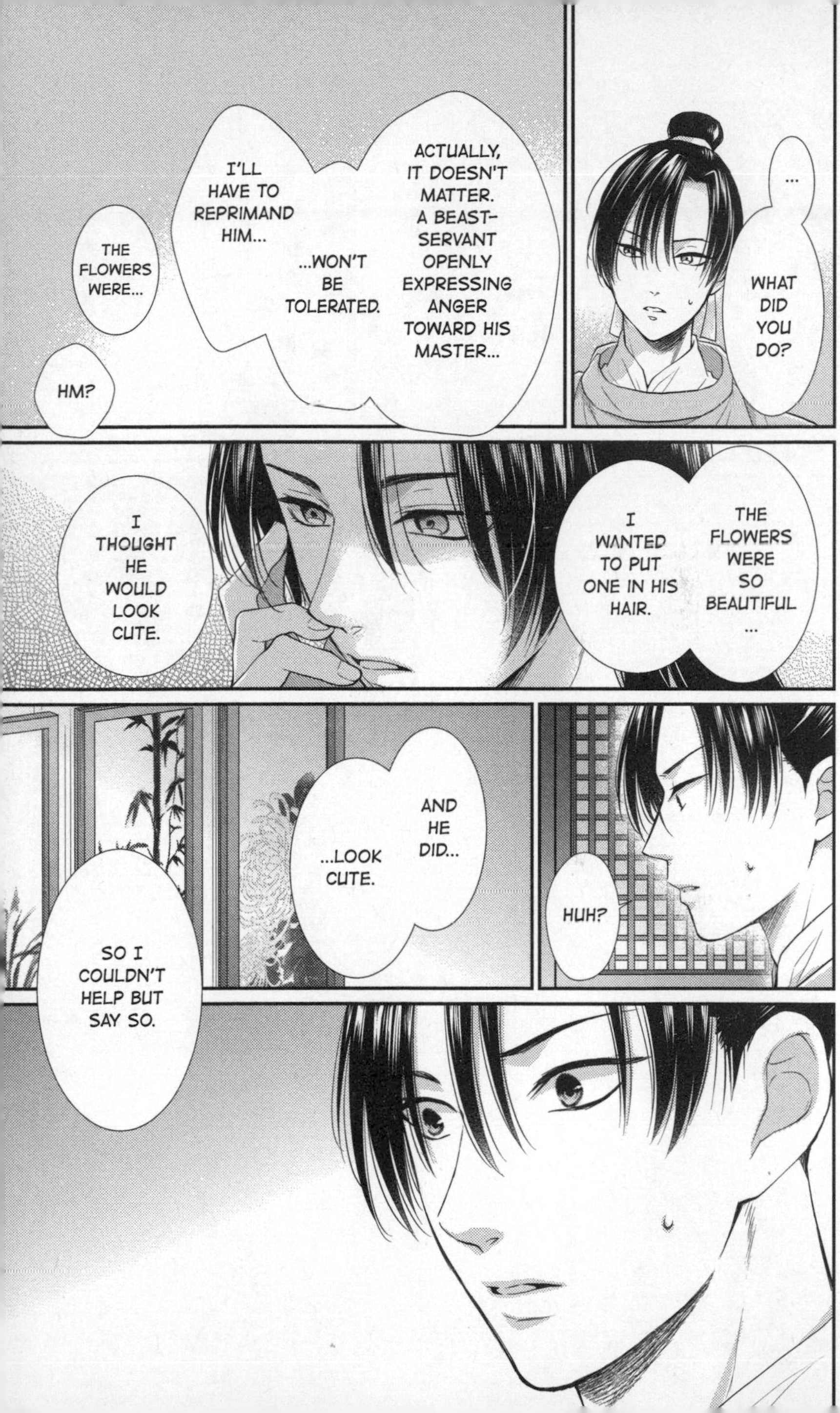
...
WHAT DID YOU DO?
ACTUALLY, IT DOESN'T MATTER. A BEAST-SERVANT OPENLY EXPRESSING ANGER TOWARD HIS MASTER...
...WON'T BE TOLERATED.
I'LL HAVE TO REPRIMAND HIM...
THE FLOWERS WERE...
HM?
THE FLOWERS WERE SO BEAUTIFUL...
I WANTED TO PUT ONE IN HIS HAIR.
I THOUGHT HE WOULD LOOK CUTE.
HUH?
AND HE DID...
...LOOK CUTE.
SO I COULDN'T HELP BUT SAY SO.

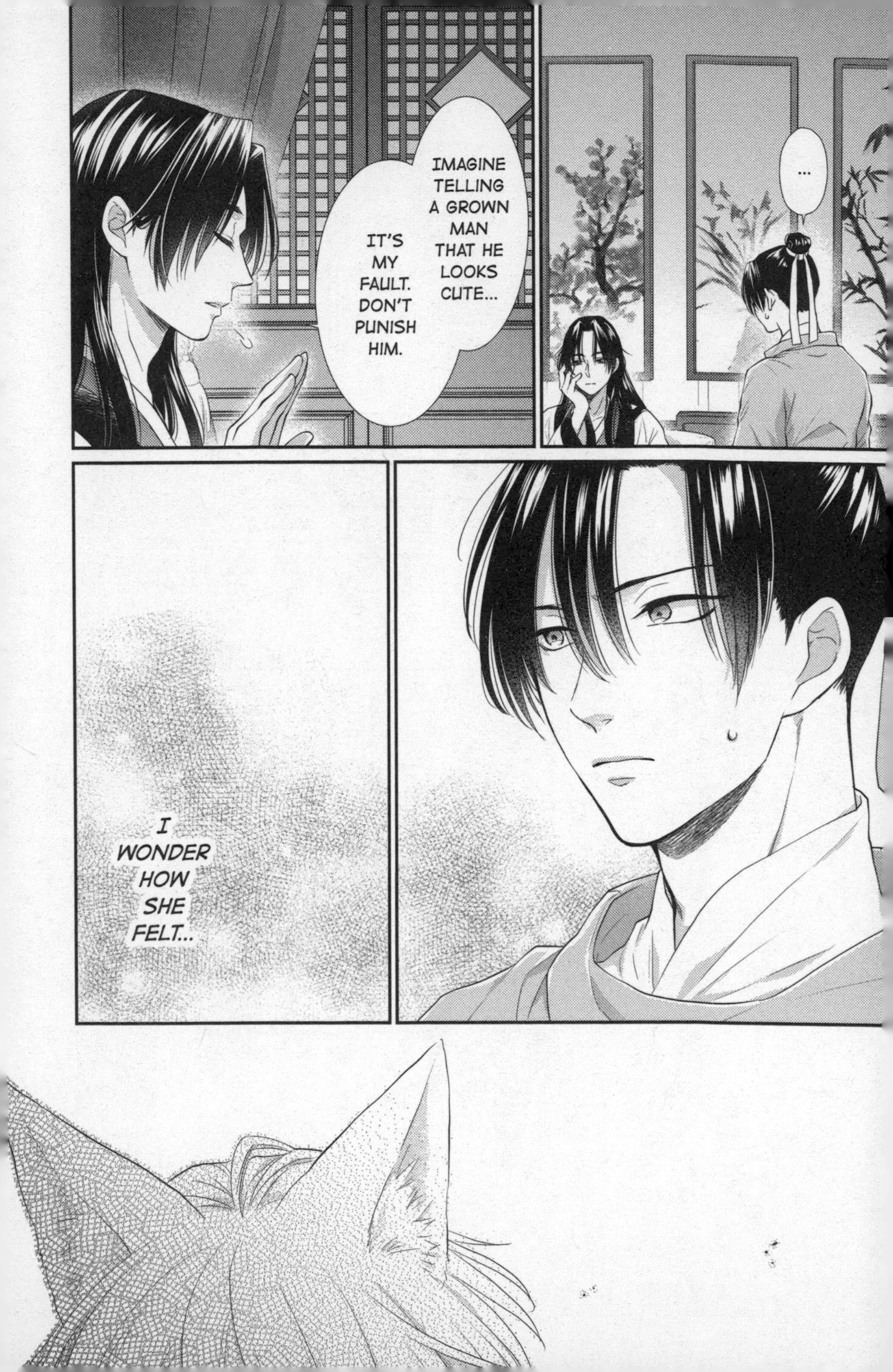
...
IMAGINE TELLING A GROWN MAN THAT HE LOOKS CUTE...
IT'S MY FAULT. DON'T PUNISH HIM.
I WONDER HOW SHE FELT...

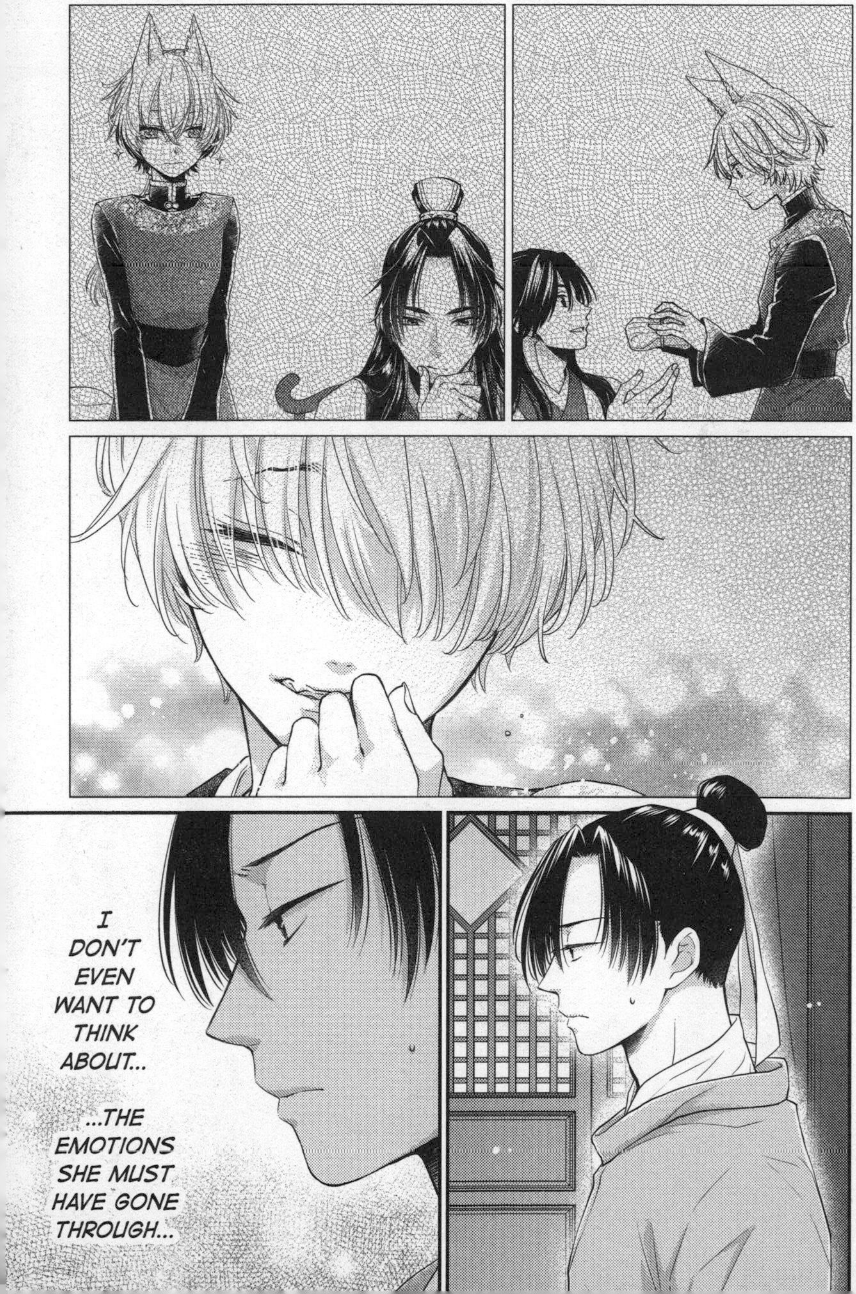
I DON'T EVEN WANT TO THINK ABOUT...
...THE EMOTIONS SHE MUST HAVE GONE THROUGH...

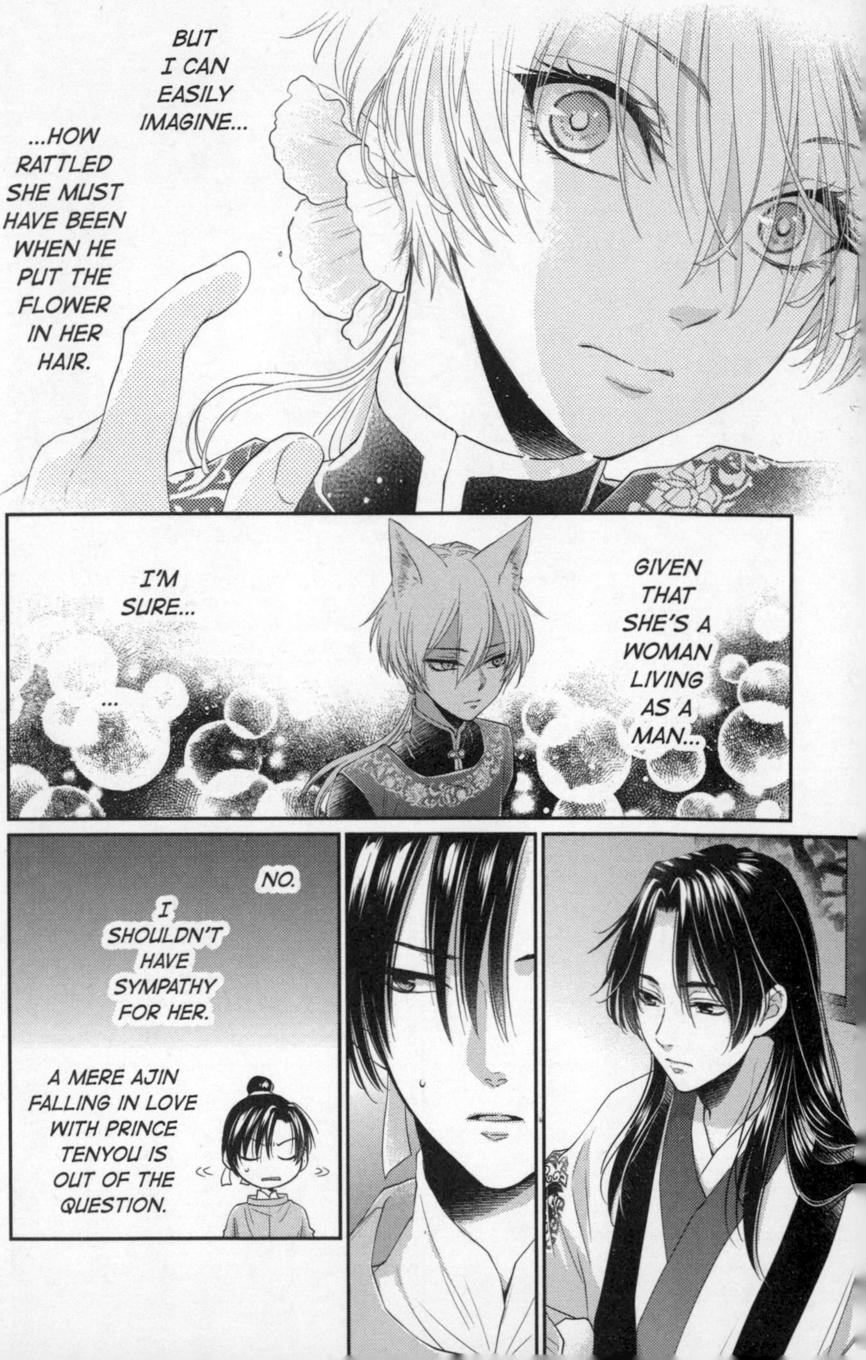
BUT I CAN EASILY IMAGINE...
...HOW RATTLED SHE MUST HAVE BEEN WHEN HE PUT THE FLOWER IN HER HAIR.
GIVEN THAT SHE'S A WOMAN LIVING AS A MAN...
I'M SURE...
...
NO.
I SHOULDN'T HAVE SYMPATHY FOR HER.
A MERE AJIN FALLING IN LOVE WITH PRINCE TENYOU IS OUT OF THE QUESTION.

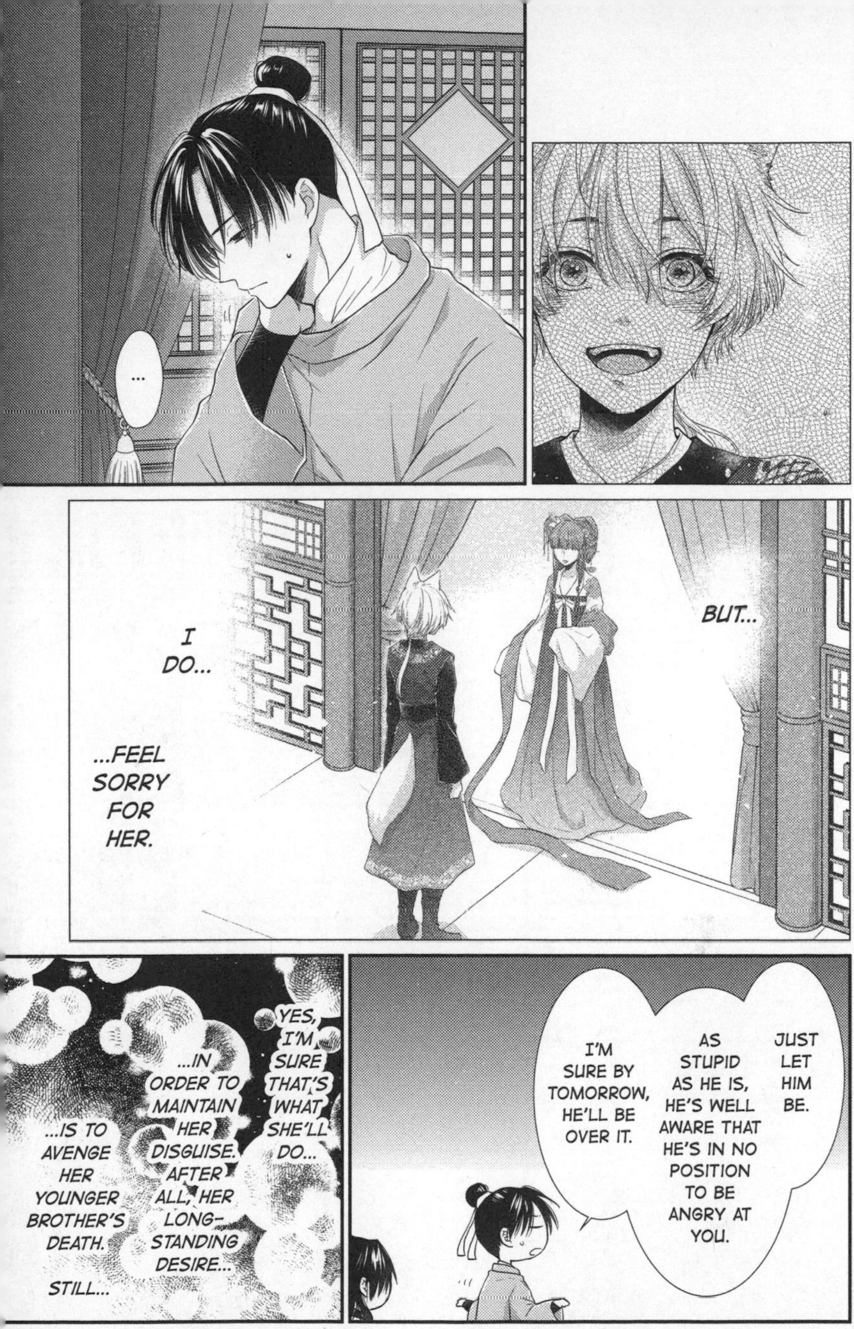
...
BUT...
I DO...
...FEEL SORRY FOR HER.
JUST LET HIM BE.
AS STUPID AS HE IS, HE'S WELL AWARE THAT HE'S IN NO POSITION TO BE ANGRY AT YOU.
I'M SURE BY TOMORROW, HE'LL BE OVER IT.
YES, I'M SURE THAT'S WHAT SHE'LL DO...
...IN ORDER TO MAINTAIN HER DISGUISE. AFTER ALL, HER LONG-STANDING DESIRE...
...IS TO AVENGE HER YOUNGER BROTHER'S DEATH.
STILL...

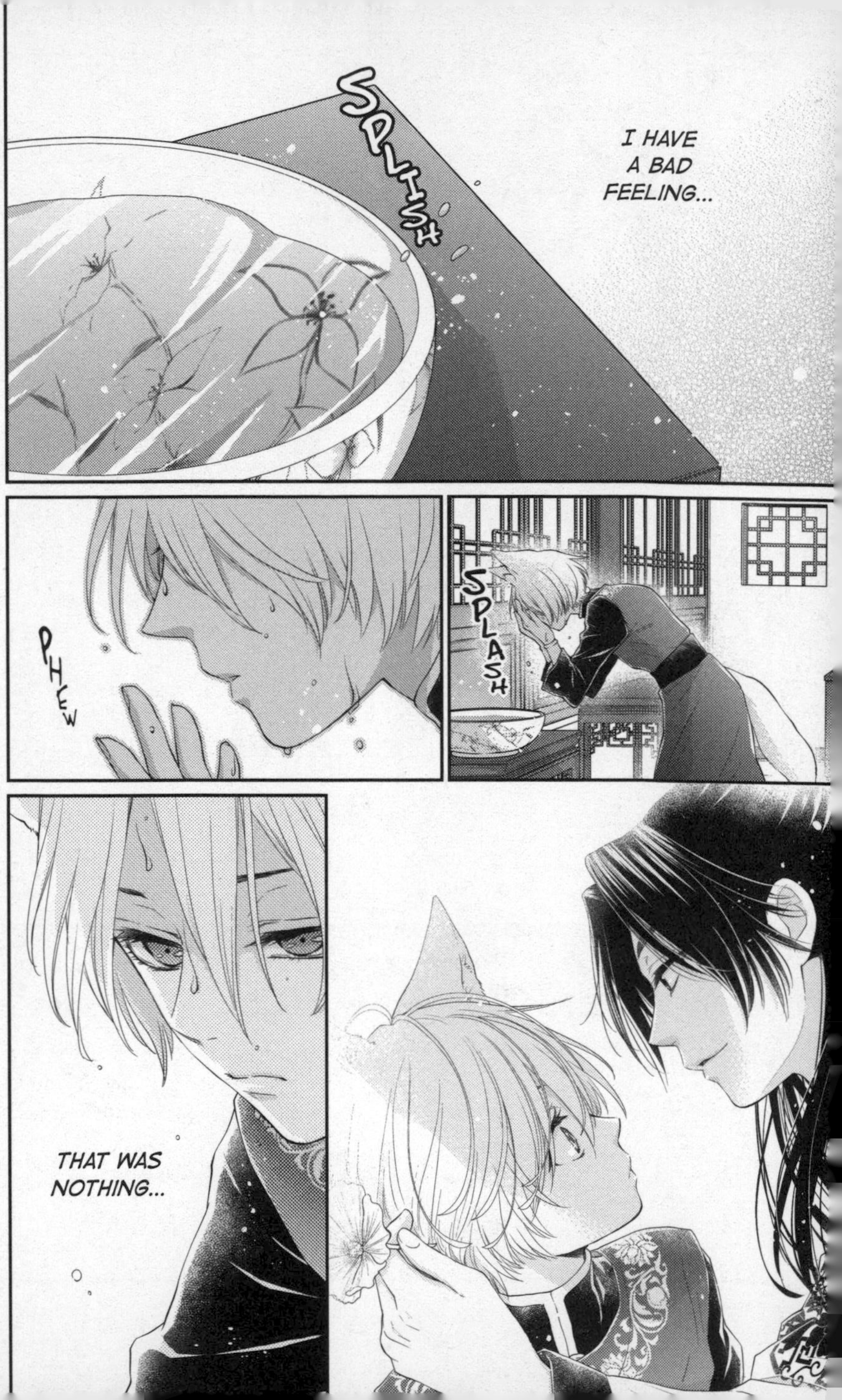
I HAVE A BAD FEELING...
SPLISH
SPLASH
PHEW
THAT WAS NOTHING...

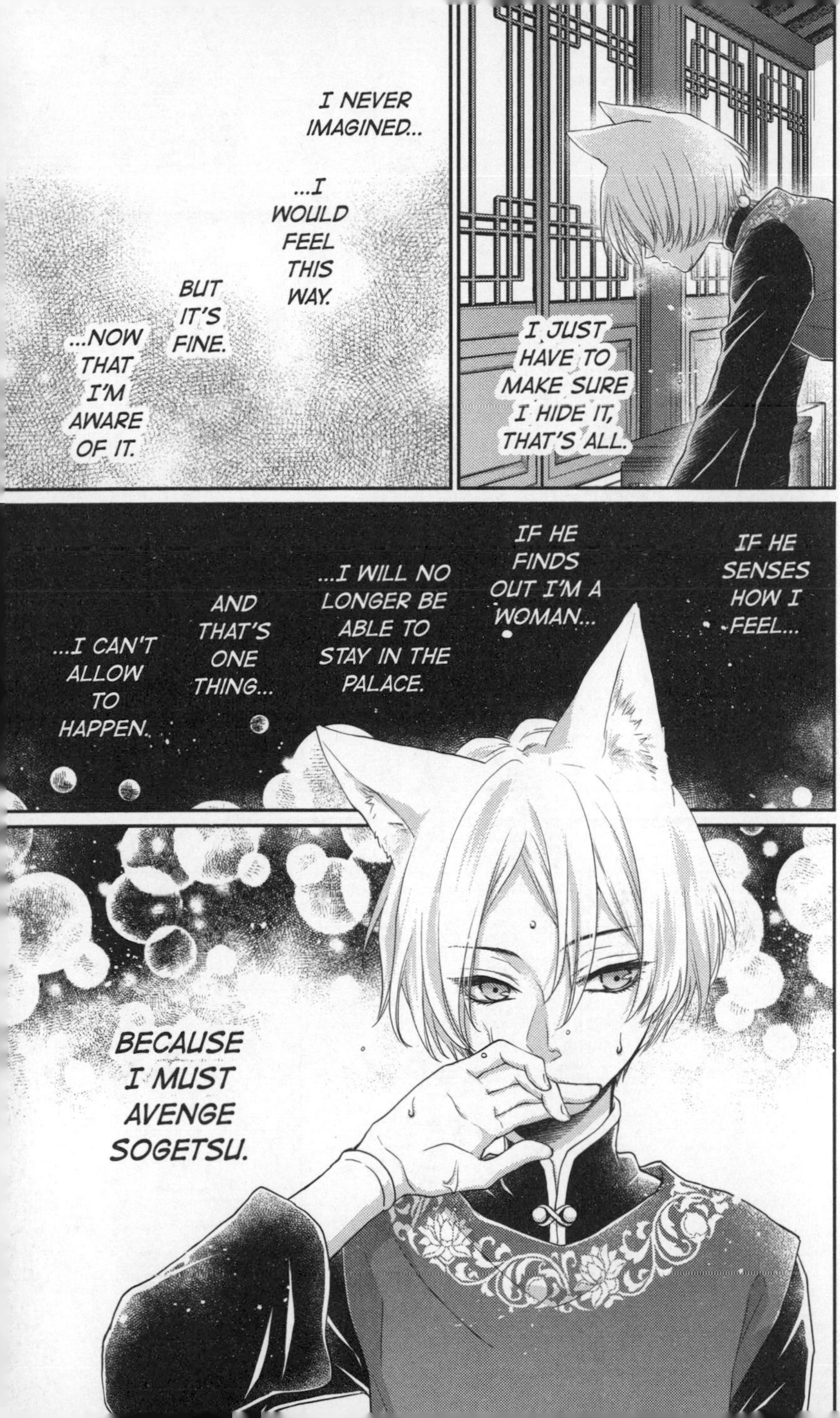
I JUST HAVE TO MAKE SURE I HIDE IT, THAT'S ALL.
I NEVER IMAGINED...
...I WOULD FEEL THIS WAY.
BUT IT'S FINE.
...NOW THAT I'M AWARE OF IT.
IF HE SENSES HOW I FEEL...
IF HE FINDS OUT I'M A WOMAN...
...I WILL NO LONGER BE ABLE TO STAY IN THE PALACE.
AND THAT'S ONE THING...
...I CAN'T ALLOW TO HAPPEN.
BECAUSE I MUST AVENGE SOGETSU.

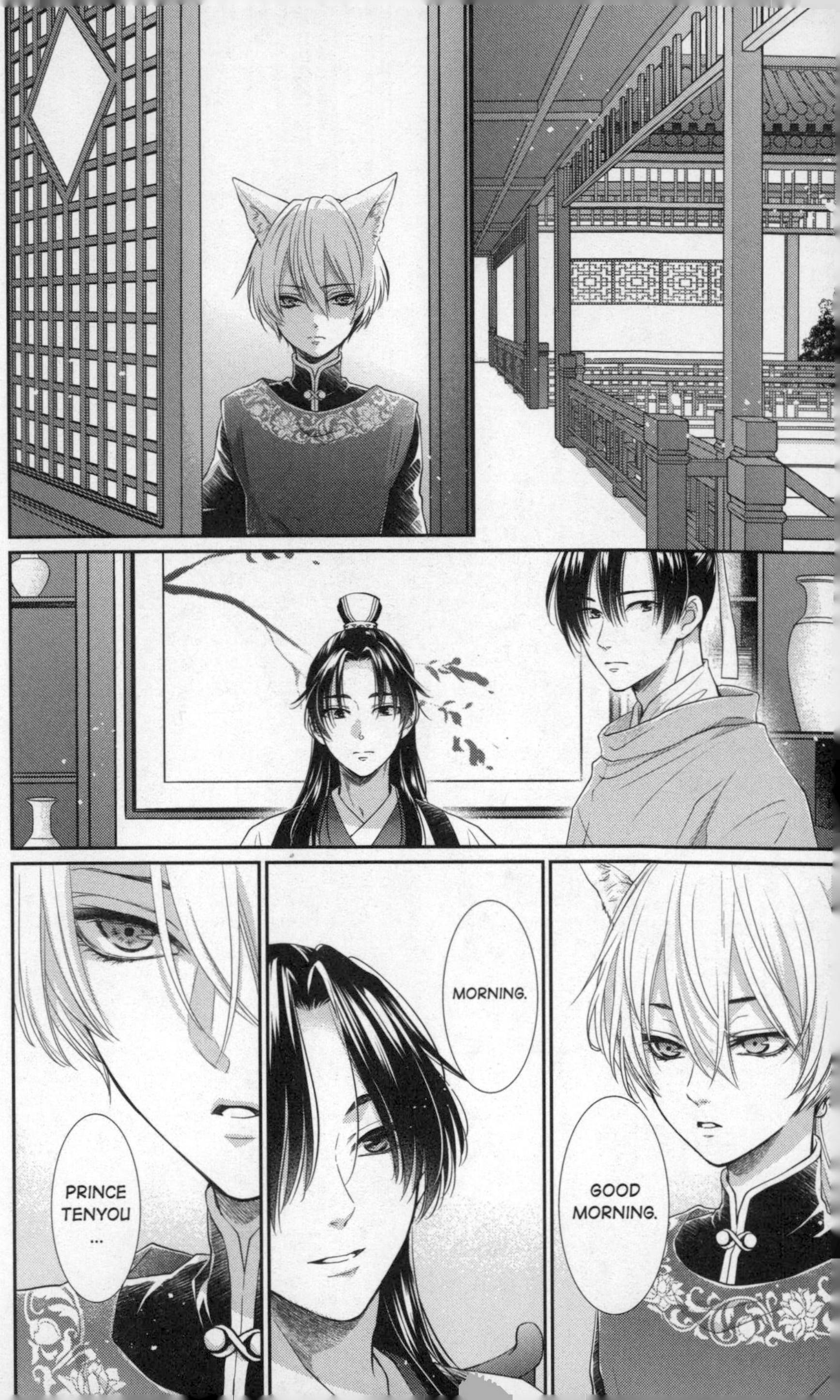
GOOD MORNING.
MORNING.
PRINCE TENYOU ...

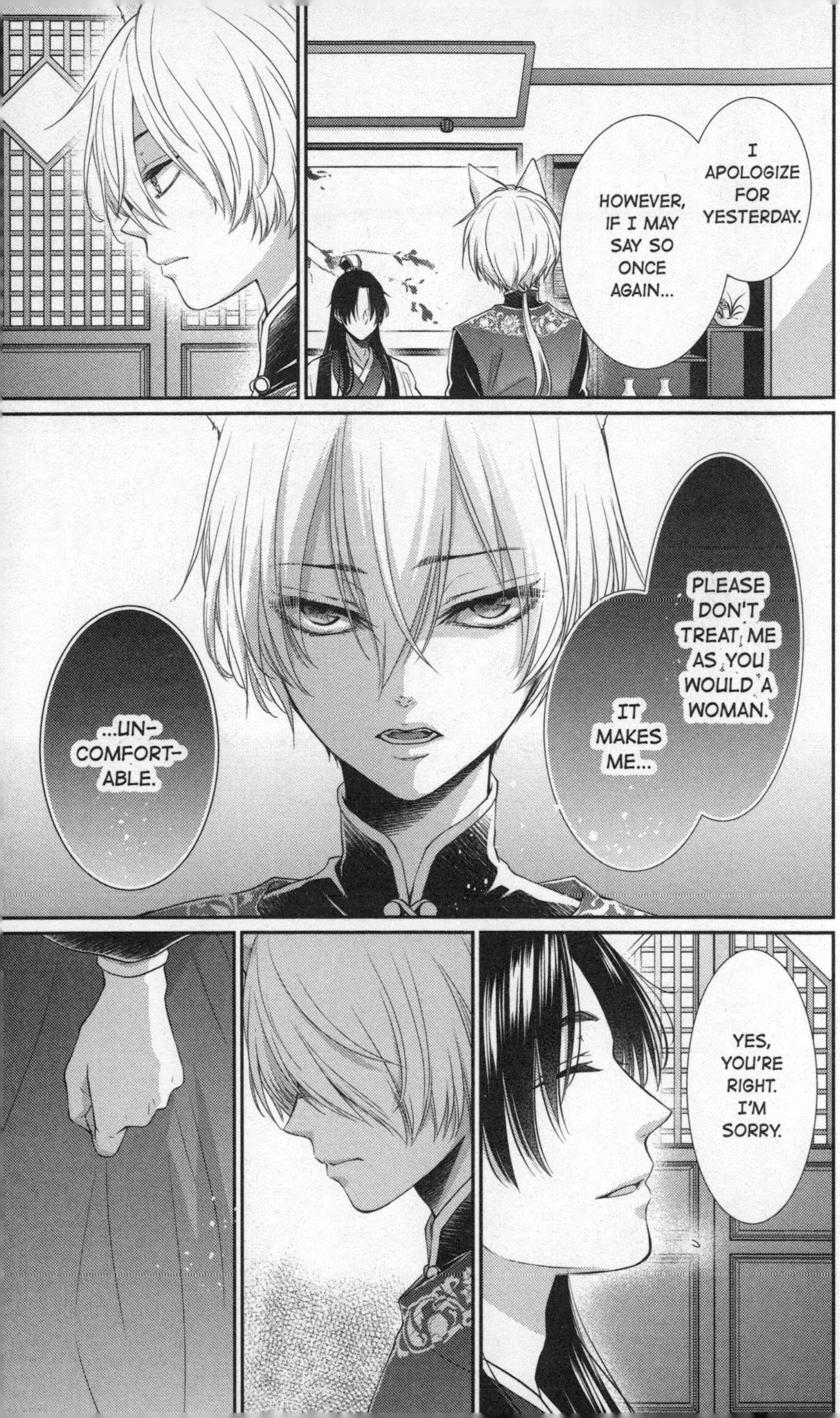
I APOLOGIZE FOR YESTERDAY.
HOWEVER, IF I MAY SAY SO ONCE AGAIN...
PLEASE DON'T TREAT ME AS YOU WOULD A WOMAN.
IT MAKES ME...
...UN-COMFORT-ABLE.
YES, YOU'RE RIGHT. I'M SORRY.

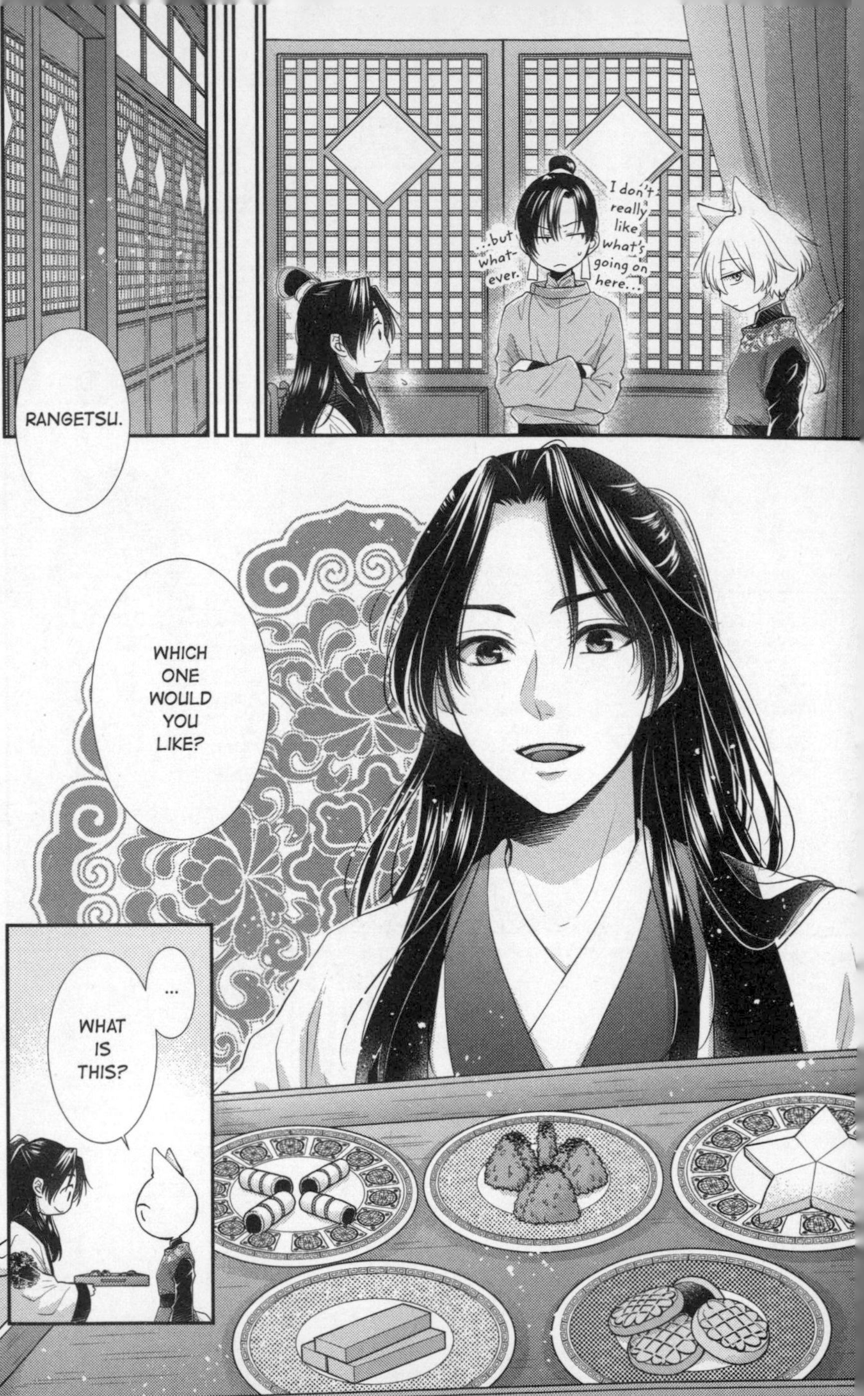

I don't really like what's going on here...
...but whatever.
RANGETSU.
WHICH ONE WOULD YOU LIKE?
... WHAT IS THIS?

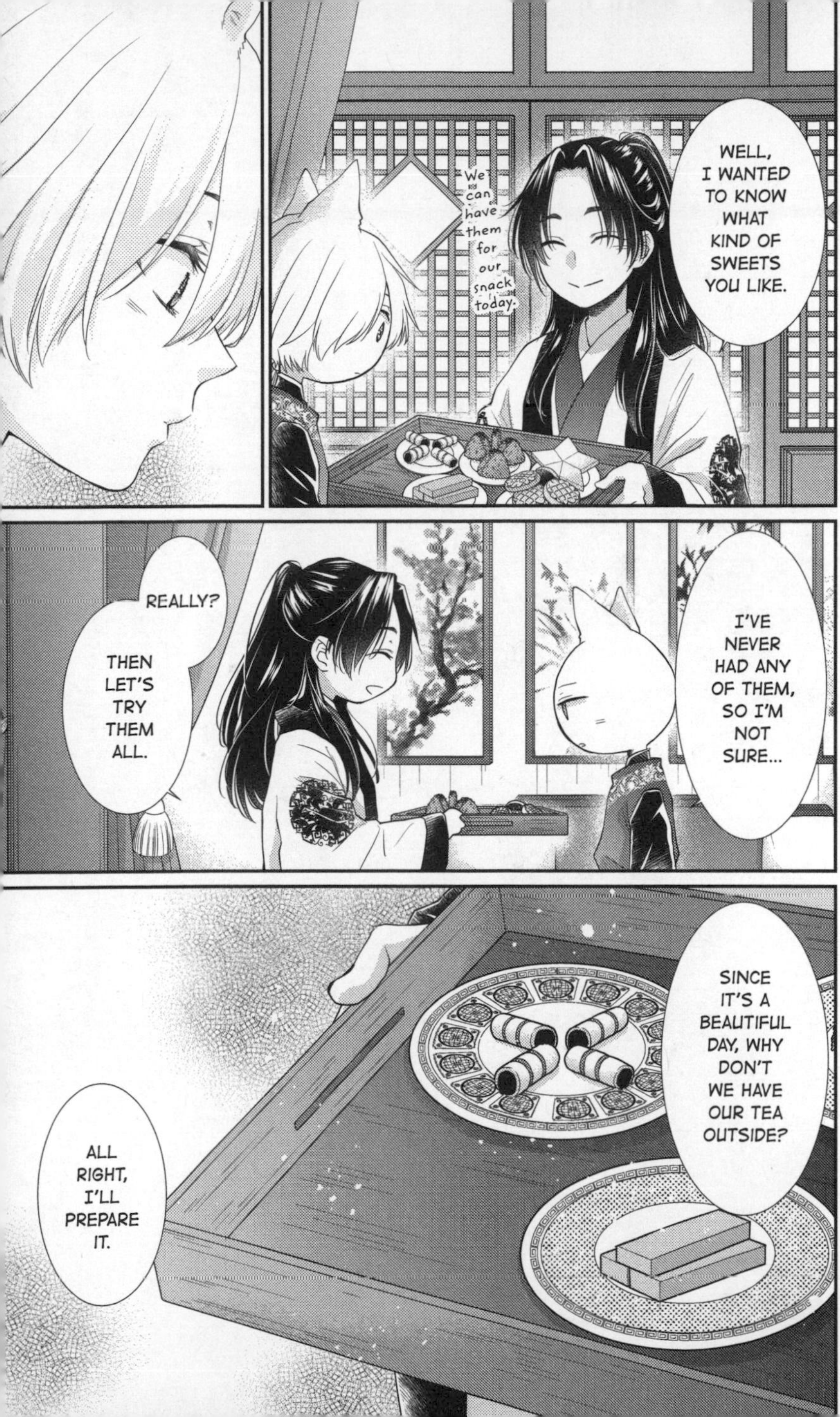
WELL, I WANTED TO KNOW WHAT KIND OF SWEETS YOU LIKE.
We can have them for our snack today.
I'VE NEVER HAD ANY OF THEM, SO I'M NOT SURE...
REALLY?
THEN LET'S TRY THEM ALL.
SINCE IT'S A BEAUTIFUL DAY, WHY DON'T WE HAVE OUR TEA OUTSIDE?
ALL RIGHT, I'LL PREPARE IT.

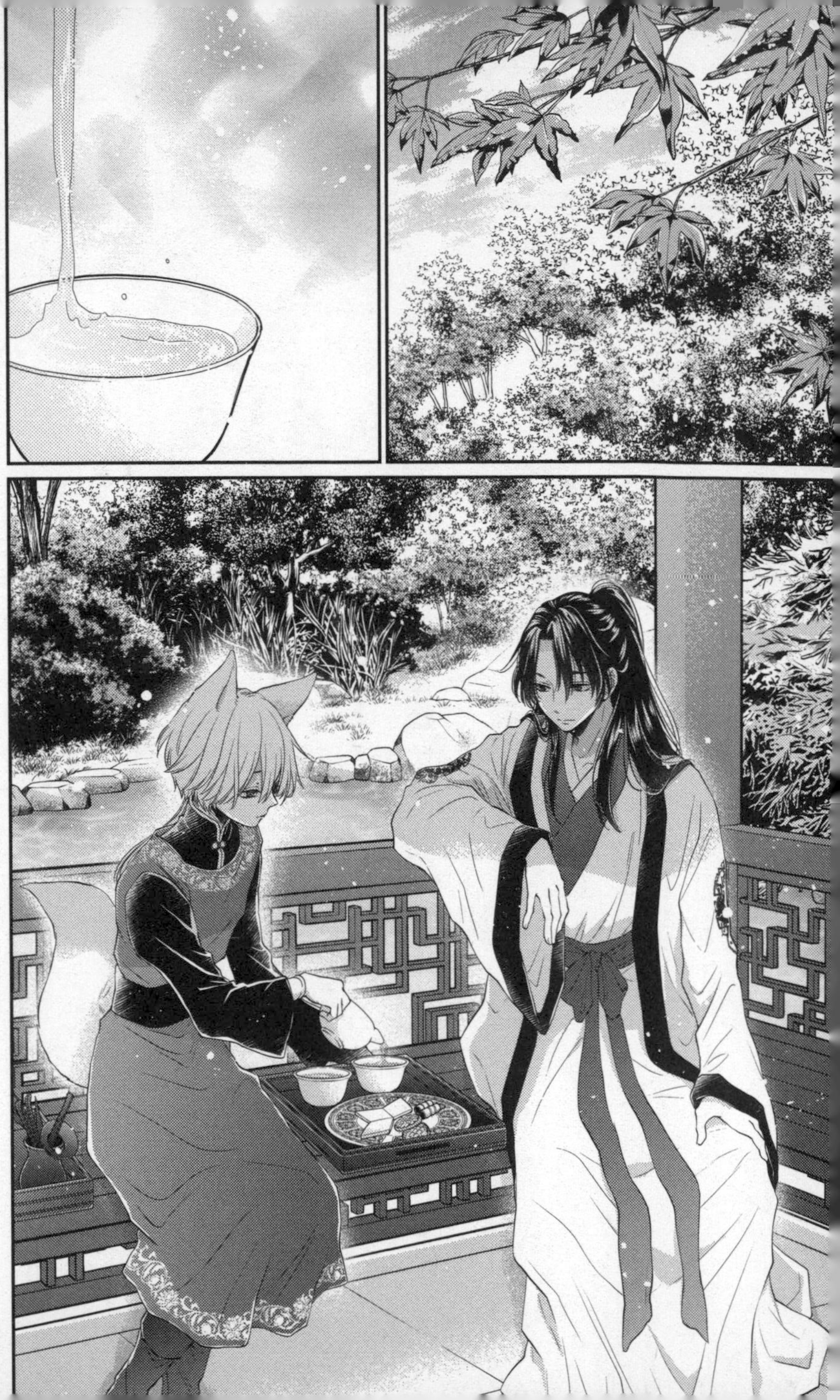

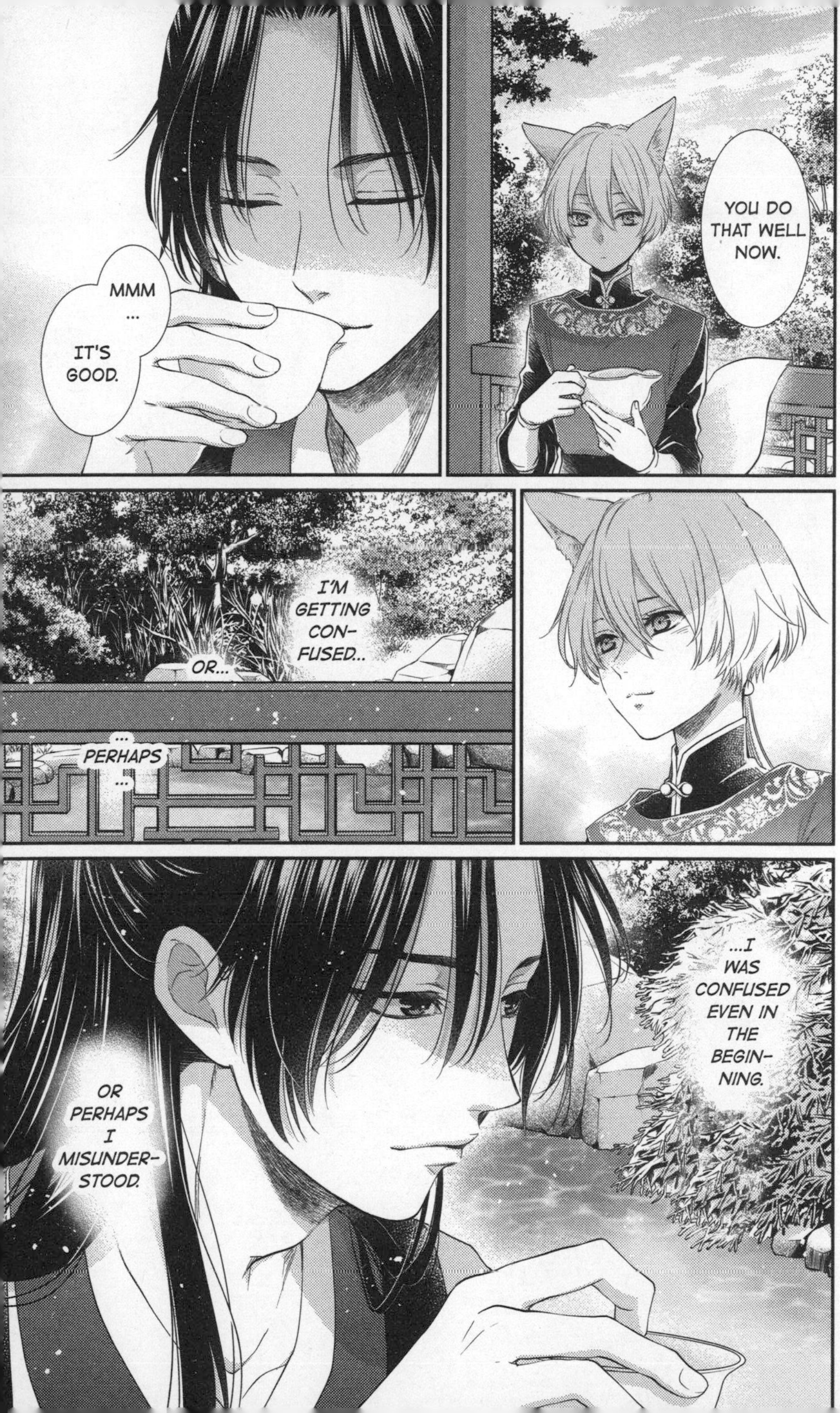
YOU DO THAT WELL NOW.
MMM ... IT'S GOOD.
I'M GETTING CON-FUSED...
OR...
... PERHAPS ...
...I WAS CONFUSED EVEN IN THE BEGIN-NING.
OR PERHAPS I MISUNDER-STOOD.

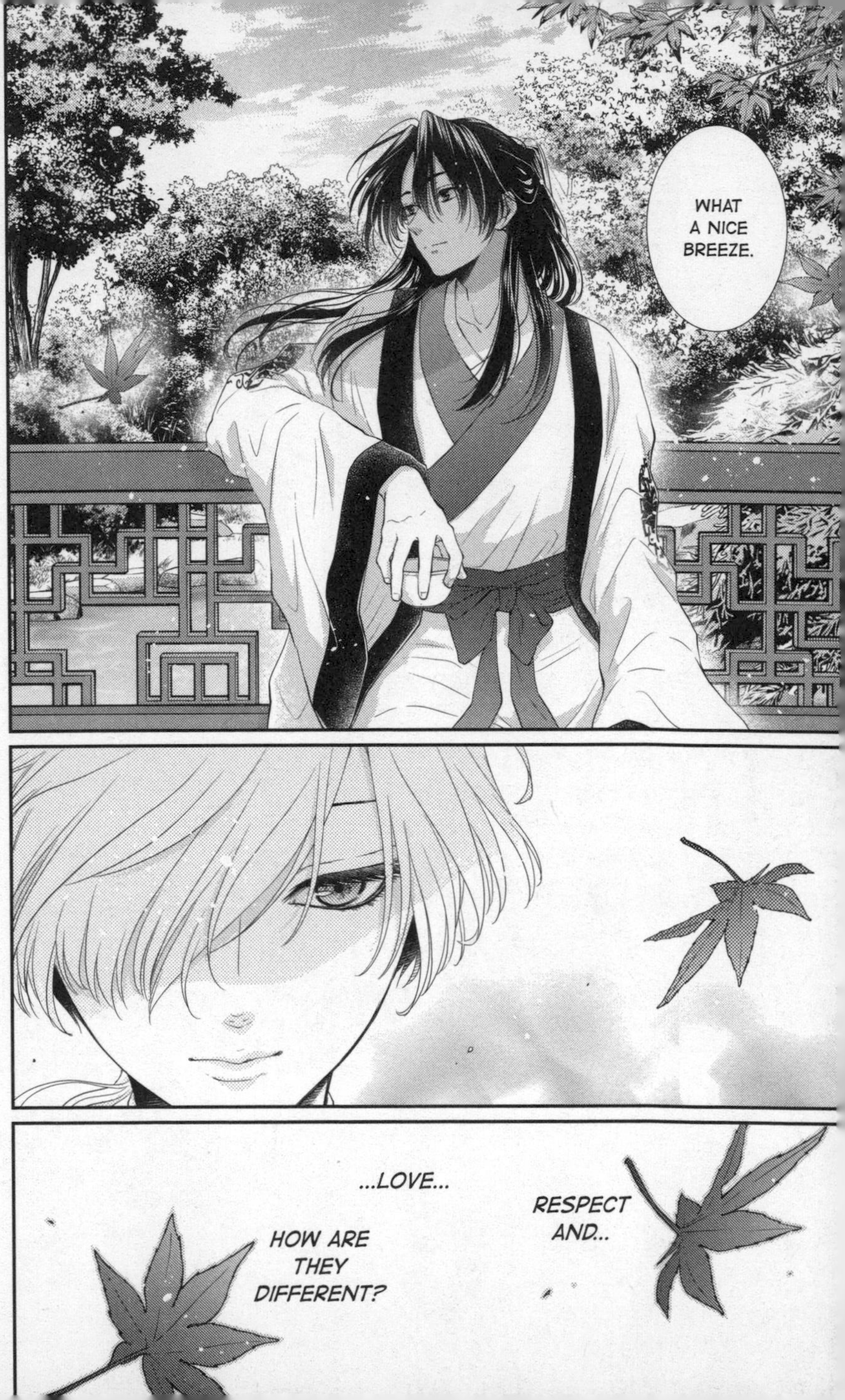
WHAT A NICE BREEZE.
RESPECT AND...
...LOVE...
HOW ARE THEY DIFFERENT?

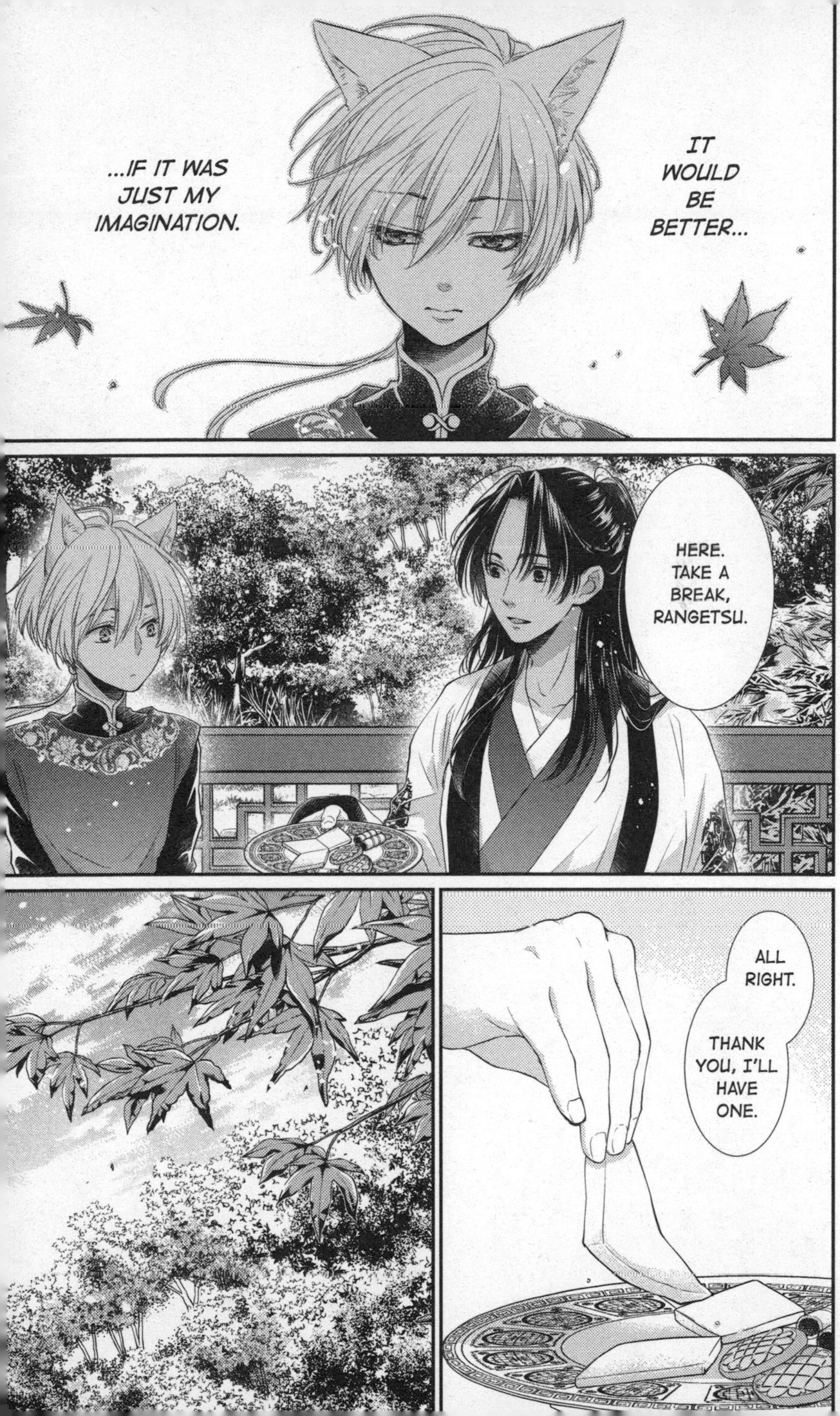
IT WOULD BE BETTER...
...IF IT WAS JUST MY IMAGINATION.
HERE. TAKE A BREAK, RANGETSU.
ALL RIGHT.
THANK YOU, I'LL HAVE ONE.

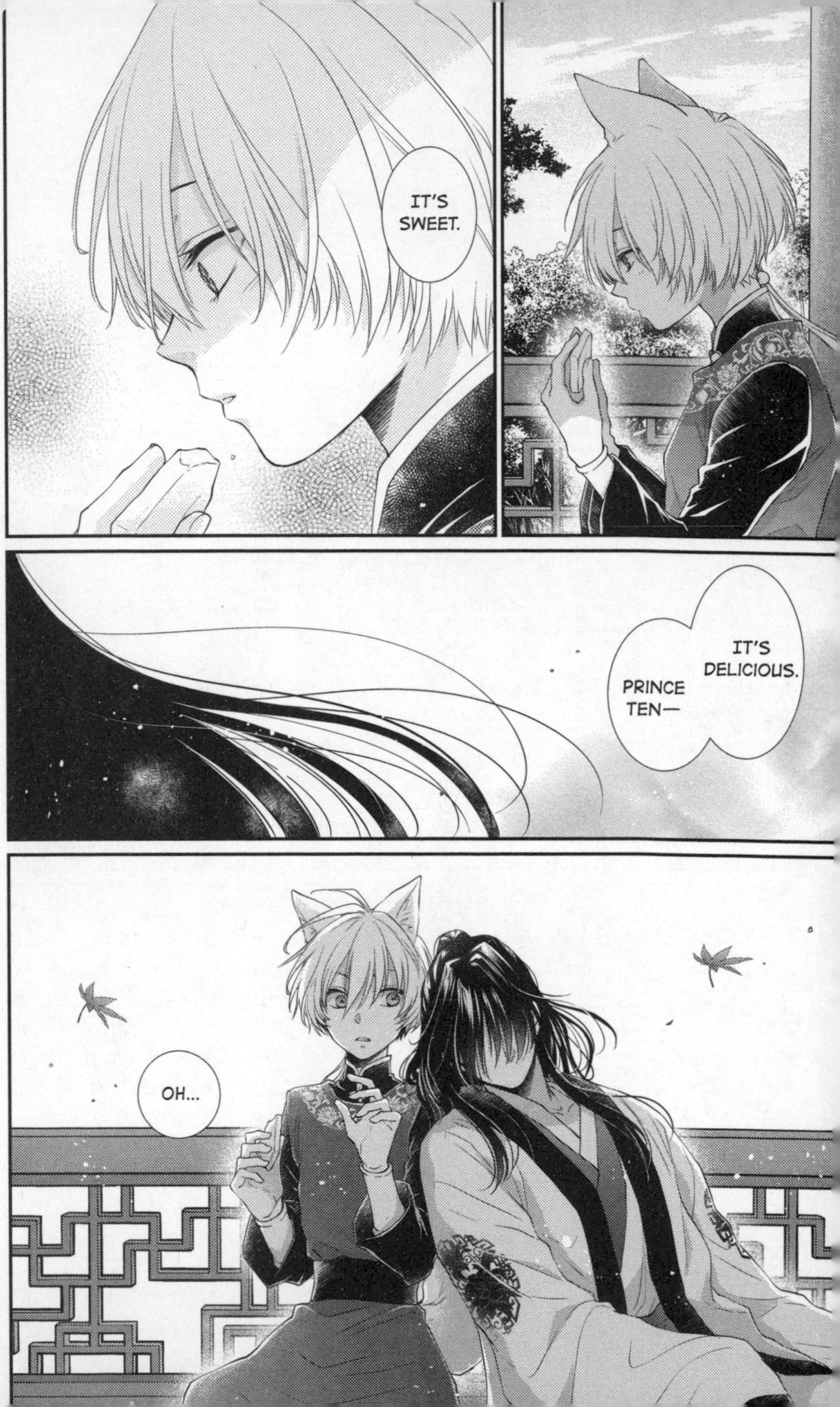
IT'S SWEET.
IT'S DELICIOUS.
PRINCE TEN—
OH...

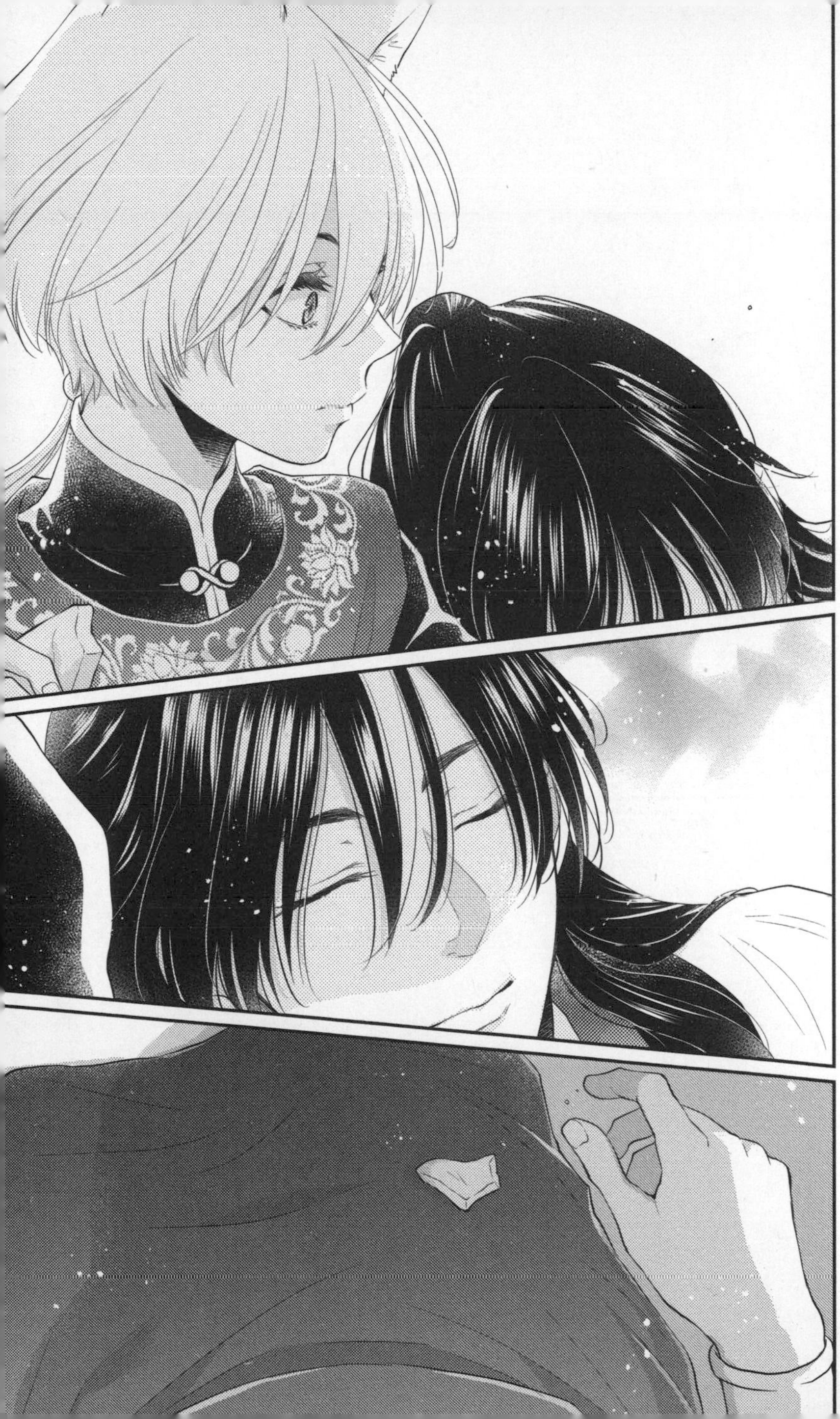

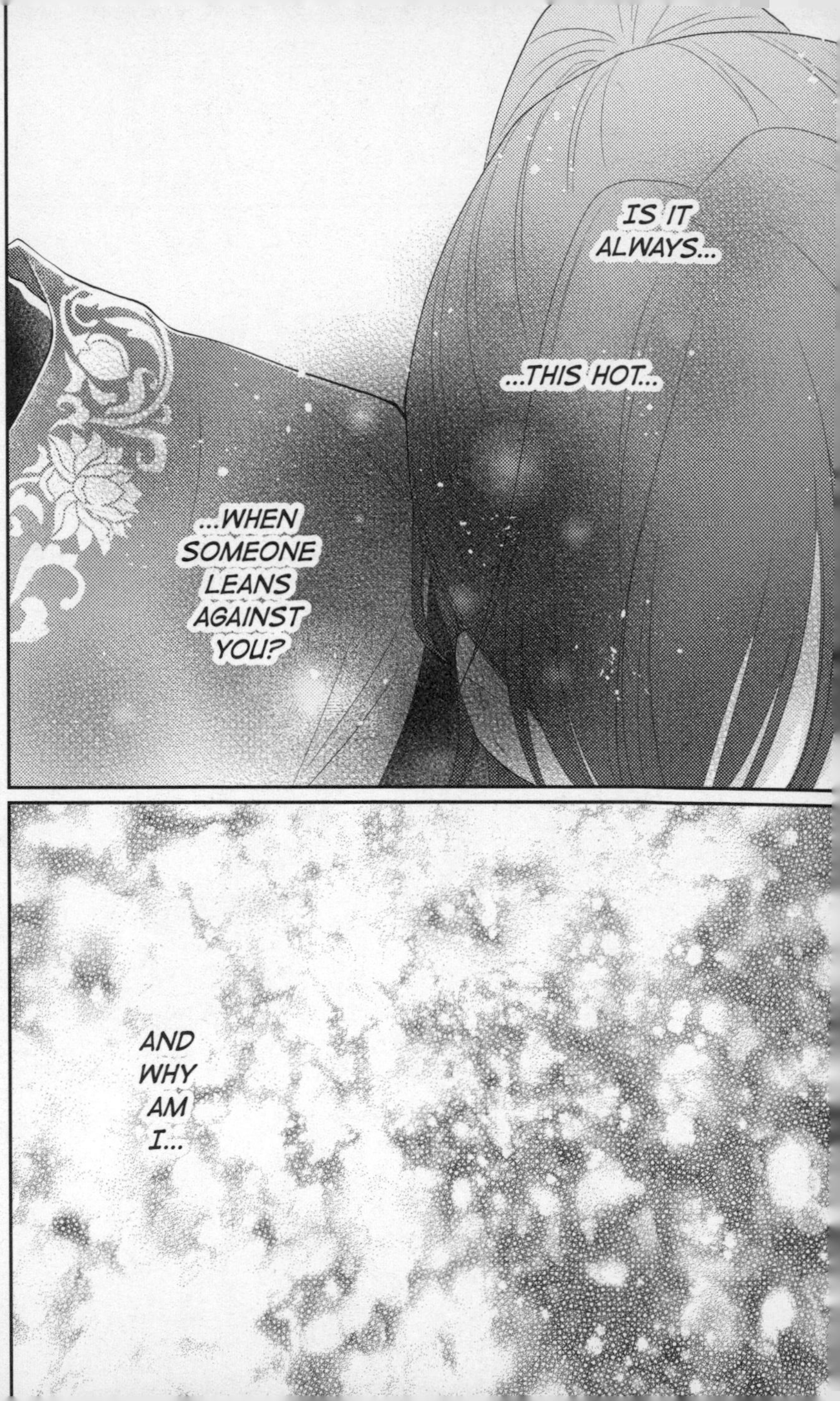
IS IT ALWAYS...
...THIS HOT...
...WHEN SOMEONE LEANS AGAINST YOU?
AND WHY AM I...

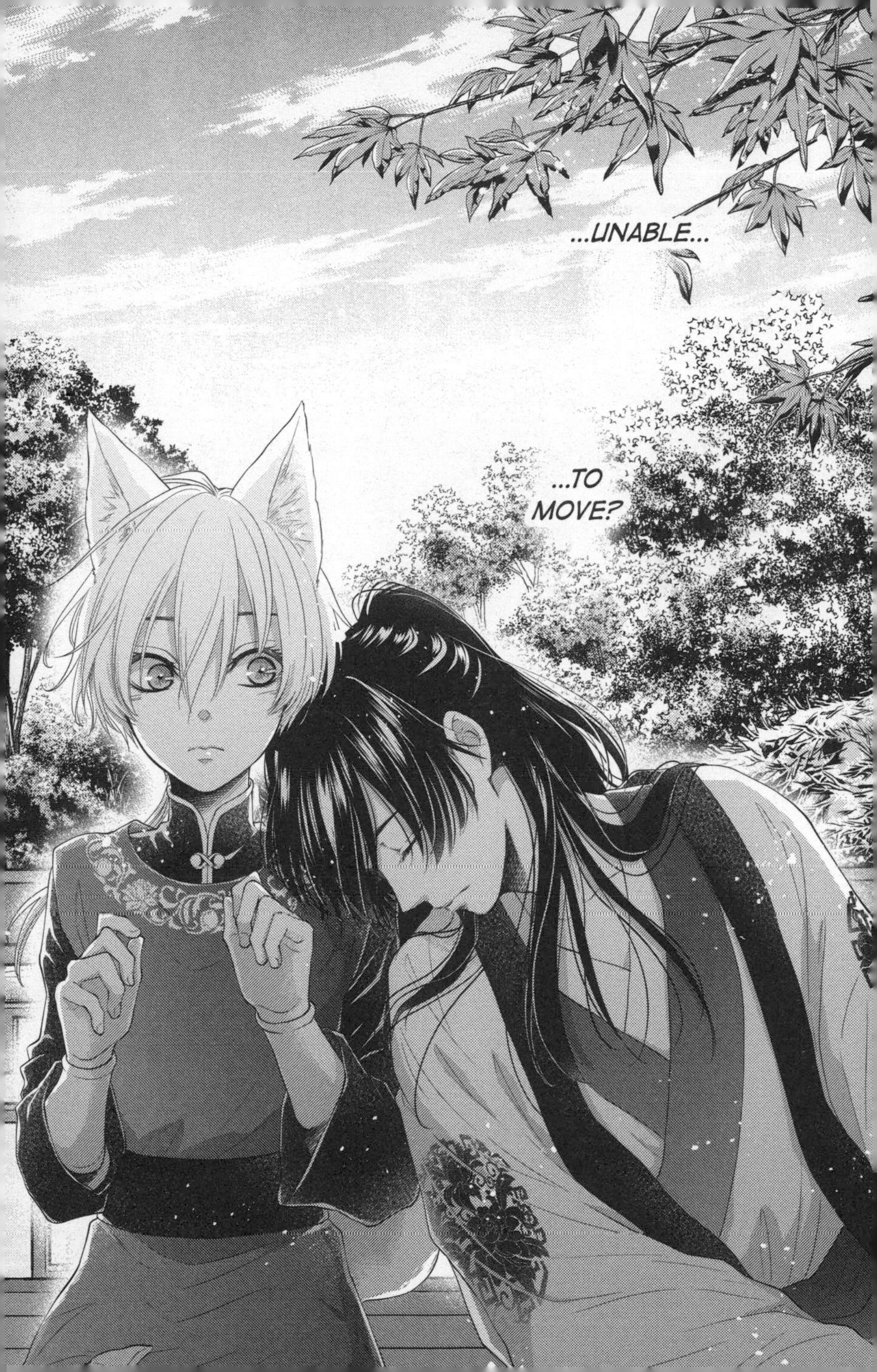
...UNABLE...
...TO MOVE?

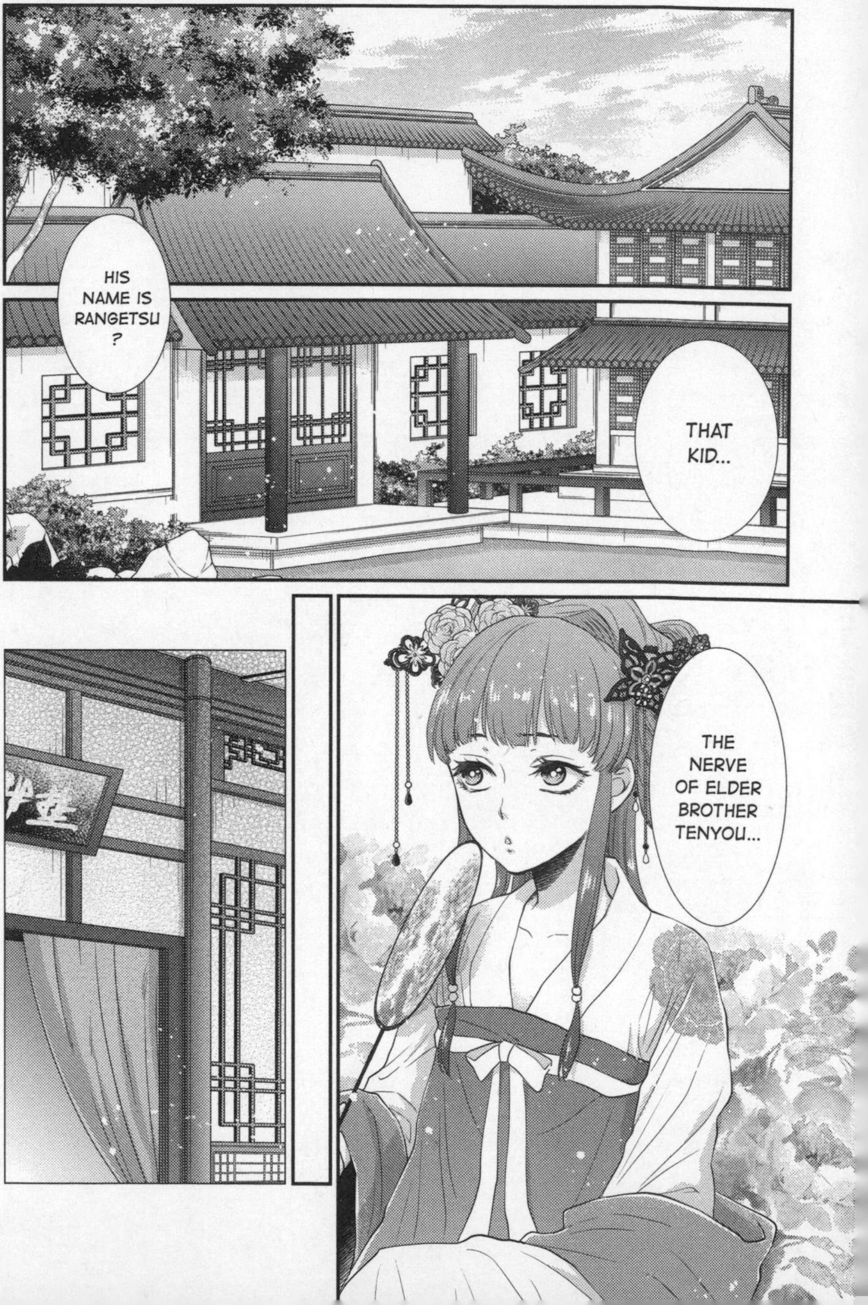
HIS NAME IS RANGETSU ?
THAT KID...
THE NERVE OF ELDER BROTHER TENYOU...

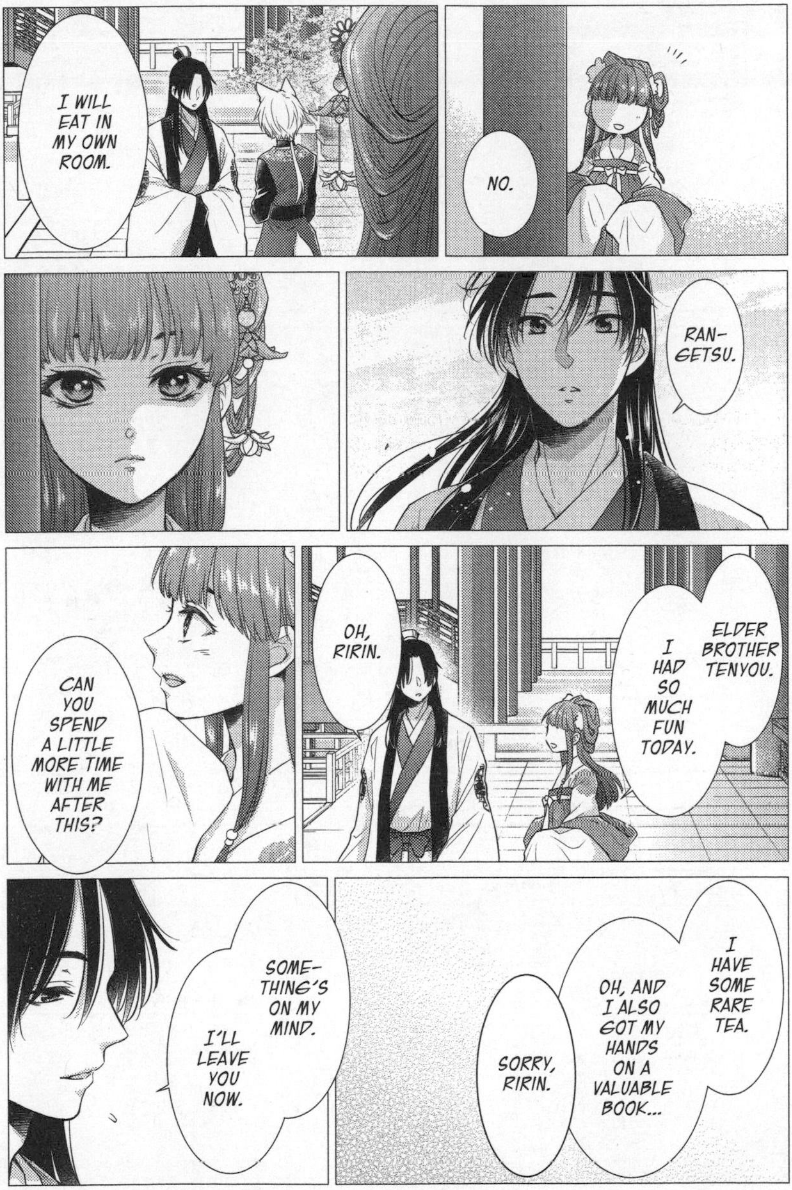
NO.
I WILL EAT IN MY OWN ROOM.
RAN-GETSU.
ELDER BROTHER TENYOU.
I HAD SO MUCH FUN TODAY.
OH, RIRIN.
CAN YOU SPEND A LITTLE MORE TIME WITH ME AFTER THIS?
I HAVE SOME RARE TEA.
OH, AND I ALSO GOT MY HANDS ON A VALUABLE BOOK...
SORRY, RIRIN.
SOMETHING'S ON MY MIND.
I'LL LEAVE YOU NOW.

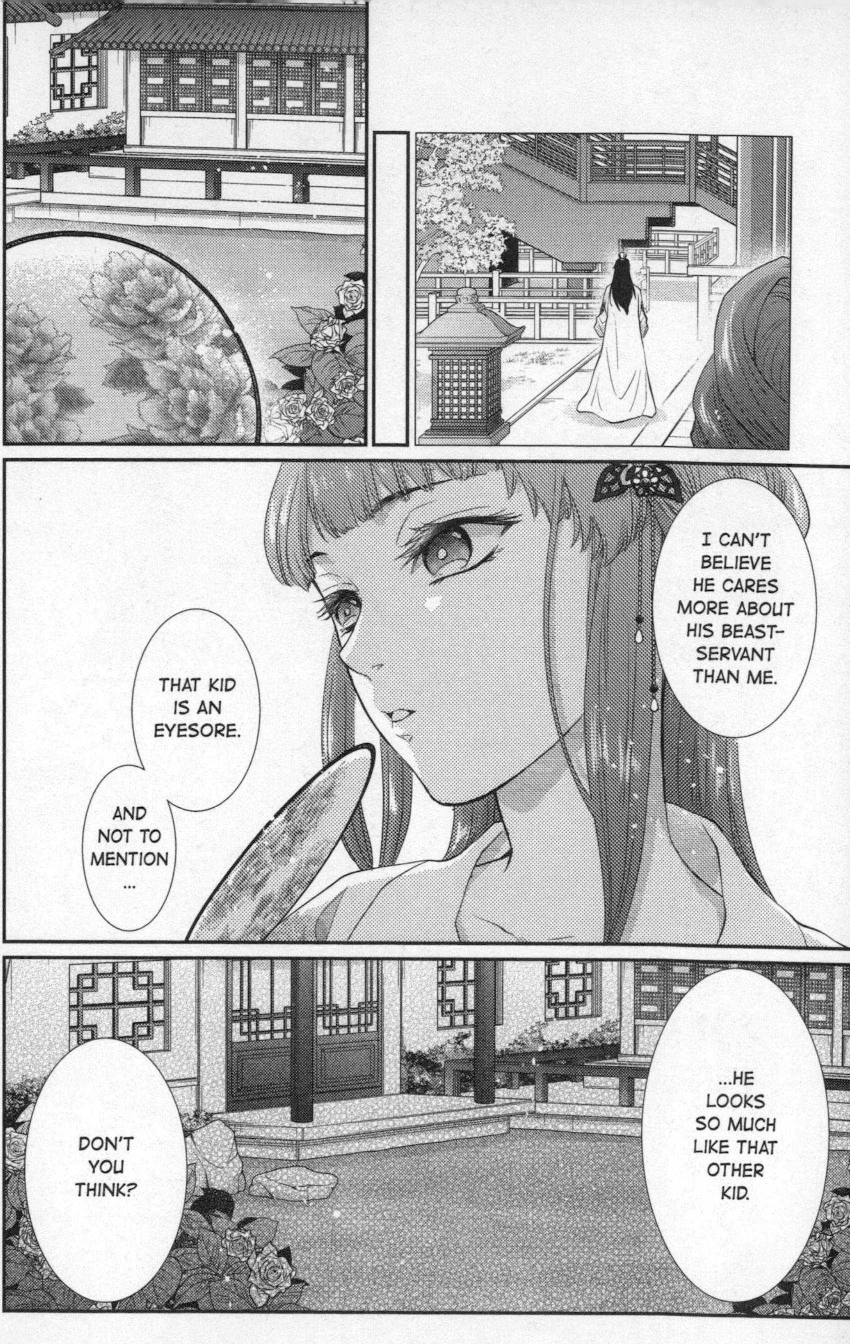
I CAN'T BELIEVE HE CARES MORE ABOUT HIS BEAST-SERVANT THAN ME.
THAT KID IS AN EYESORE.
AND NOT TO MENTION ...
...HE LOOKS SO MUCH LIKE THAT OTHER KID.
DON'T YOU THINK?

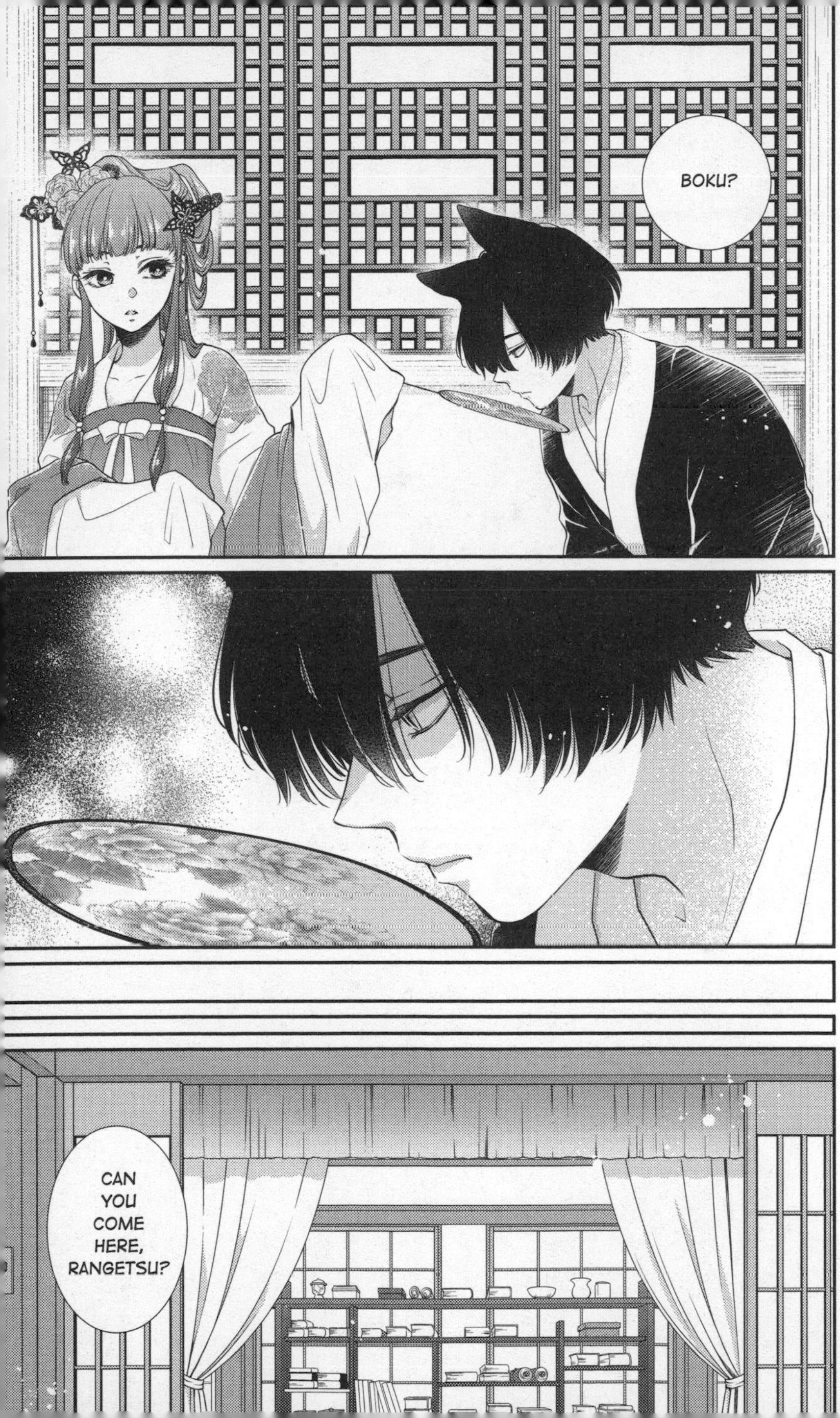
BOKU?
CAN YOU COME HERE, RANGETSU?

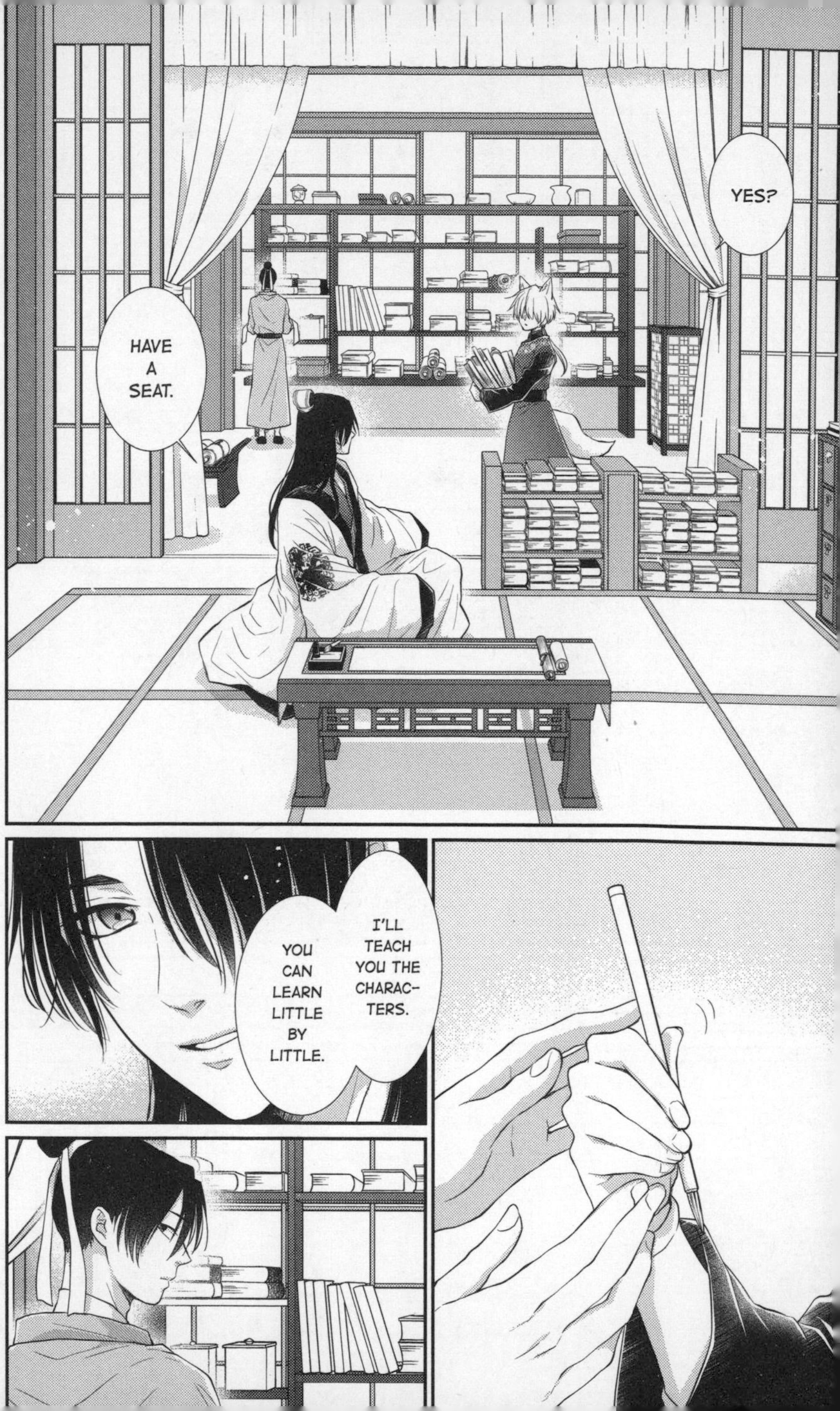
YES?
HAVE A SEAT.
I'LL TEACH YOU THE CHARAC-TERS.
YOU CAN LEARN LITTLE BY LITTLE.

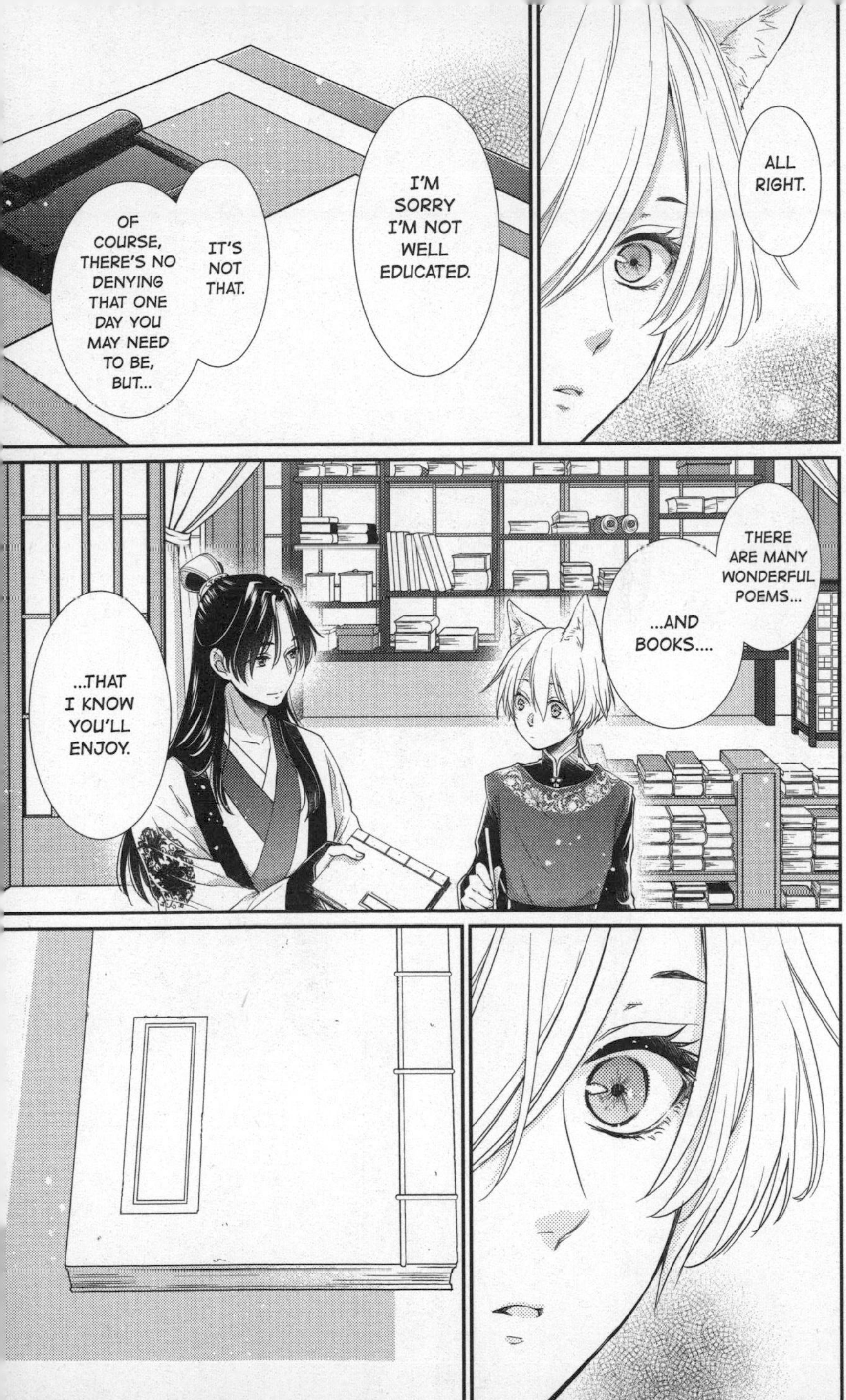
ALL RIGHT.
I'M SORRY I'M NOT WELL EDUCATED.
IT'S NOT THAT.
OF COURSE, THERE'S NO DENYING THAT ONE DAY YOU MAY NEED TO BE, BUT...
THERE ARE MANY WONDERFUL POEMS...
...AND BOOKS....
...THAT I KNOW YOU'LL ENJOY.

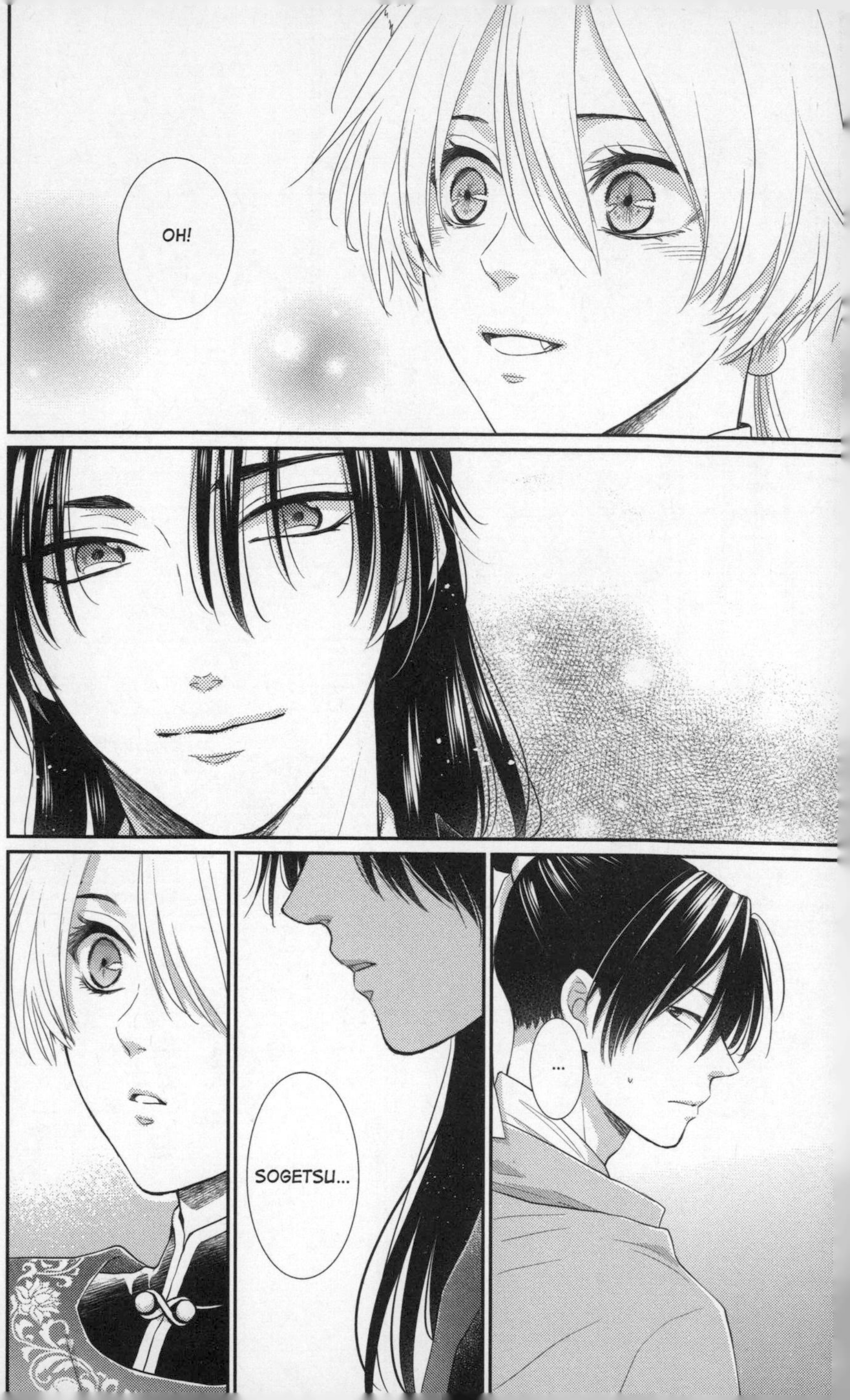
OH!
...
SOGETSU...

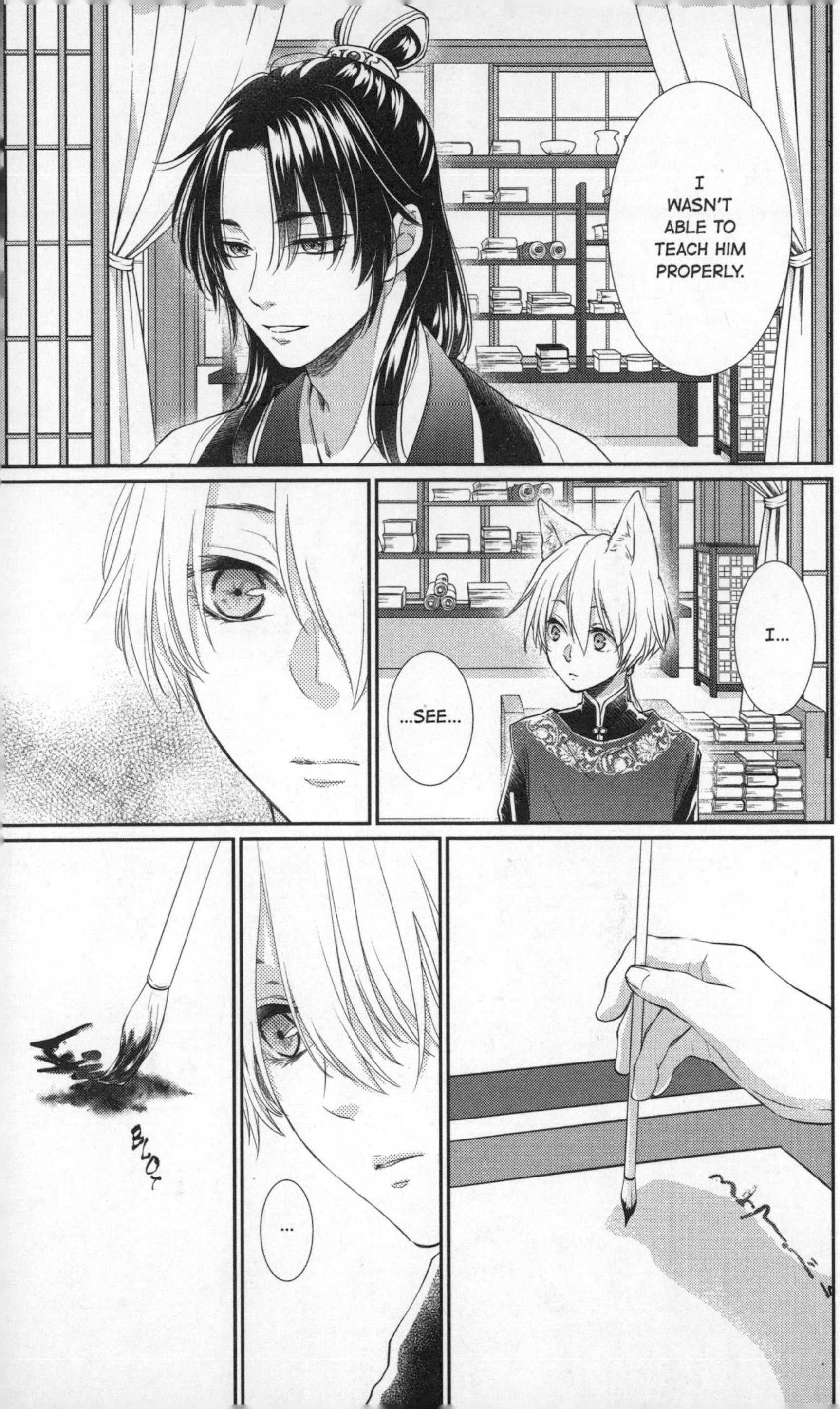
I WASN'T ABLE TO TEACH HIM PROPERLY.
I...
...SEE...
...
BLOT

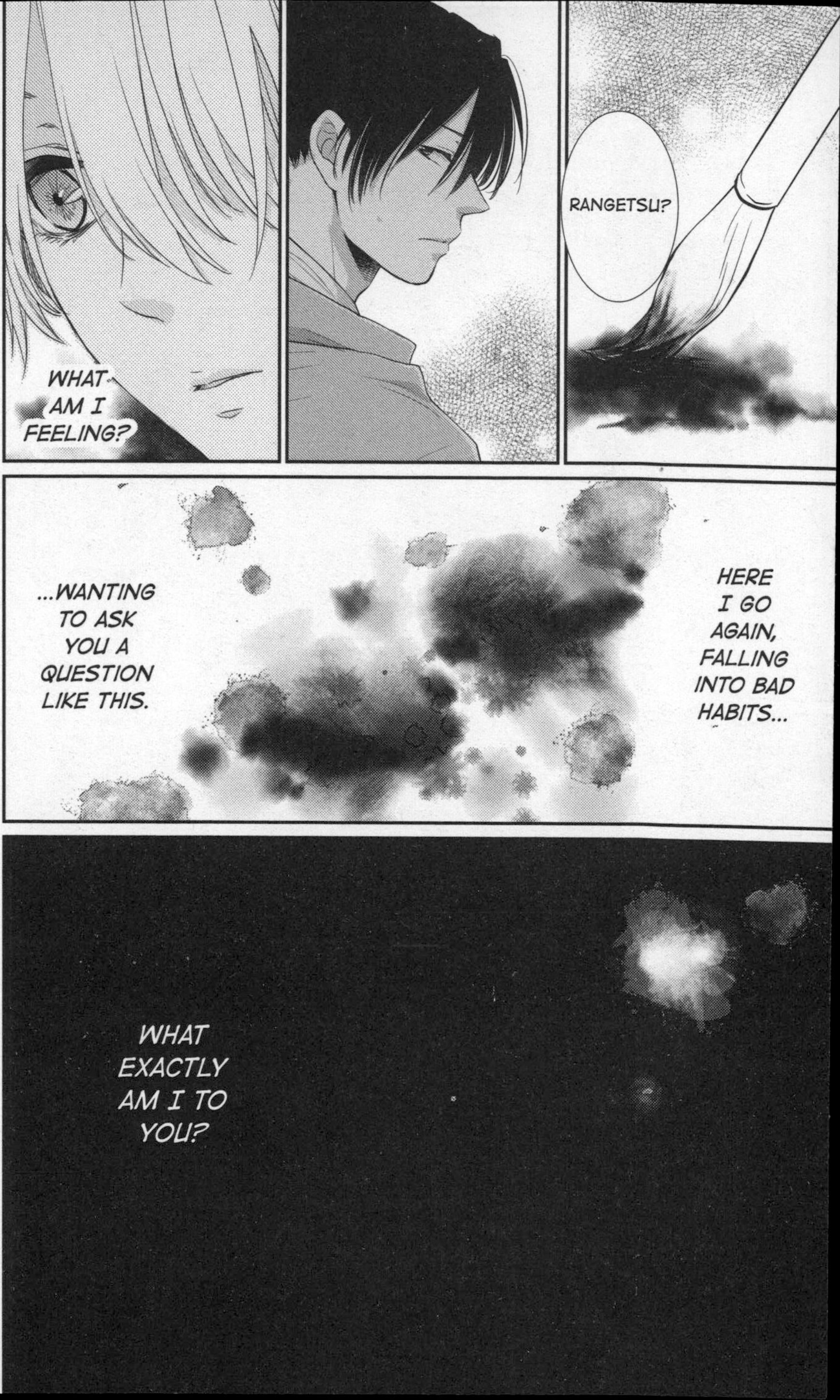
RANGETSU?
WHAT AM I FEELING?
HERE I GO AGAIN, FALLING INTO BAD HABITS...
...WANTING TO ASK YOU A QUESTION LIKE THIS.
WHAT EXACTLY AM I TO YOU?

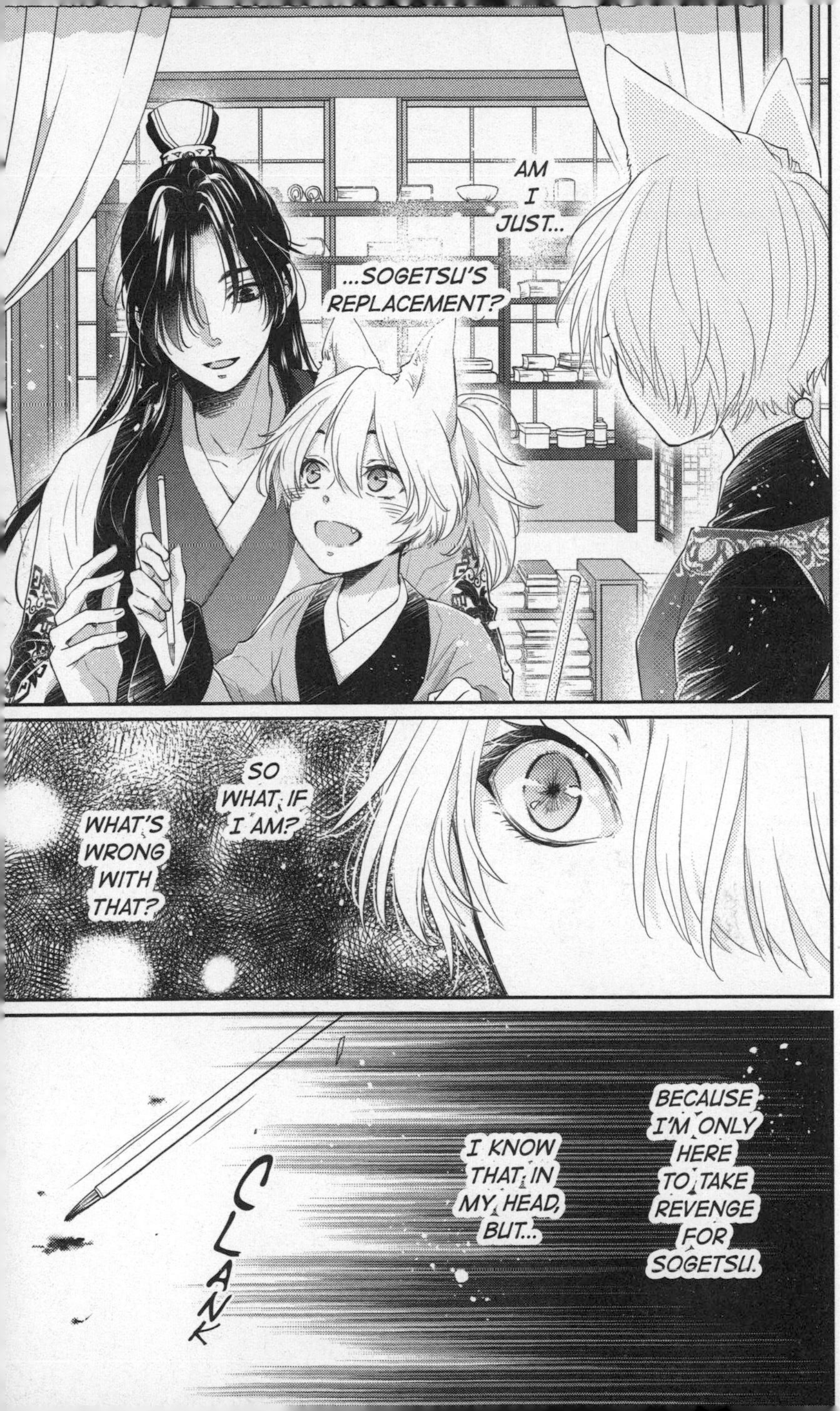
AM I JUST...
...SOGETSU'S REPLACEMENT?
SO WHAT IF I AM?
WHAT'S WRONG WITH THAT?
BECAUSE I'M ONLY HERE TO TAKE REVENGE FOR SOGETSU.
I KNOW THAT IN MY HEAD, BUT...
CLANK

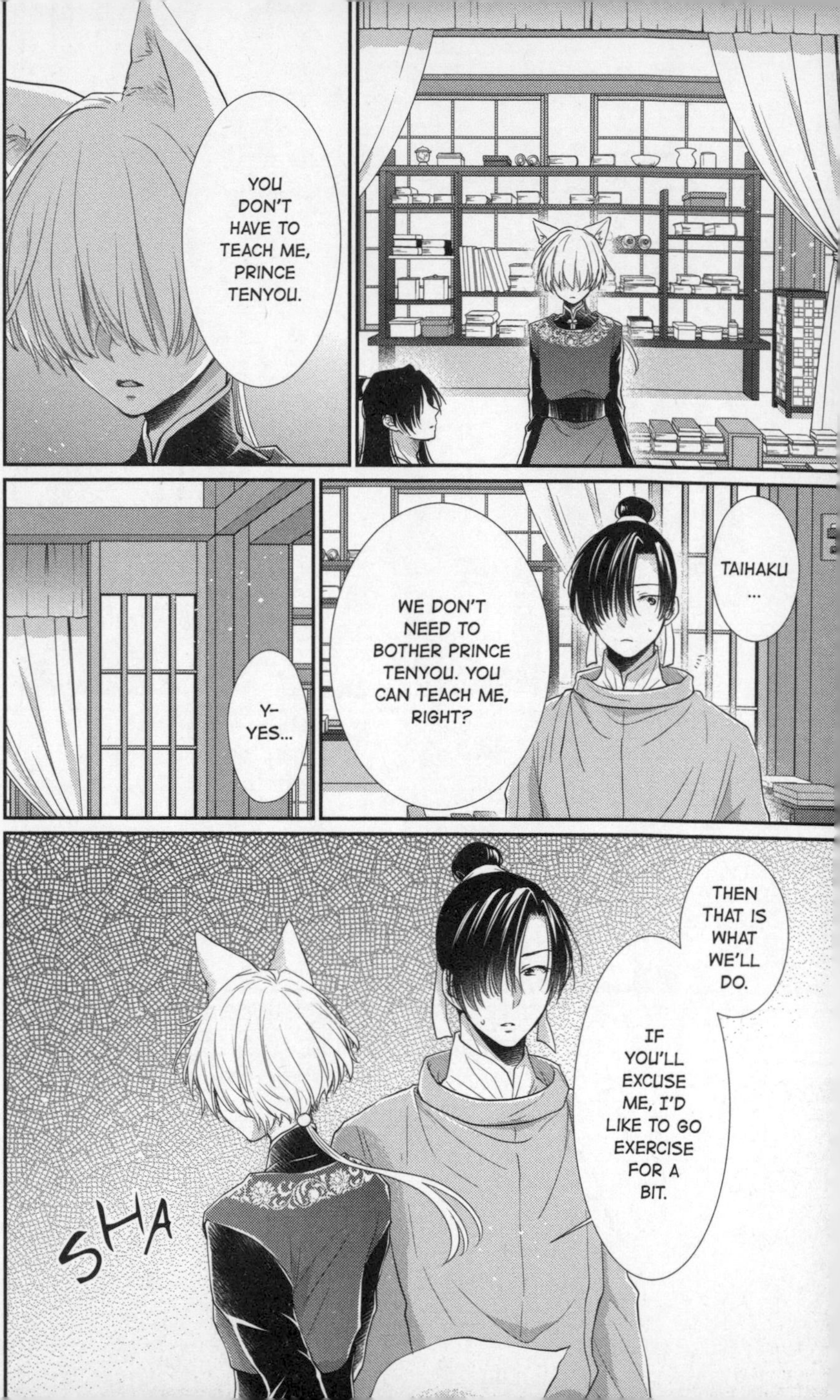
YOU DON'T HAVE TO TEACH ME, PRINCE TENYOU.
TAIHAKU ...
WE DON'T NEED TO BOTHER PRINCE TENYOU. YOU CAN TEACH ME, RIGHT?
Y- YES...
THEN THAT IS WHAT WE'LL DO.
IF YOU'LL EXCUSE ME, I'D LIKE TO GO EXERCISE FOR A BIT.
SHA

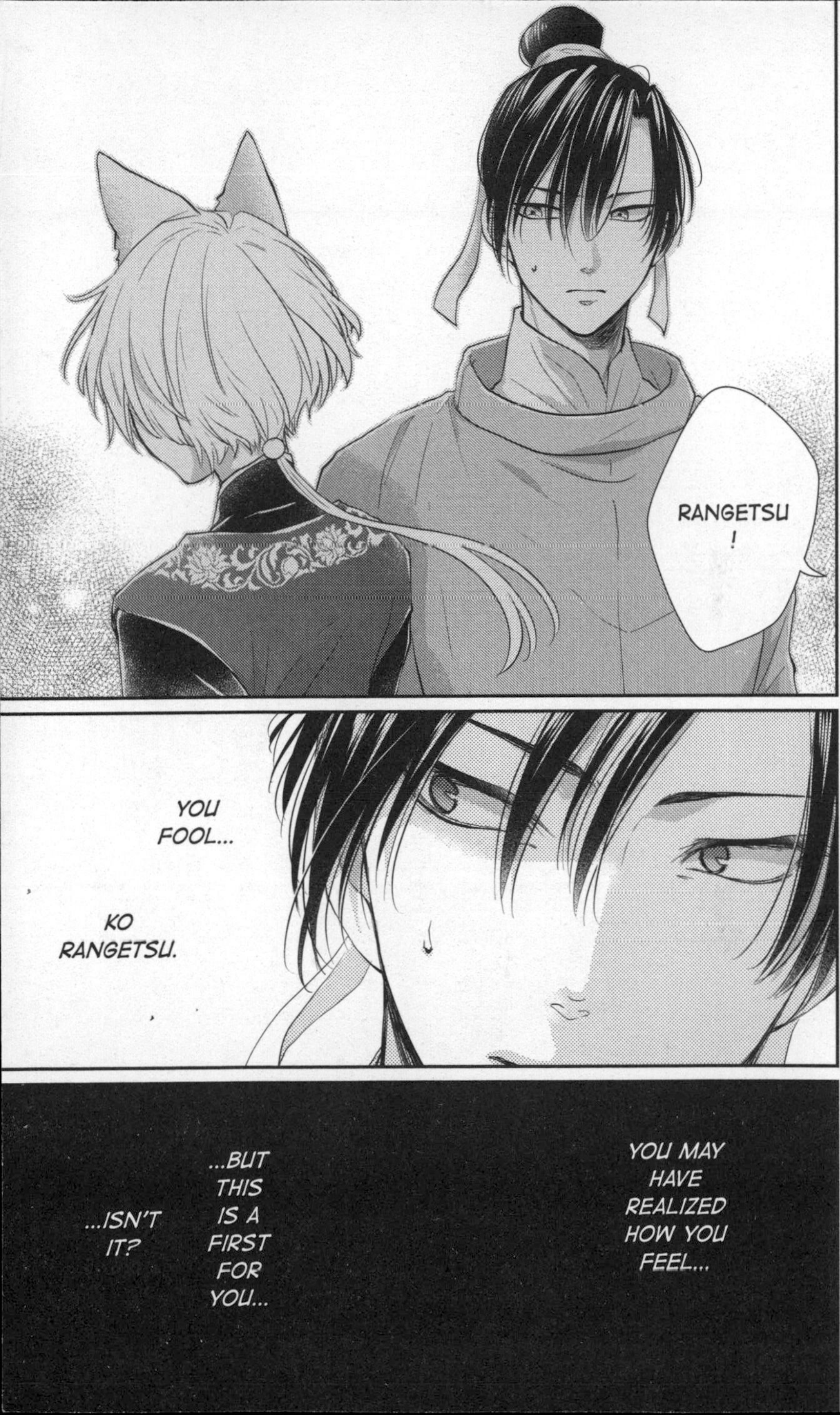
RANGETSU!
YOU FOOL...
KO RANGETSU.
YOU MAY HAVE REALIZED HOW YOU FEEL...
...BUT THIS IS A FIRST FOR YOU...
...ISN'T IT?

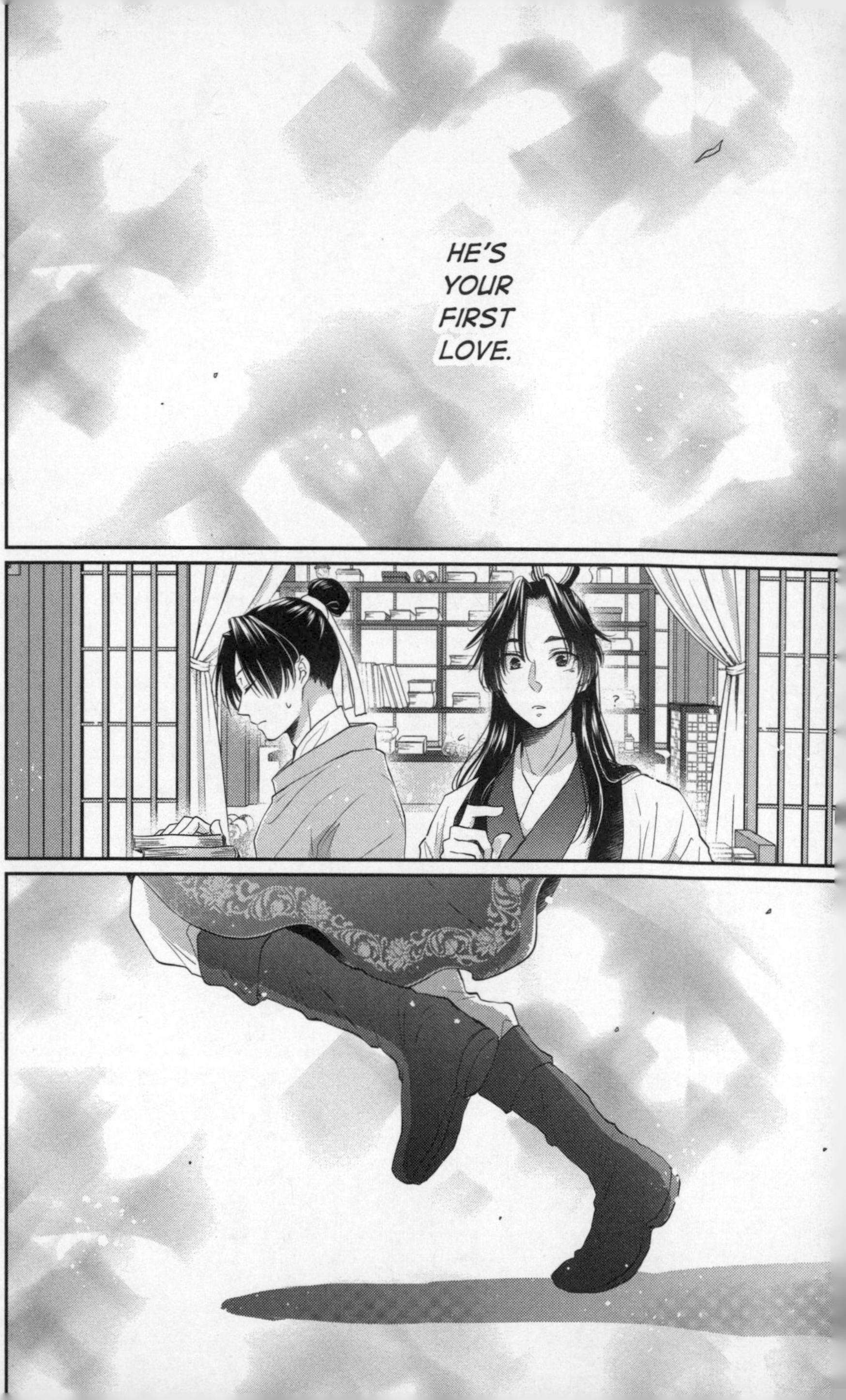
HE'S YOUR FIRST LOVE.
?

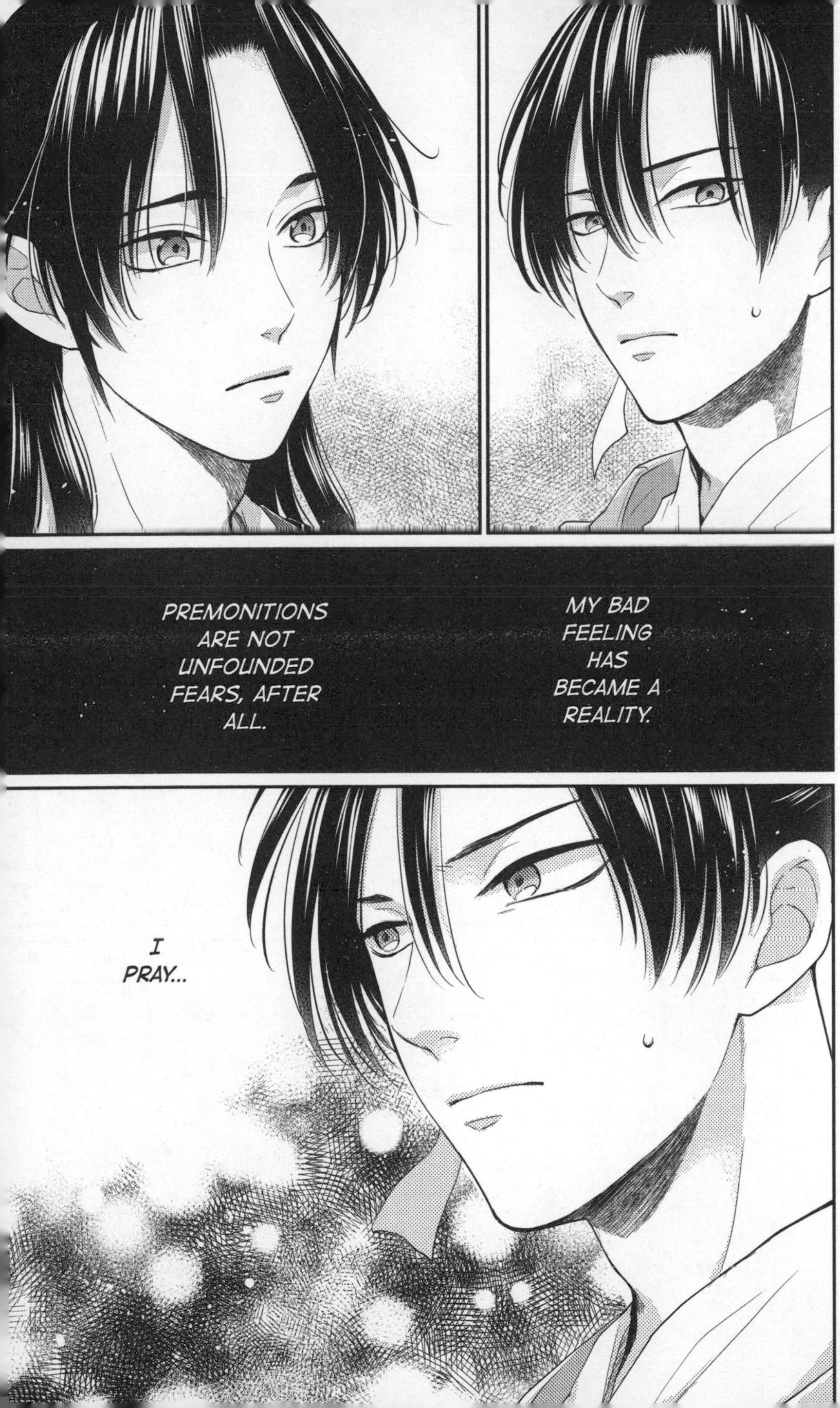
MY BAD FEELING HAS BECAME A REALITY.
PREMONITIONS ARE NOT UNFOUNDED FEARS, AFTER ALL.
I PRAY...

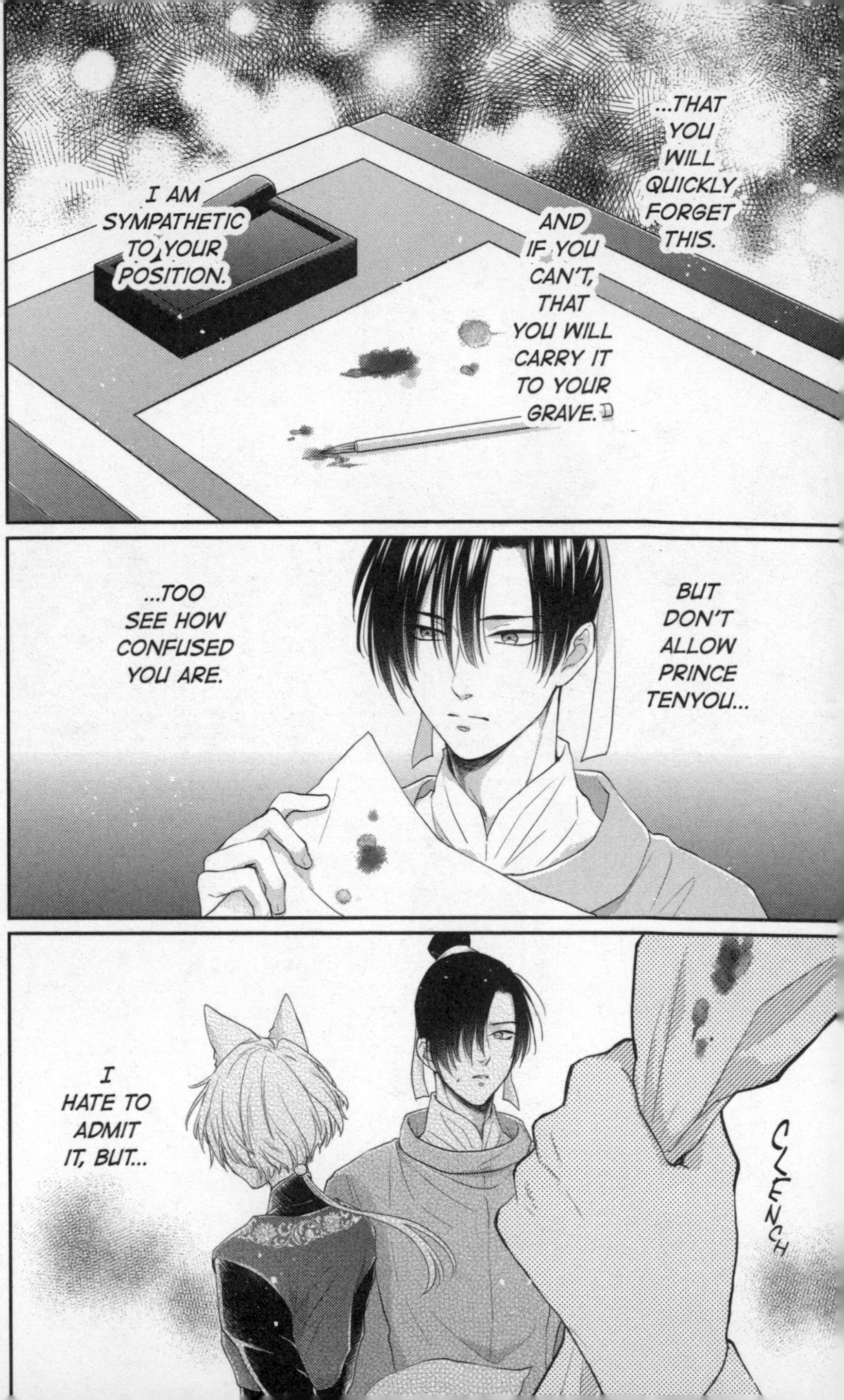
...THAT YOU WILL QUICKLY FORGET THIS.
AND IF YOU CAN'T, THAT YOU WILL CARRY IT TO YOUR GRAVE.
I AM SYMPATHETIC TO YOUR POSITION.
BUT DON'T ALLOW PRINCE TENYOU...
...TOO SEE HOW CONFUSED YOU ARE.
CLENCH
I HATE TO ADMIT IT, BUT...

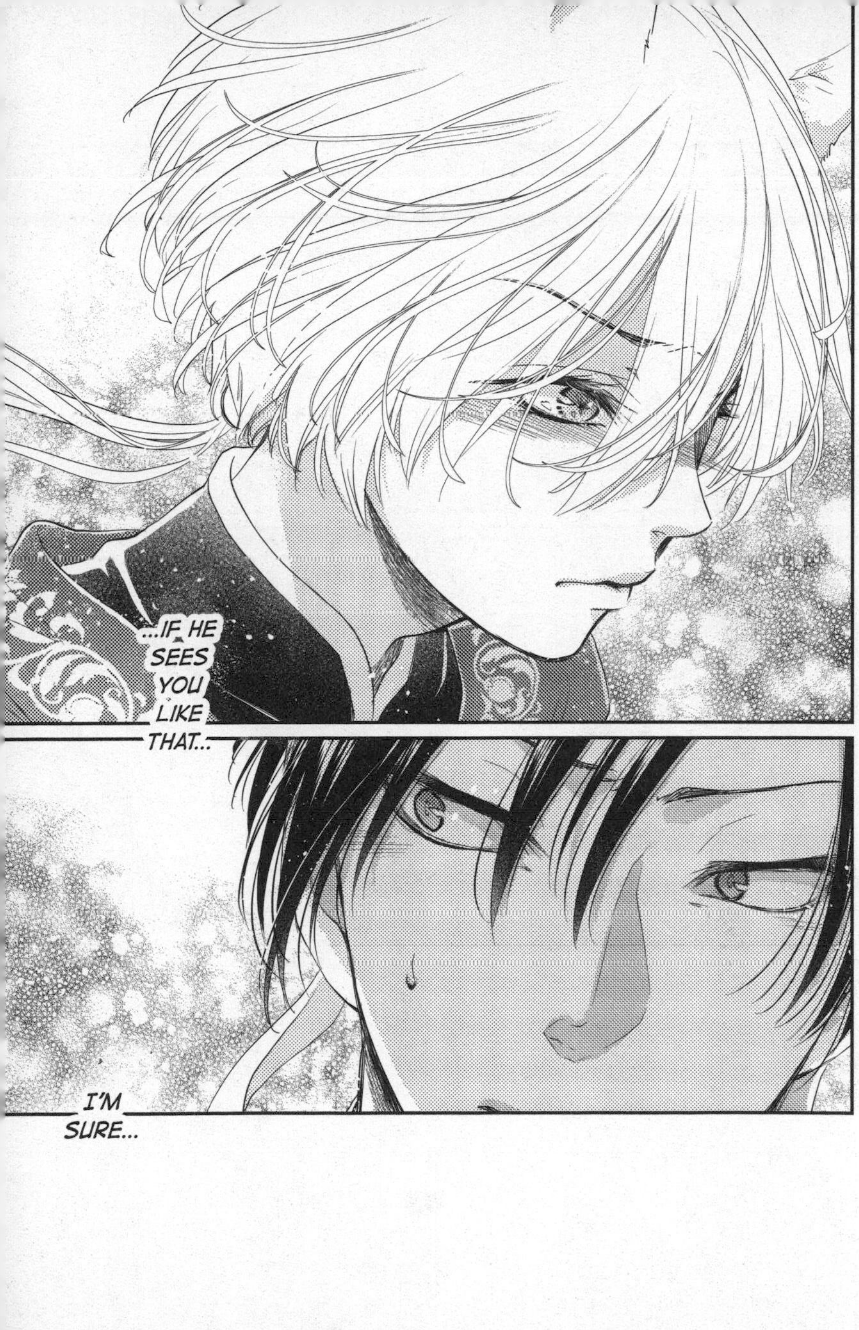
...IF HE SEES YOU LIKE THAT...
I'M SURE...

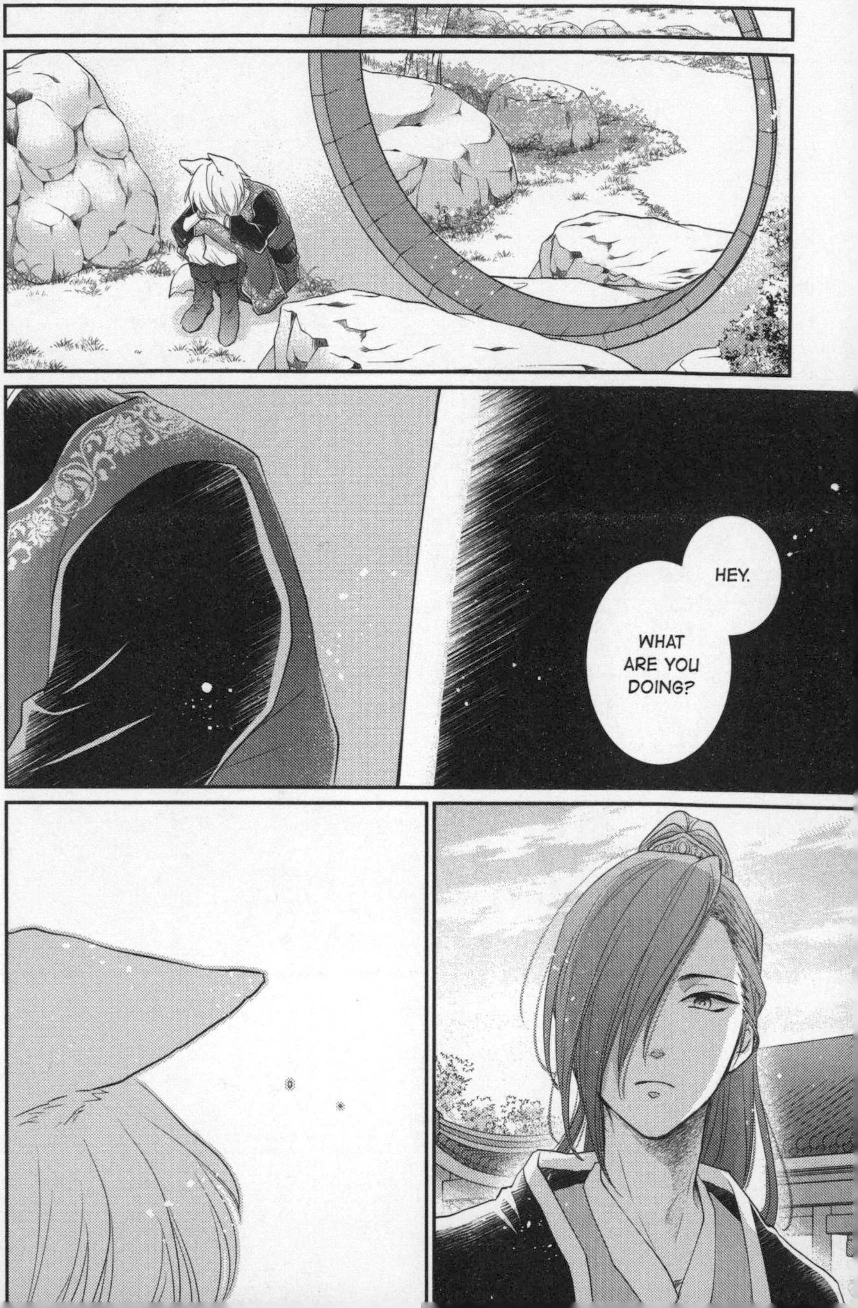
HEY.
WHAT ARE YOU DOING?

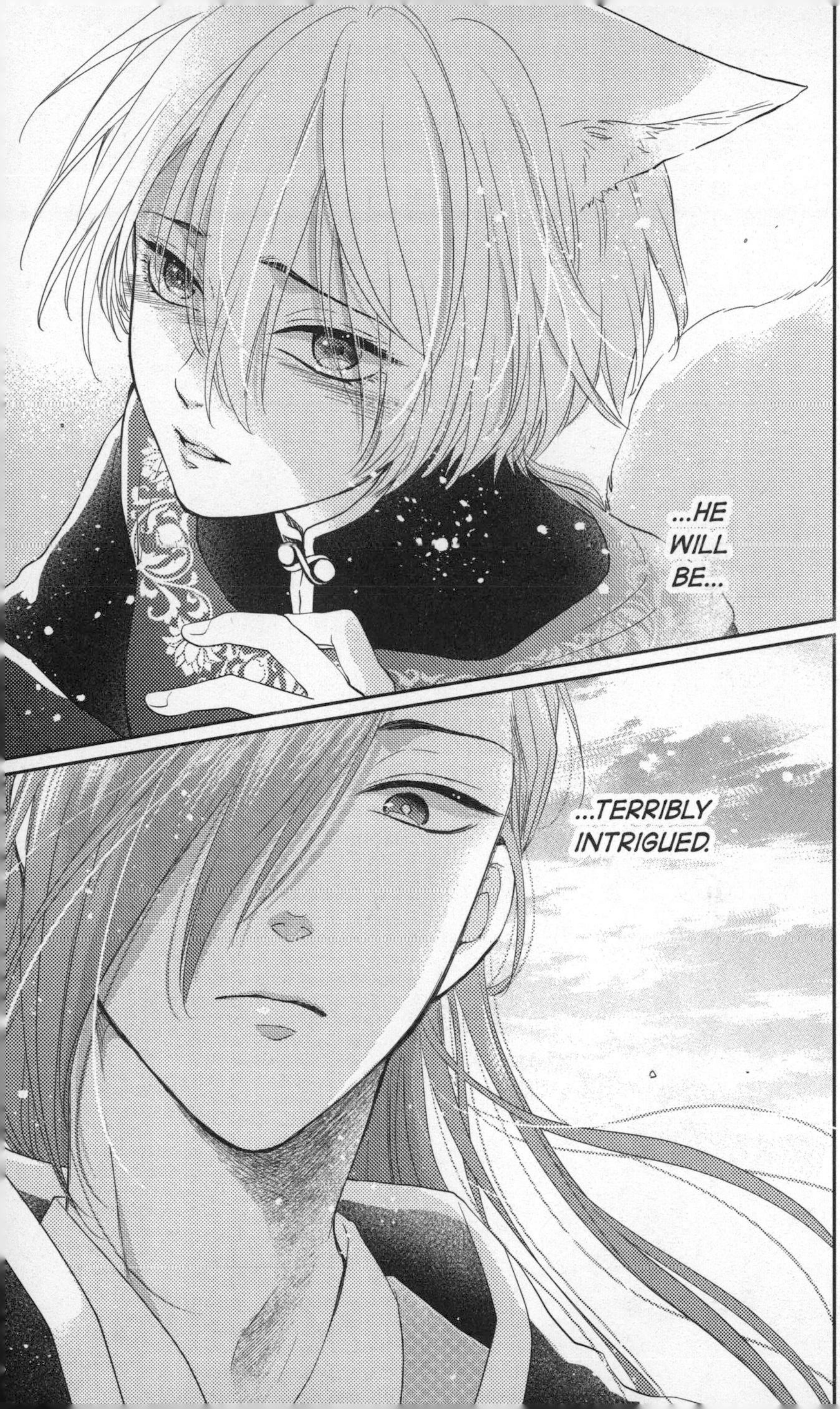
...HE WILL BE...
...TERRIBLY INTRIGUED.

THE KING'S Beast 麗

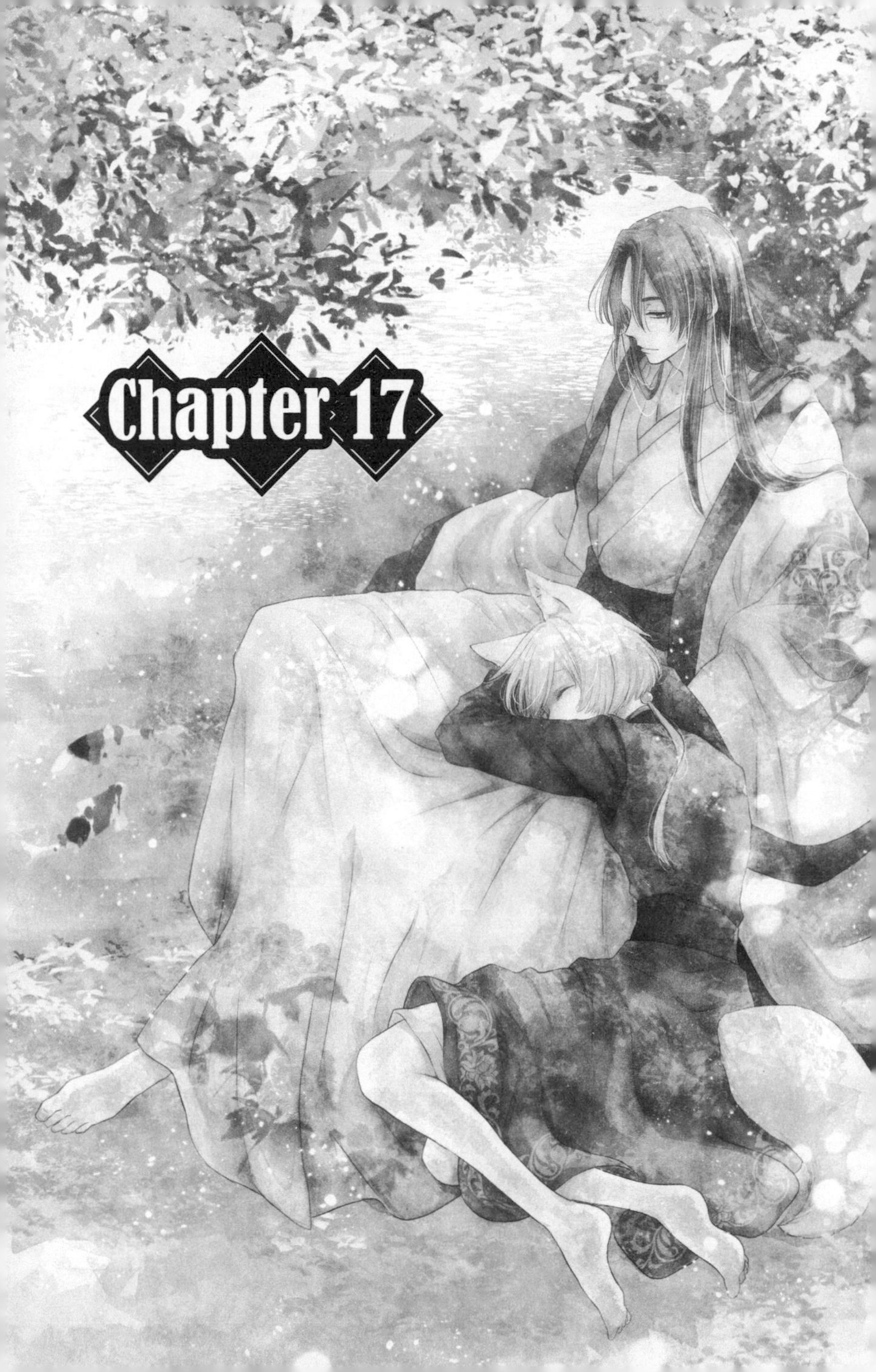
Chapter 17

THE
KING'S
Beast

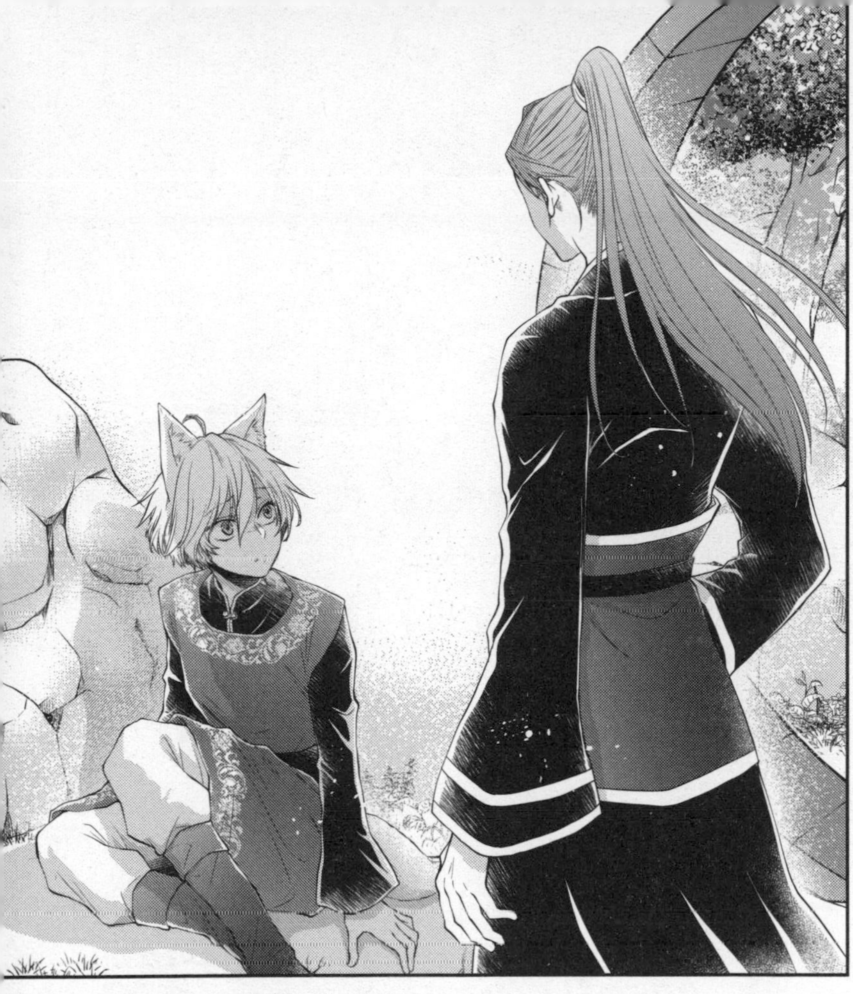

THE KING'S Beast

麗

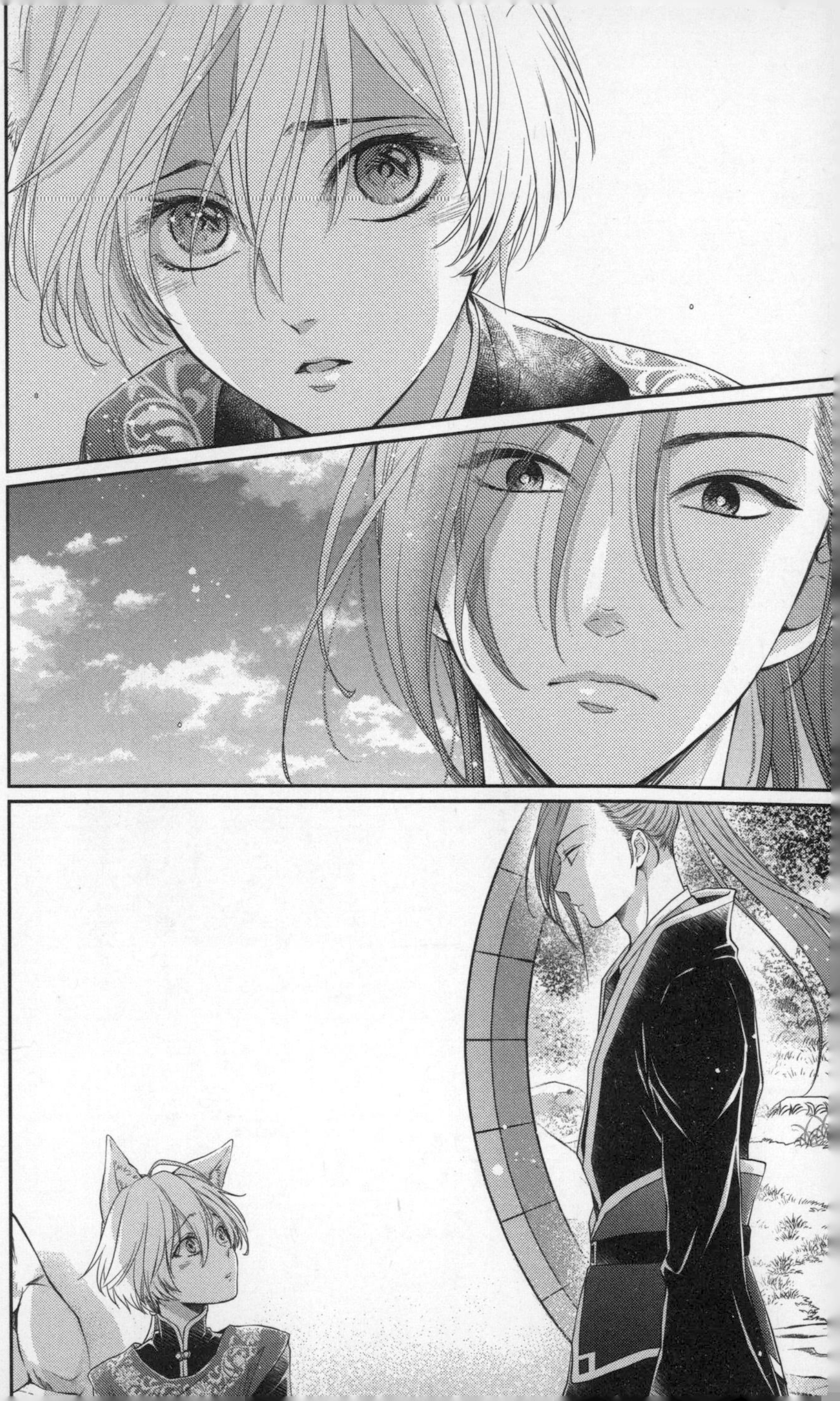

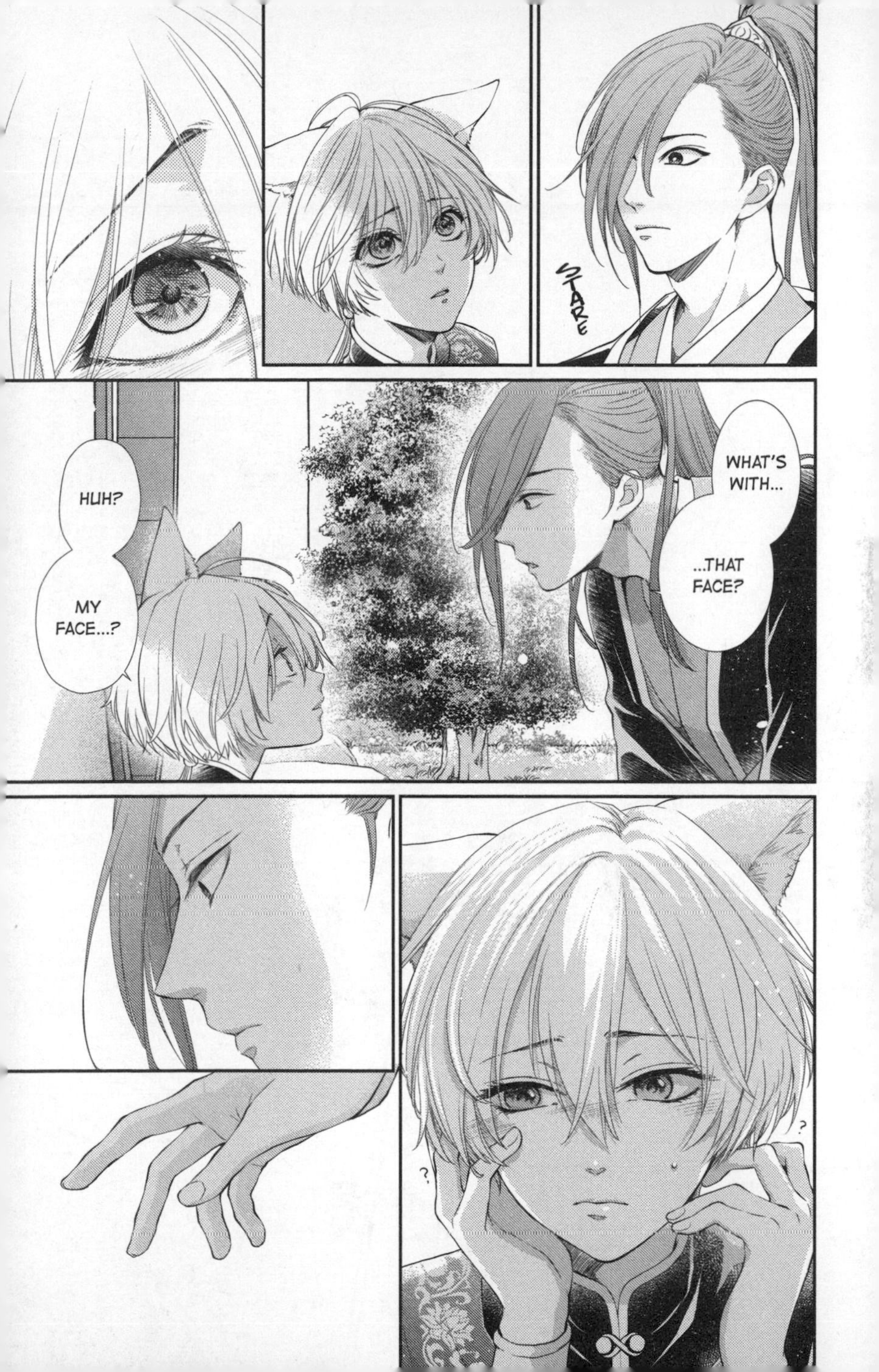
STARE
WHAT'S WITH...
...THAT FACE?
HUH?
MY FACE...?
?
?

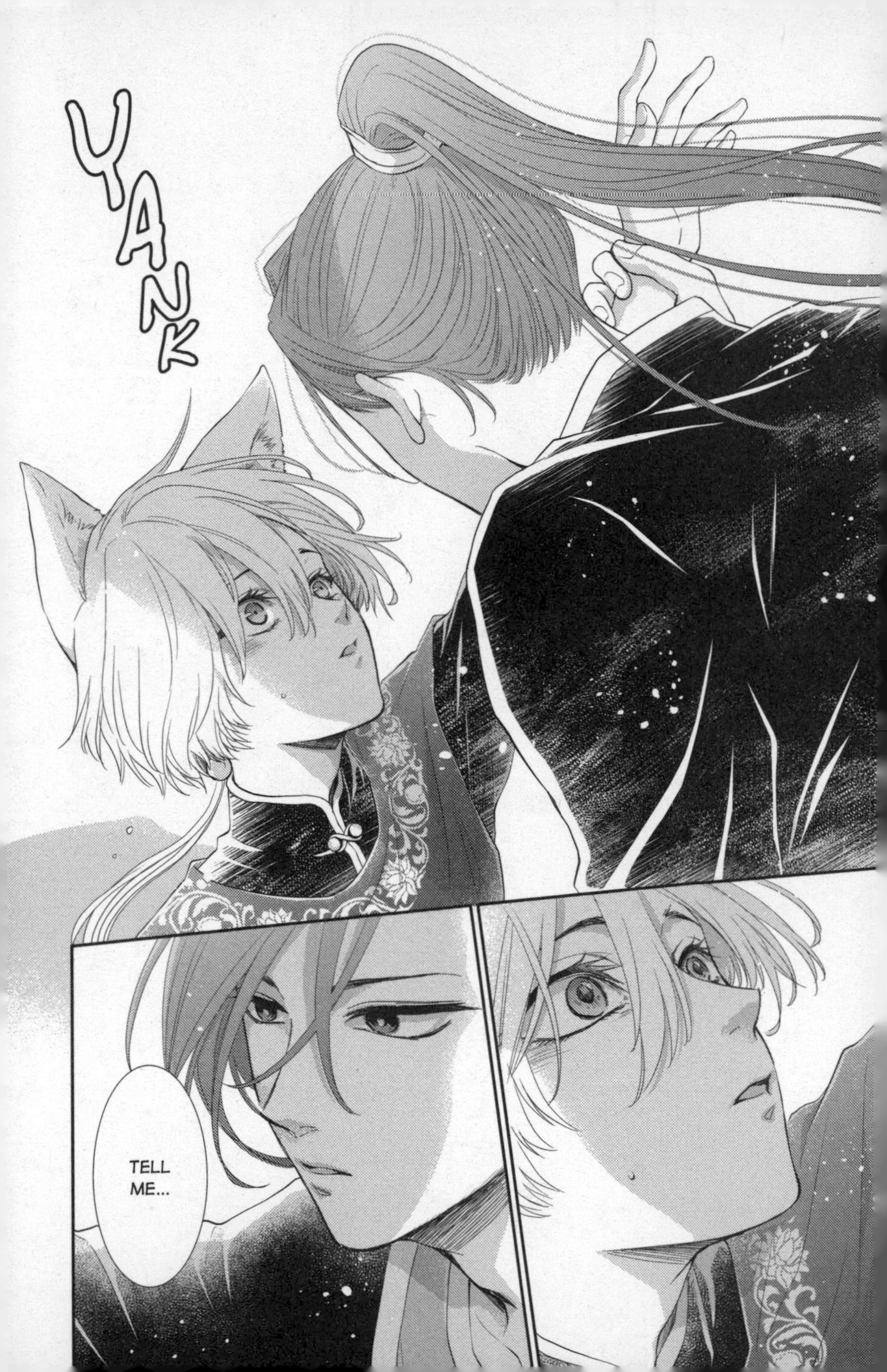
YANK
TELL ME...

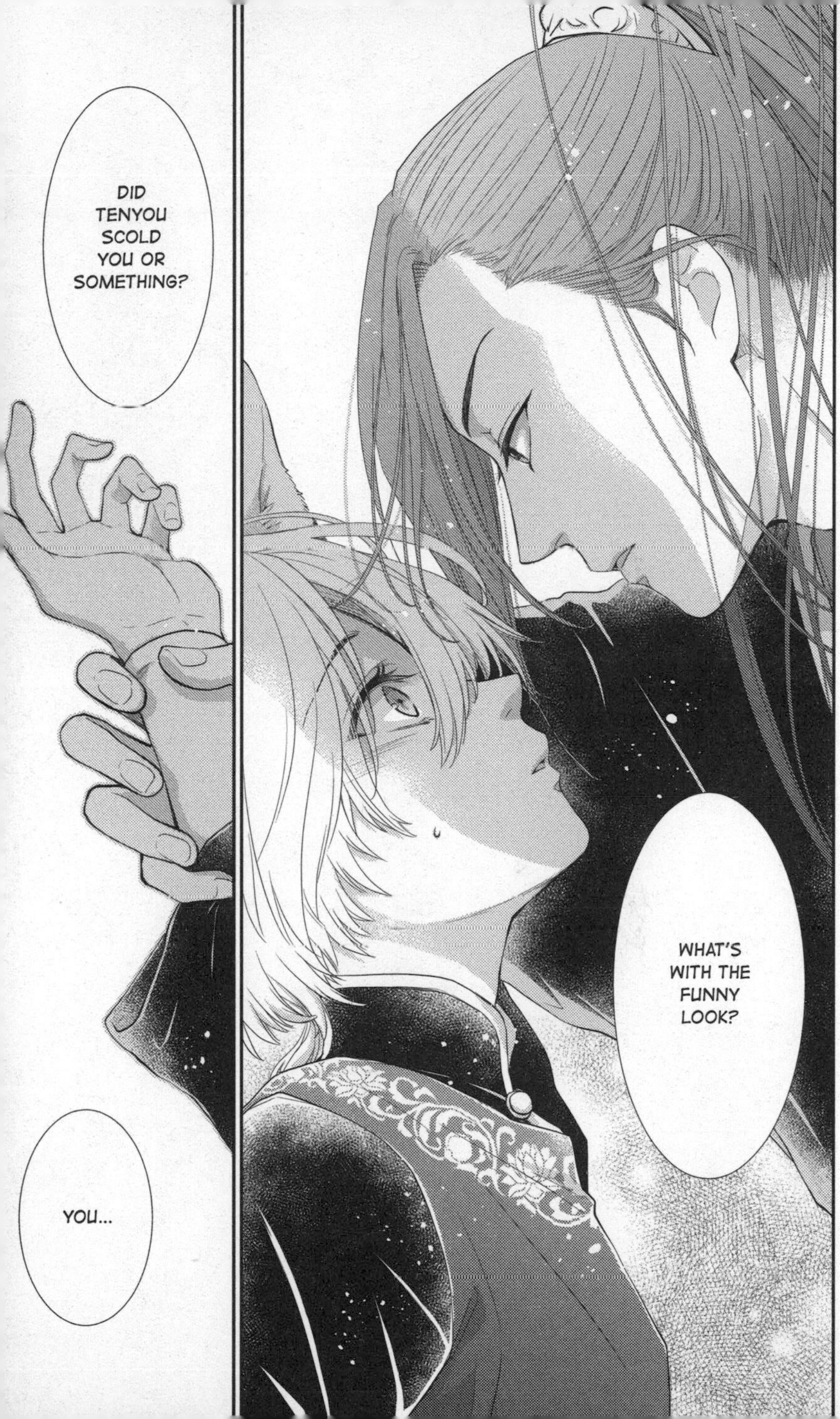
WHAT'S WITH THE FUNNY LOOK?
DID TENYOU SCOLD YOU OR SOMETHING?
YOU...

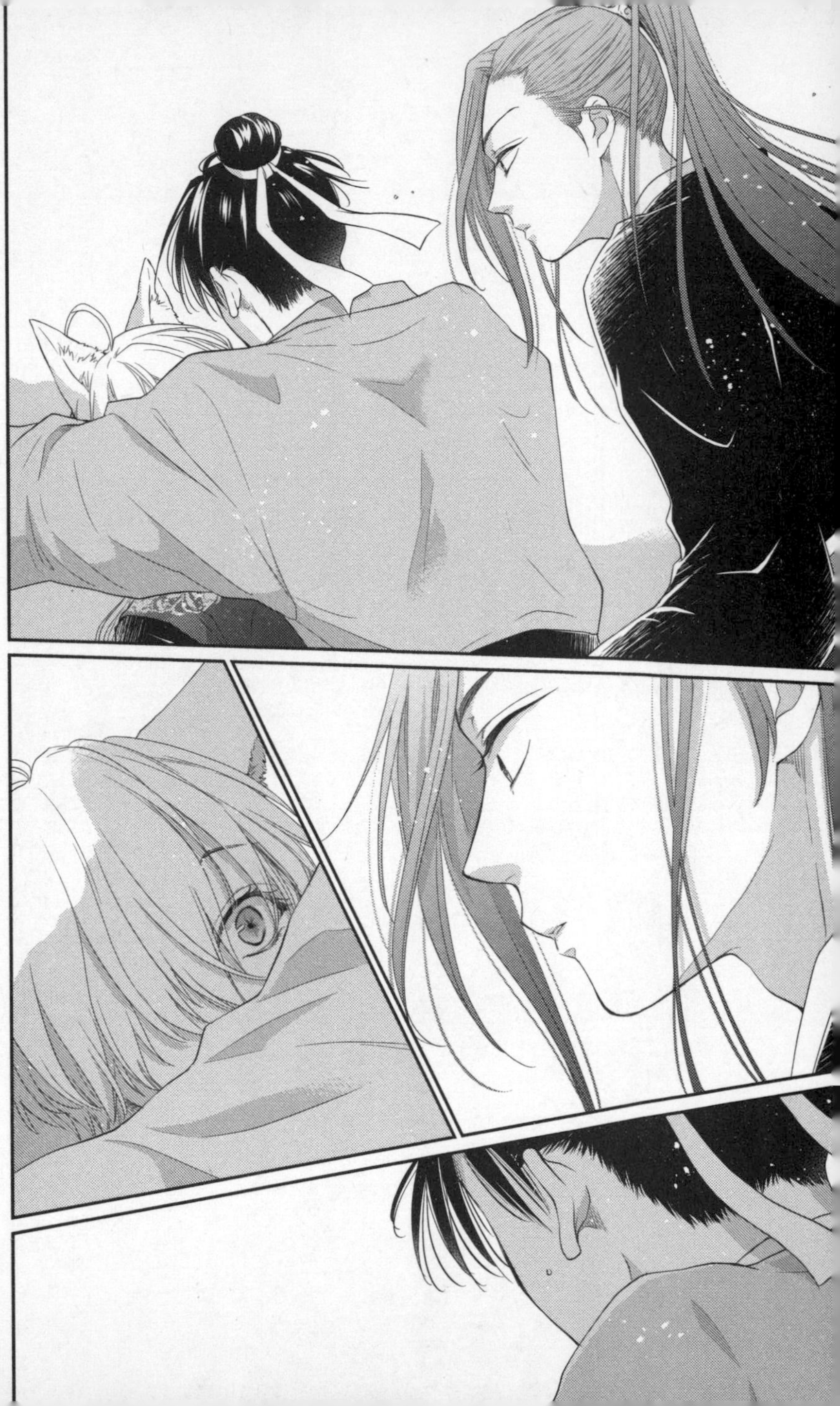

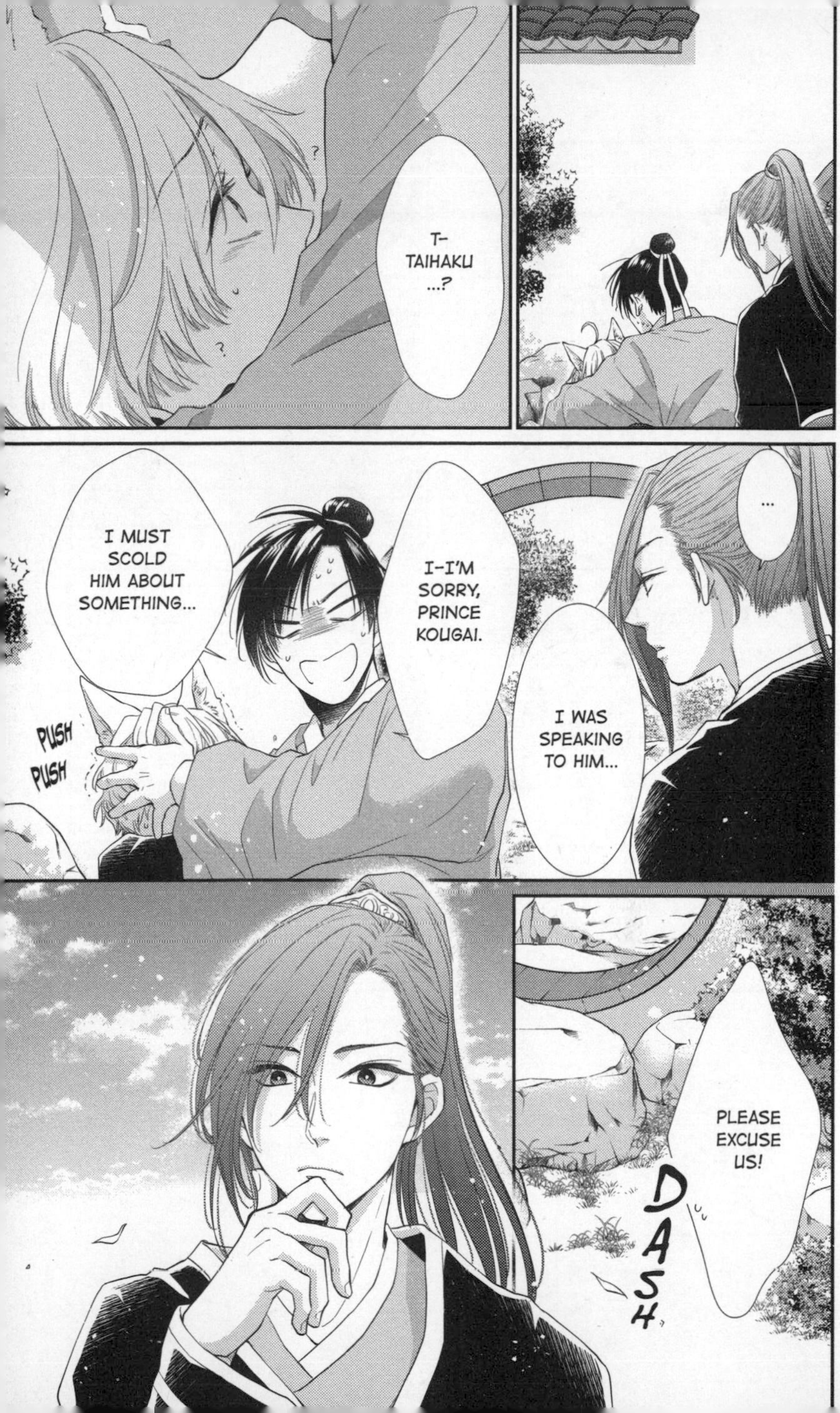
T- TAIHAKU ...?
...
I WAS SPEAKING TO HIM...
I-I'M SORRY, PRINCE KOUGAI.
I MUST SCOLD HIM ABOUT SOMETHING...
PUSH PUSH
PLEASE EXCUSE US!
DASH

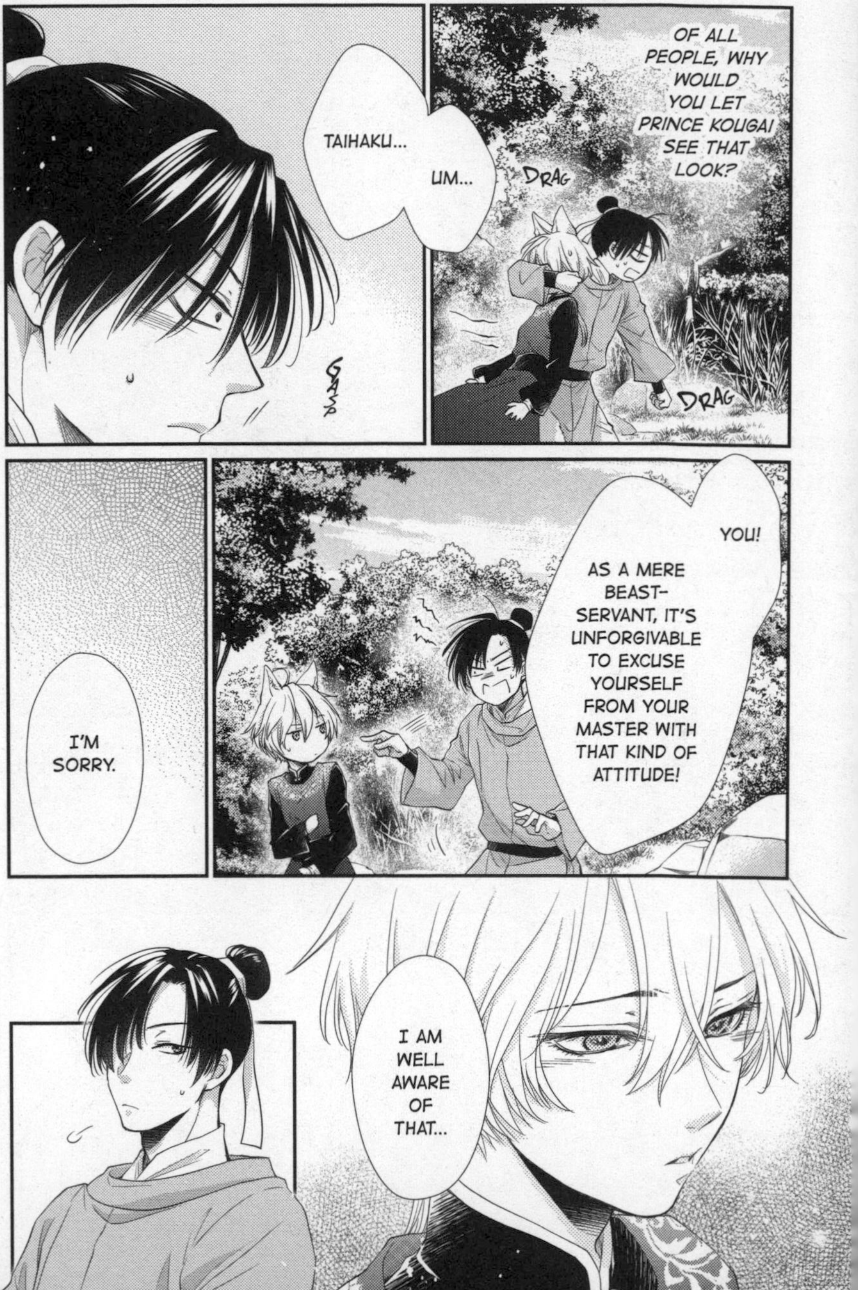
OF ALL PEOPLE, WHY WOULD YOU LET PRINCE KOUGAI SEE THAT LOOK?
DRAG
DRAG
TAIHAKU...
UM...
GASP
YOU!
AS A MERE BEAST-SERVANT, IT'S UNFORGIVABLE TO EXCUSE YOURSELF FROM YOUR MASTER WITH THAT KIND OF ATTITUDE!
I'M SORRY.
I AM WELL AWARE OF THAT...

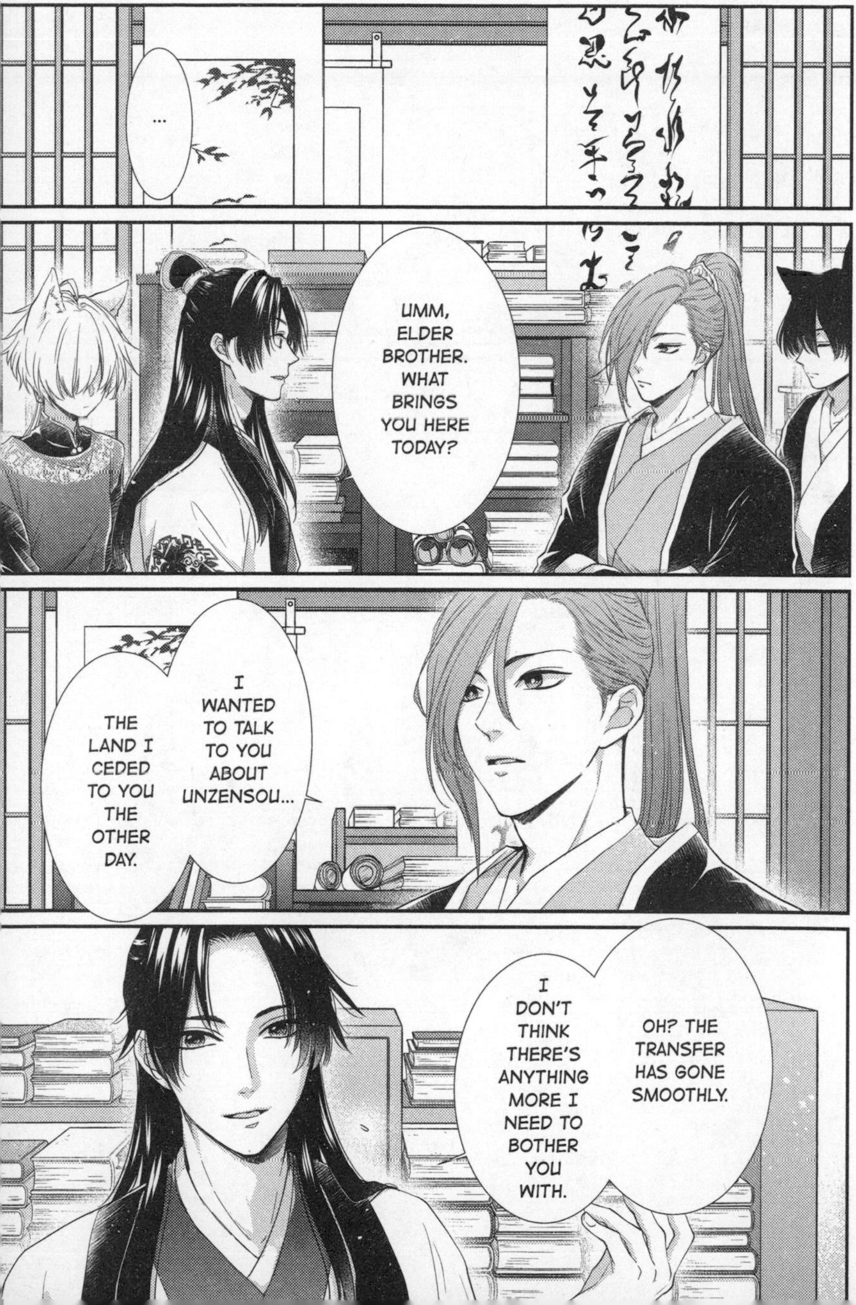
...
UMM, ELDER BROTHER. WHAT BRINGS YOU HERE TODAY?
I WANTED TO TALK TO YOU ABOUT UNZENSOU...
THE LAND I CEDED TO YOU THE OTHER DAY.
OH? THE TRANSFER HAS GONE SMOOTHLY.
I DON'T THINK THERE'S ANYTHING MORE I NEED TO BOTHER YOU WITH.

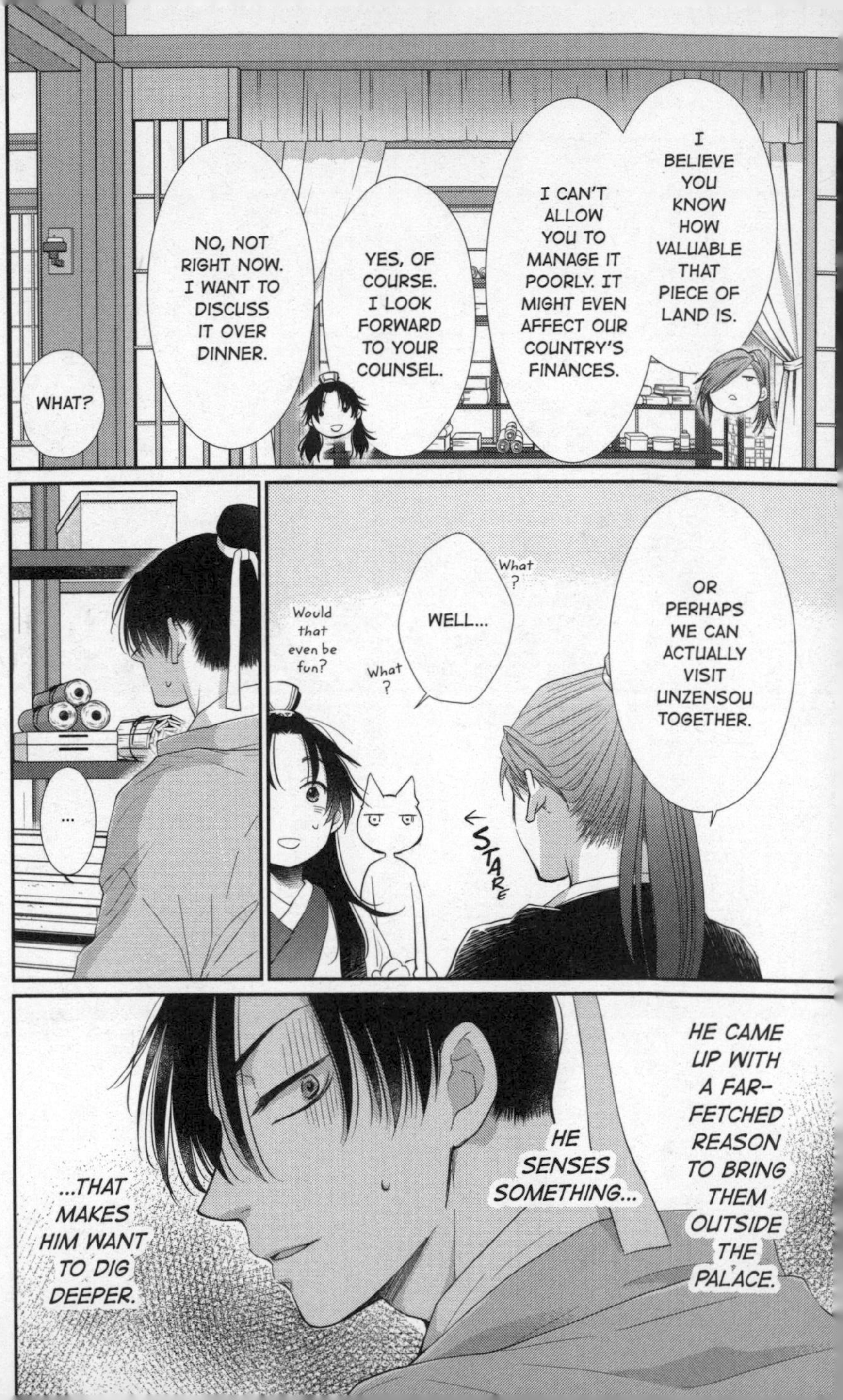
I BELIEVE YOU KNOW HOW VALUABLE THAT PIECE OF LAND IS.
I CAN'T ALLOW YOU TO MANAGE IT POORLY. IT MIGHT EVEN AFFECT OUR COUNTRY'S FINANCES.
YES, OF COURSE. I LOOK FORWARD TO YOUR COUNSEL.
NO, NOT RIGHT NOW. I WANT TO DISCUSS IT OVER DINNER.
WHAT?
OR PERHAPS WE CAN ACTUALLY VISIT UNZENSOU TOGETHER.
STARE
WELL...
What?
What?
Would that even be fun?
...
HE CAME UP WITH A FAR-FETCHED REASON TO BRING THEM OUTSIDE THE PALACE.
HE SENSES SOMETHING...
...THAT MAKES HIM WANT TO DIG DEEPER.

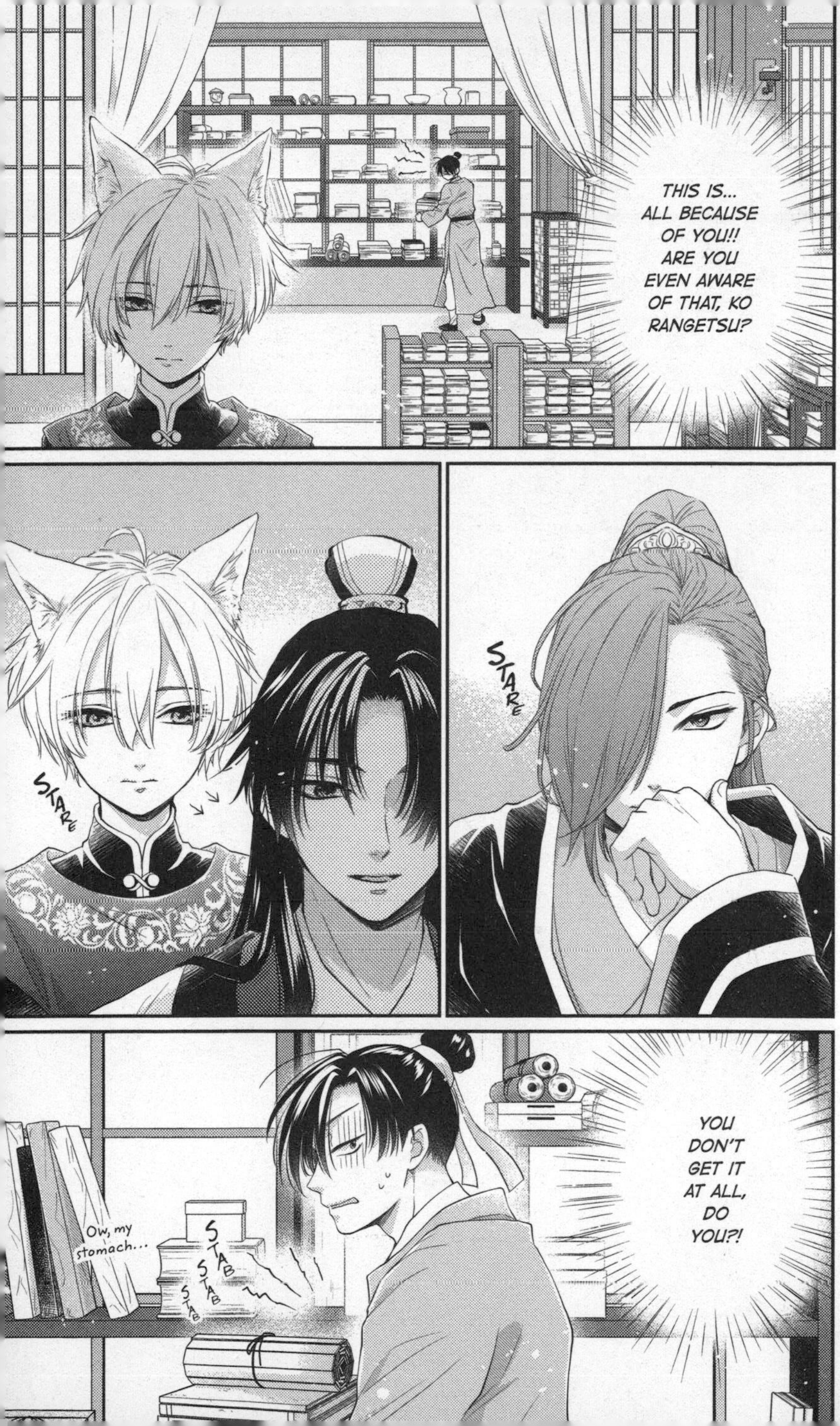
THIS IS... ALL BECAUSE OF YOU!! ARE YOU EVEN AWARE OF THAT, KO RANGETSU?
STARE
STARE
YOU DON'T GET IT AT ALL, DO YOU?!
STAB STAB STAB
Ow, my stomach...

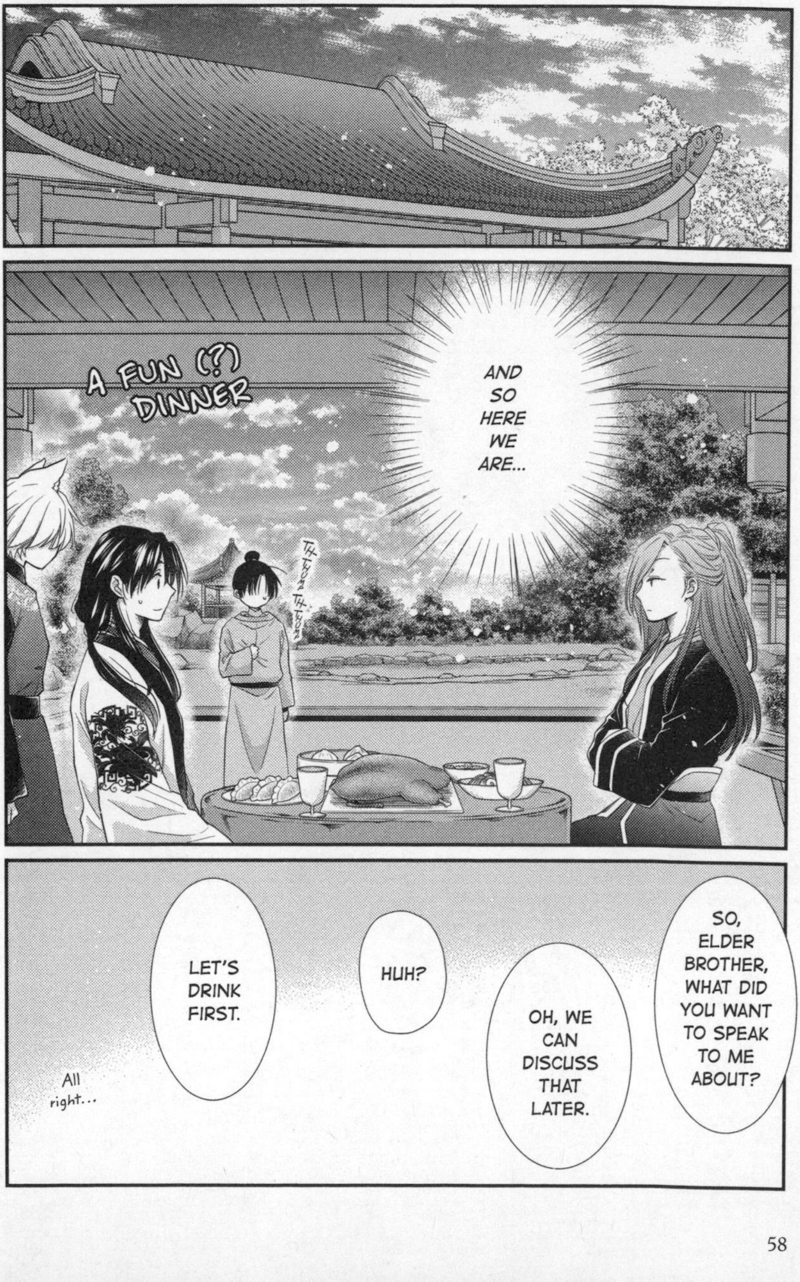
AND SO HERE WE ARE...
A FUN (?) DINNER
SO, ELDER BROTHER, WHAT DID YOU WANT TO SPEAK TO ME ABOUT?
OH, WE CAN DISCUSS THAT LATER.
HUH?
LET'S DRINK FIRST.
All right...

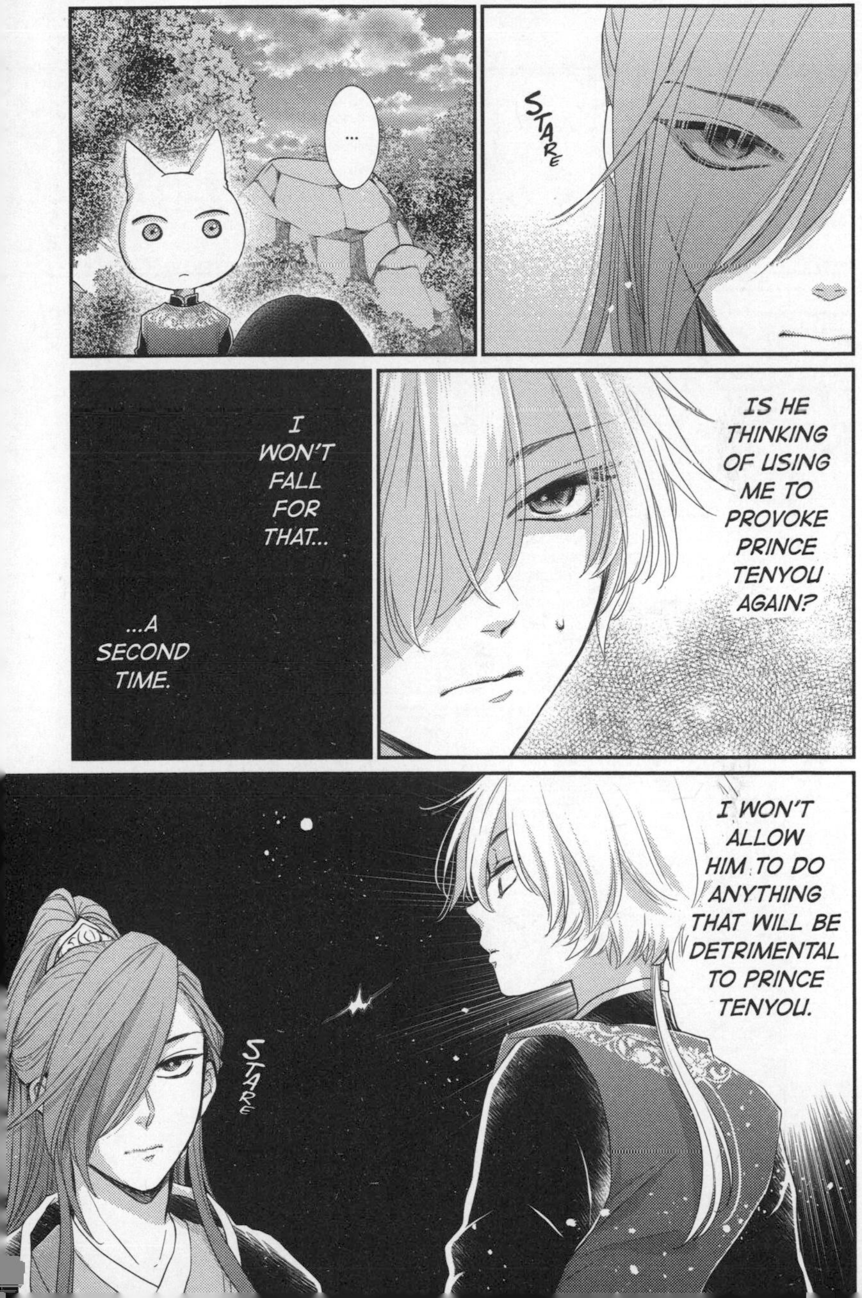
STARE
...
IS HE THINKING OF USING ME TO PROVOKE PRINCE TENYOU AGAIN?
I WON'T FALL FOR THAT...
...A SECOND TIME.
I WON'T ALLOW HIM TO DO ANYTHING THAT WILL BE DETRIMENTAL TO PRINCE TENYOU.
STARE

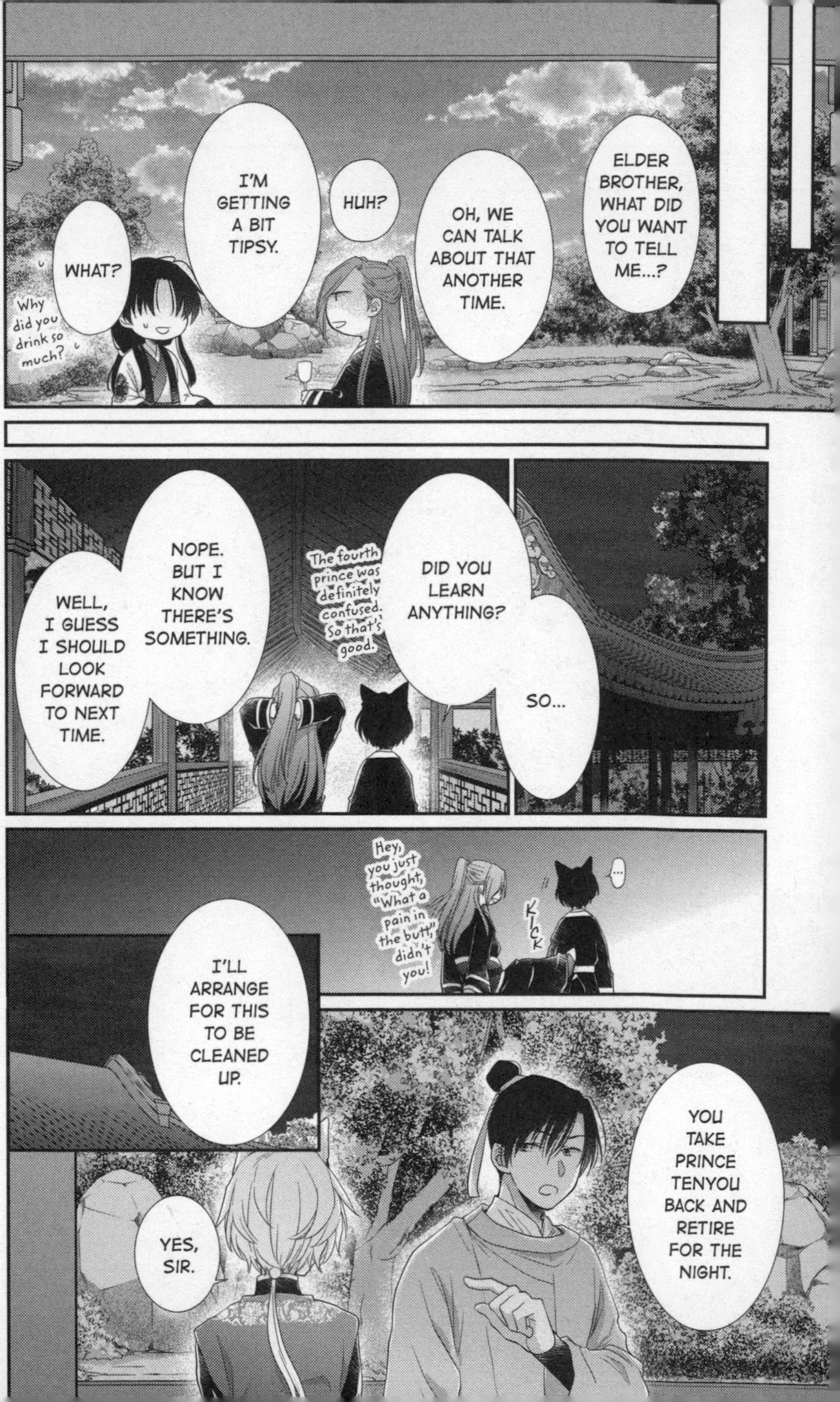
ELDER BROTHER, WHAT DID YOU WANT TO TELL ME...?
OH, WE CAN TALK ABOUT THAT ANOTHER TIME.
HUH?
I'M GETTING A BIT TIPSY.
WHAT?
Why did you drink so much?
SO...
DID YOU LEARN ANYTHING?
The fourth prince was definitely confused. So that's good.
NOPE. BUT I KNOW THERE'S SOMETHING.
WELL, I GUESS I SHOULD LOOK FORWARD TO NEXT TIME.
...
KICK
Hey, you just thought, "What a pain in the butt," didn't you!
I'LL ARRANGE FOR THIS TO BE CLEANED UP.
YOU TAKE PRINCE TENYOU BACK AND RETIRE FOR THE NIGHT.
YES, SIR.

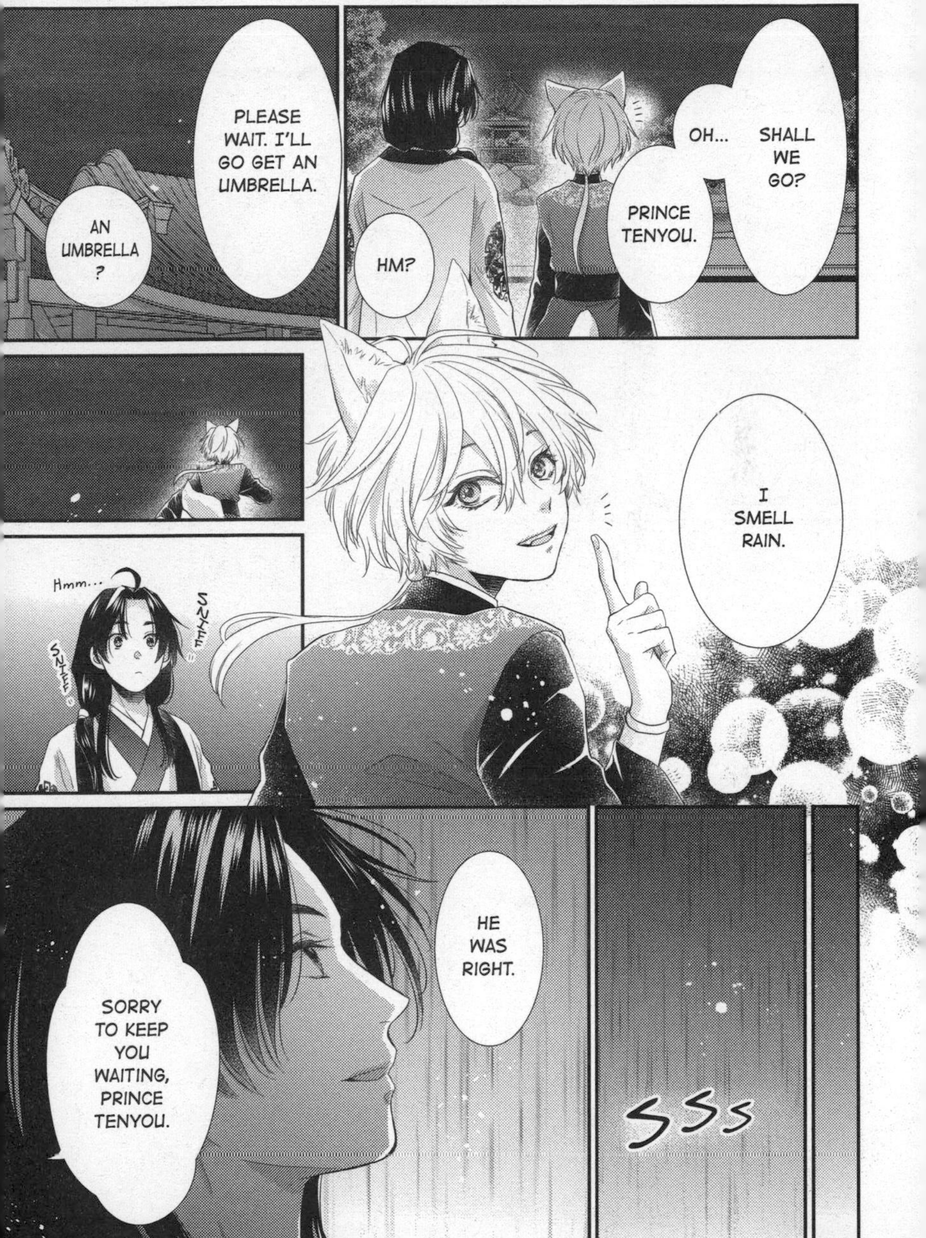
SHALL WE GO?
OH...
PRINCE TENYOU.
HM?
PLEASE WAIT. I'LL GO GET AN UMBRELLA.
AN UMBRELLA?
I SMELL RAIN.
Hmm...
SNIFF
SNIFF
SSS
HE WAS RIGHT.
SORRY TO KEEP YOU WAITING, PRINCE TENYOU.

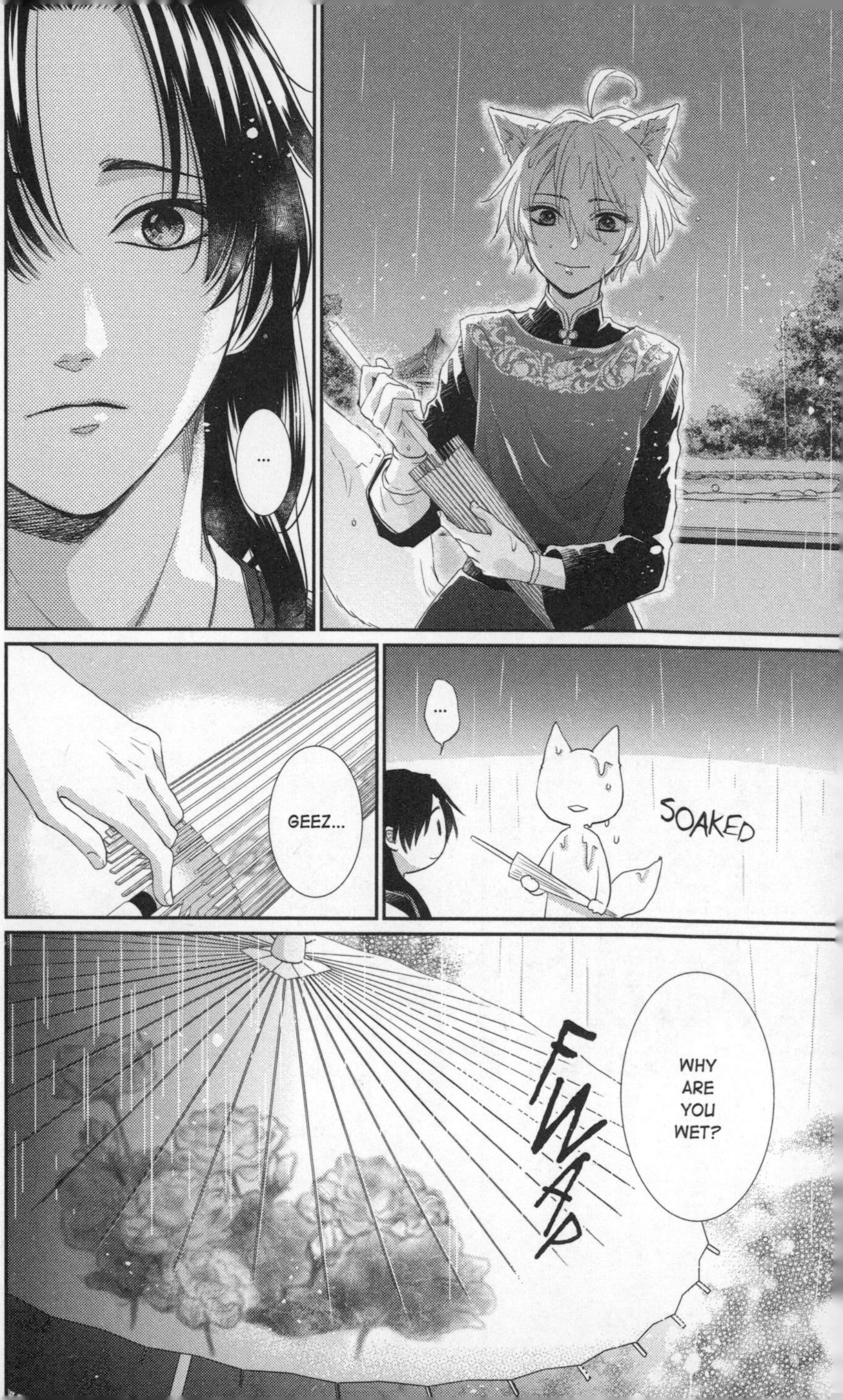
...
...
SOAKED
GEEZ...
WHY ARE YOU WET?
FWAP

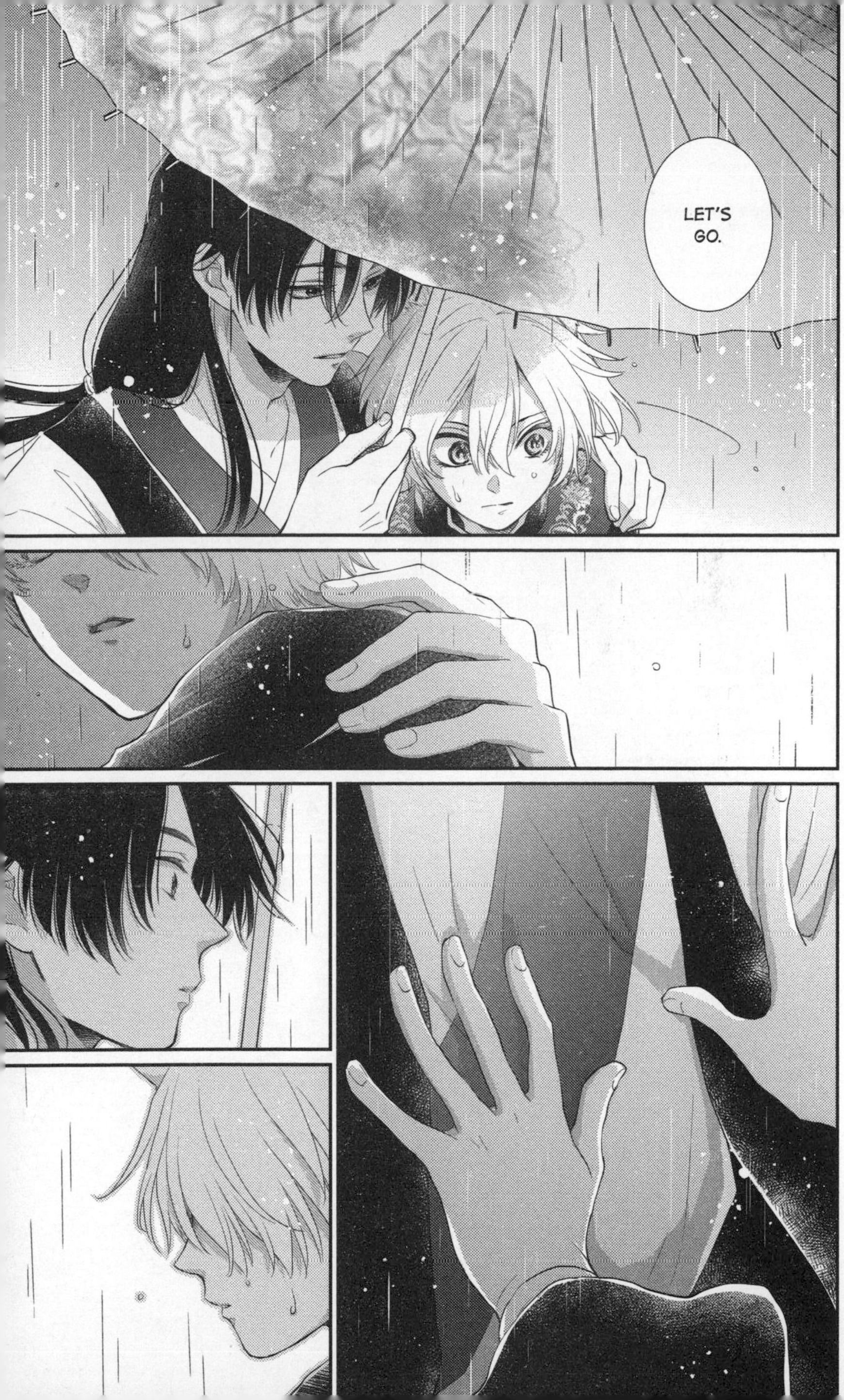
LET'S GO.

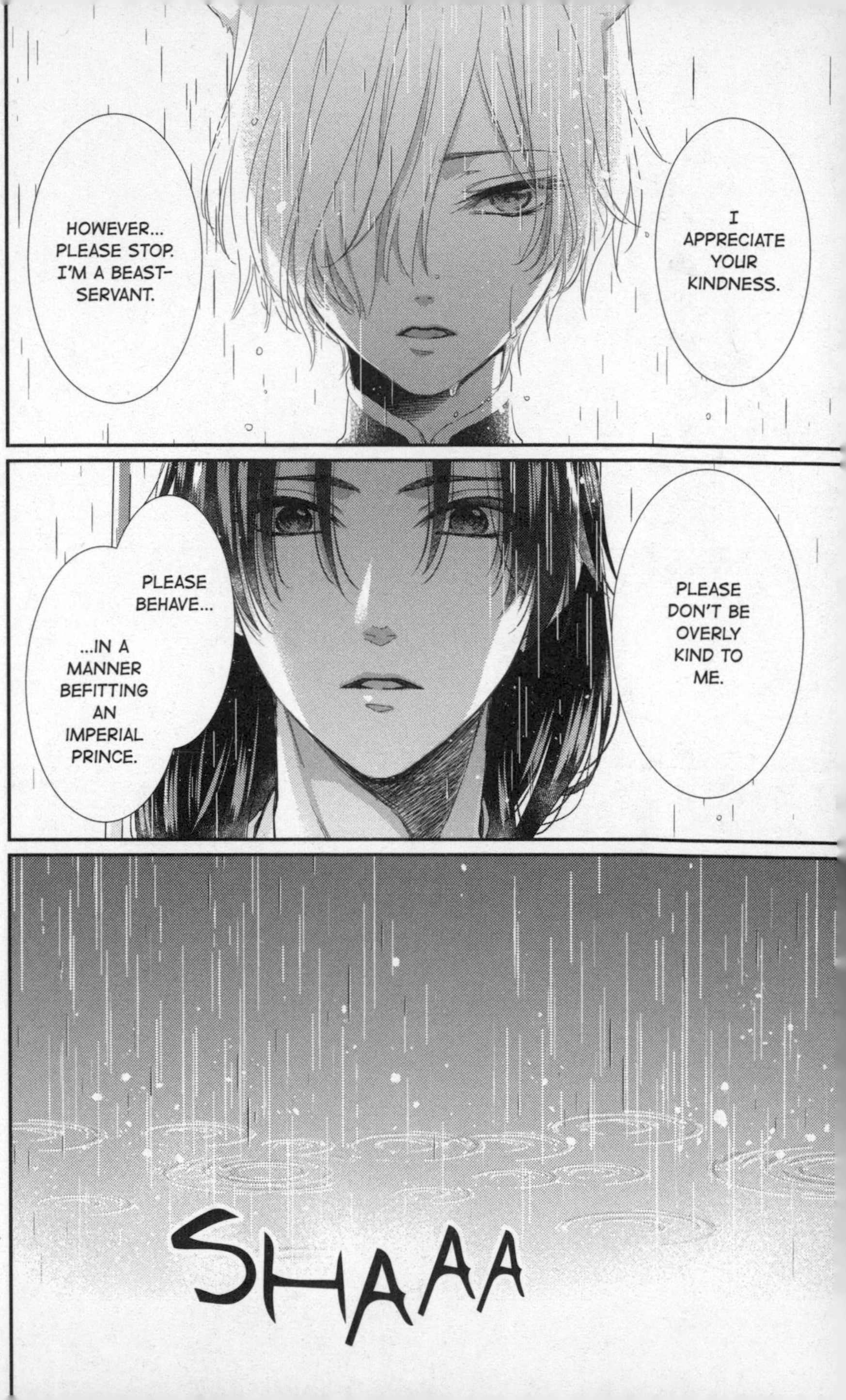
I APPRECIATE YOUR KINDNESS.
HOWEVER... PLEASE STOP. I'M A BEAST-SERVANT.
PLEASE DON'T BE OVERLY KIND TO ME.
PLEASE BEHAVE...
...IN A MANNER BEFITTING AN IMPERIAL PRINCE.
SHAAA

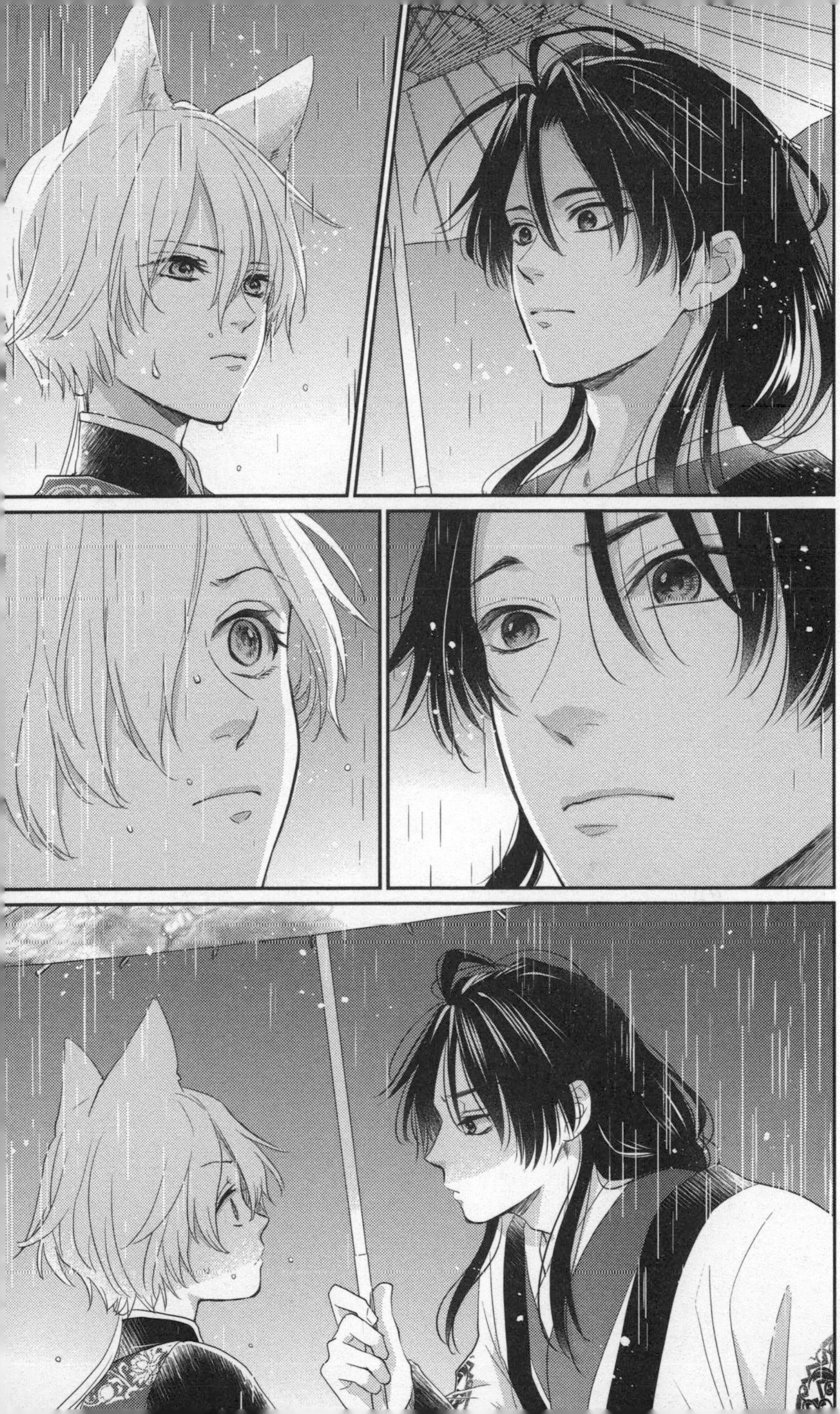

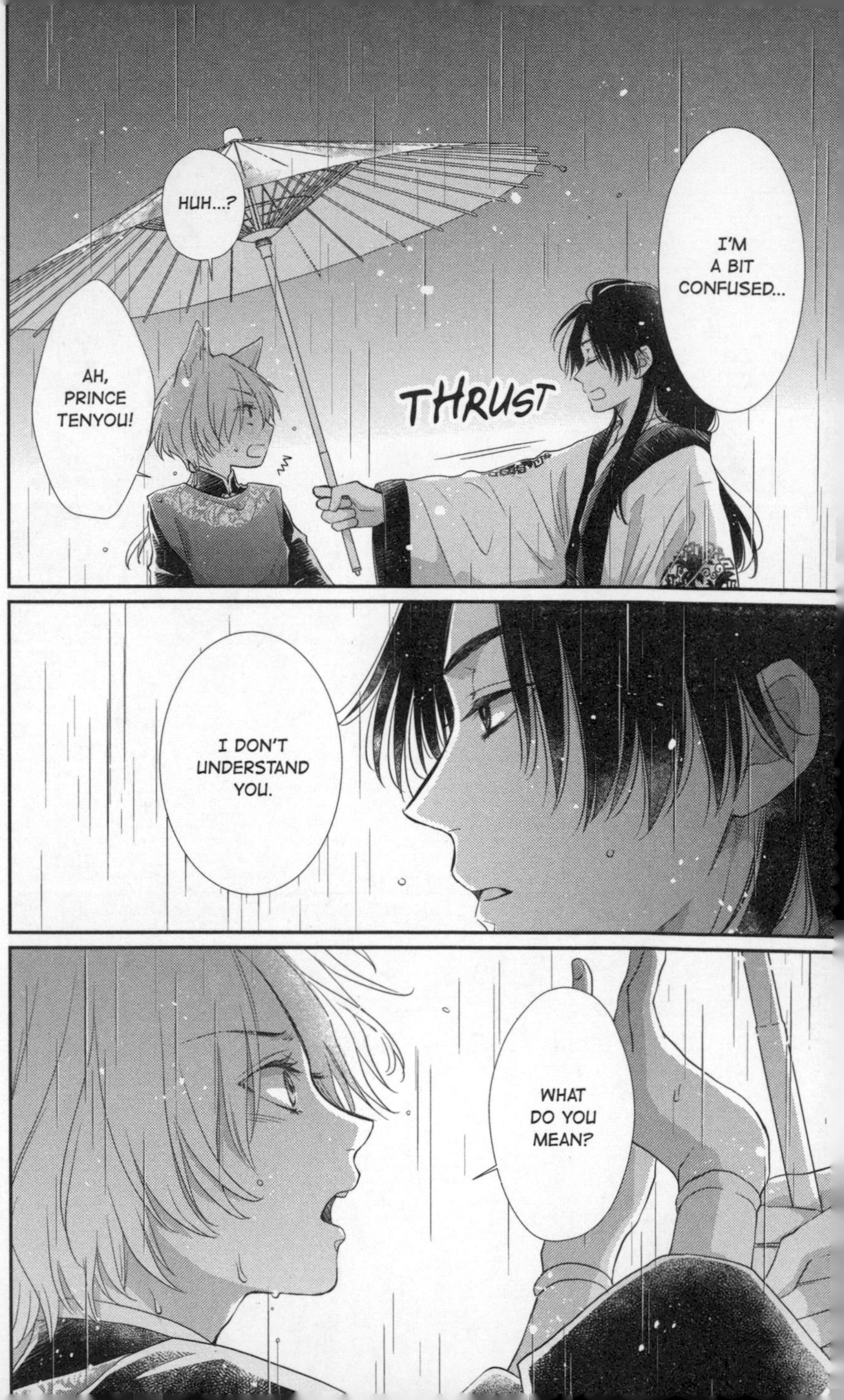
I'M A BIT CONFUSED...
HUH...?
THRUST
AH, PRINCE TENYOU!
I DON'T UNDERSTAND YOU.
WHAT DO YOU MEAN?

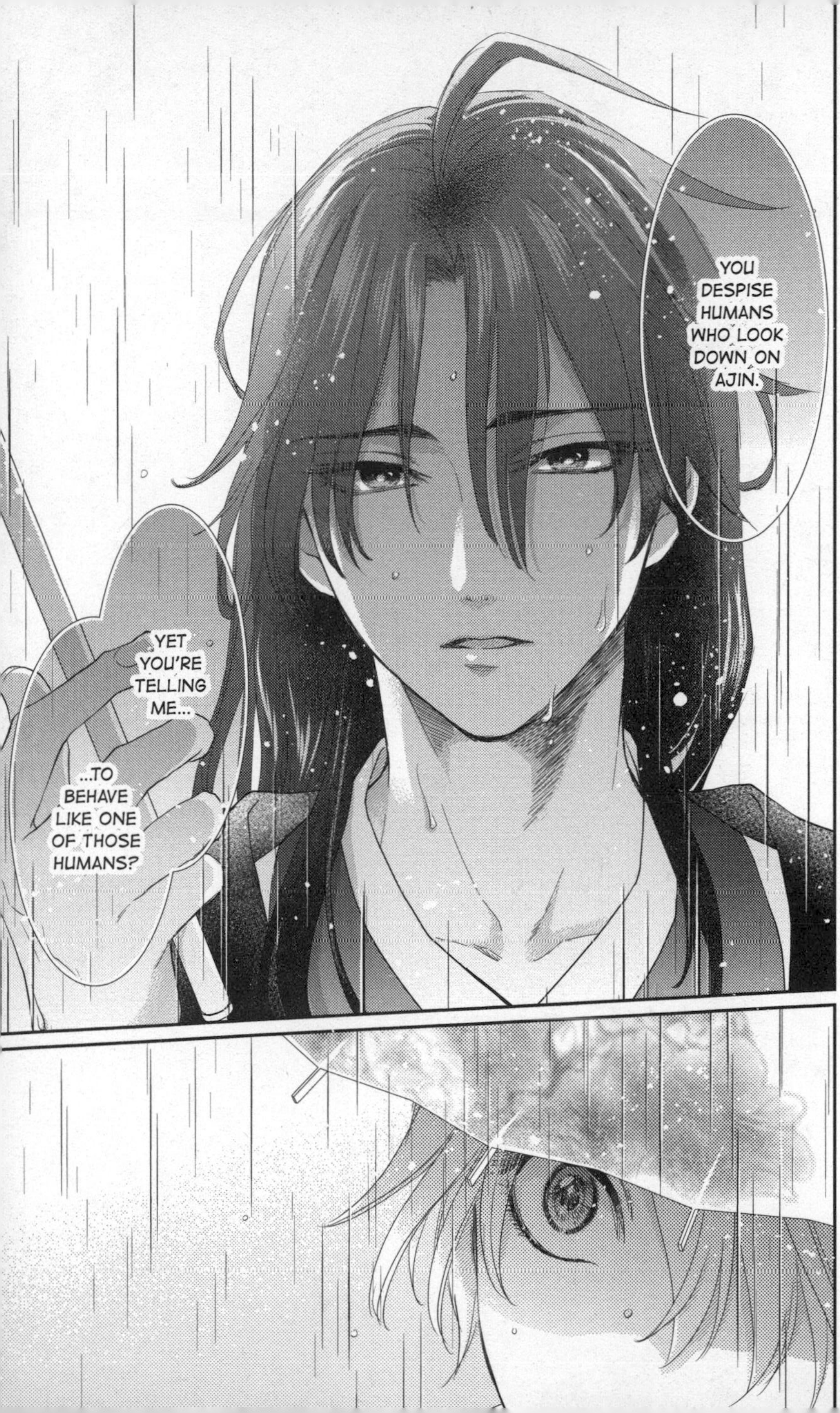
YOU DESPISE HUMANS WHO LOOK DOWN ON AJIN.
YET YOU'RE TELLING ME...
...TO BEHAVE LIKE ONE OF THOSE HUMANS?

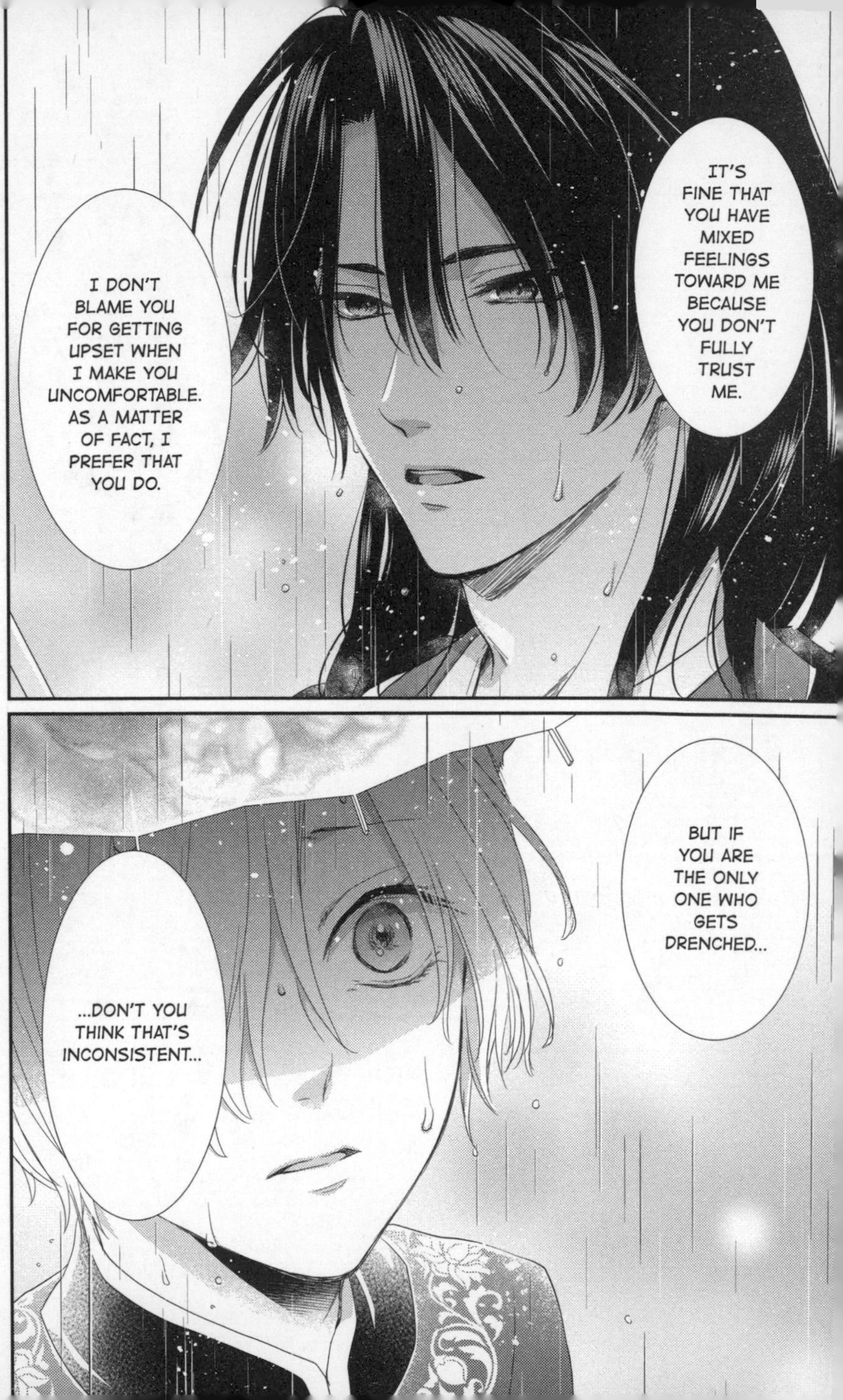
IT'S FINE THAT YOU HAVE MIXED FEELINGS TOWARD ME BECAUSE YOU DON'T FULLY TRUST ME.
I DON'T BLAME YOU FOR GETTING UPSET WHEN I MAKE YOU UNCOMFORTABLE. AS A MATTER OF FACT, I PREFER THAT YOU DO.
BUT IF YOU ARE THE ONLY ONE WHO GETS DRENCHED...
...DON'T YOU THINK THAT'S INCONSISTENT...

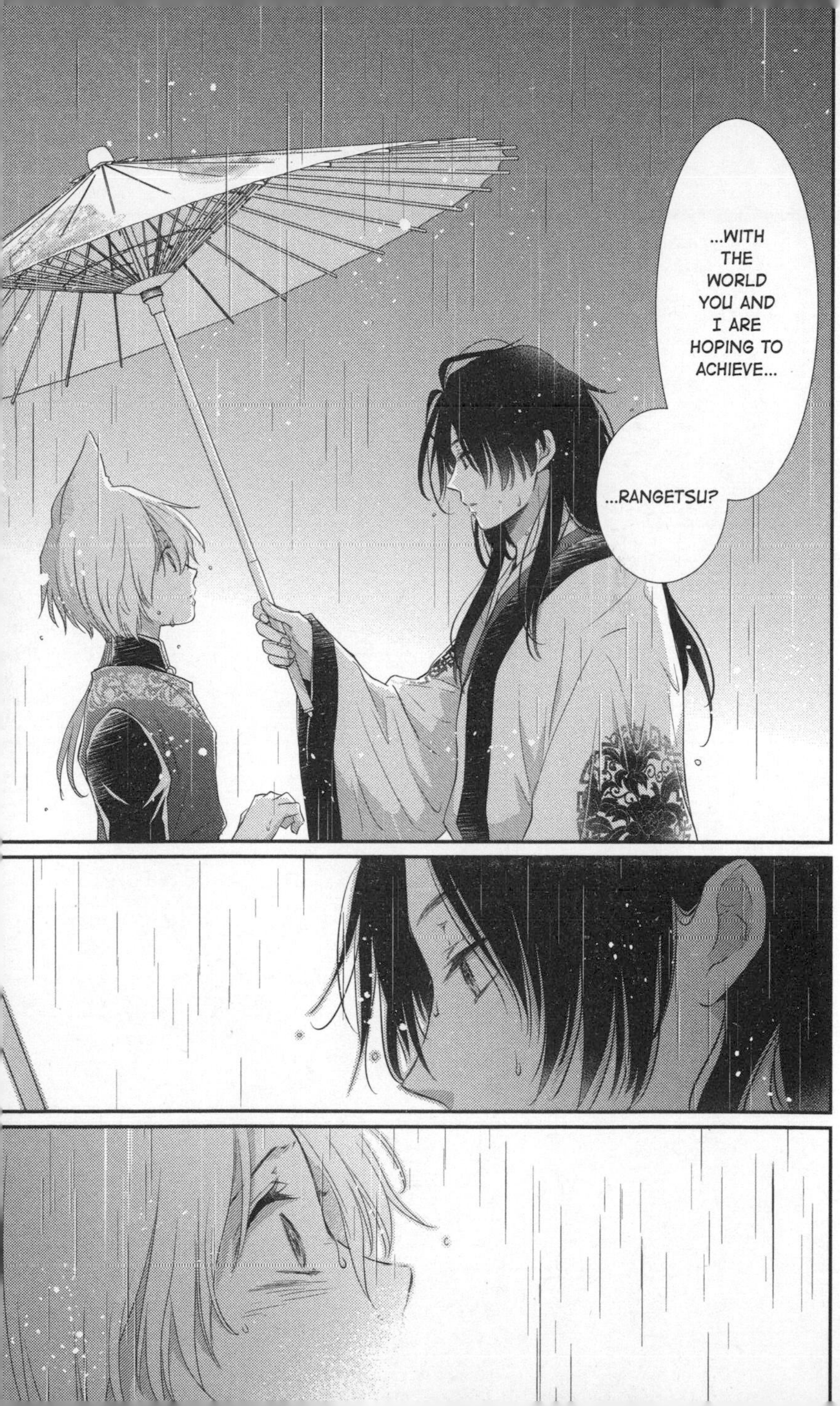
...WITH THE WORLD YOU AND I ARE HOPING TO ACHIEVE...
...RANGETSU?

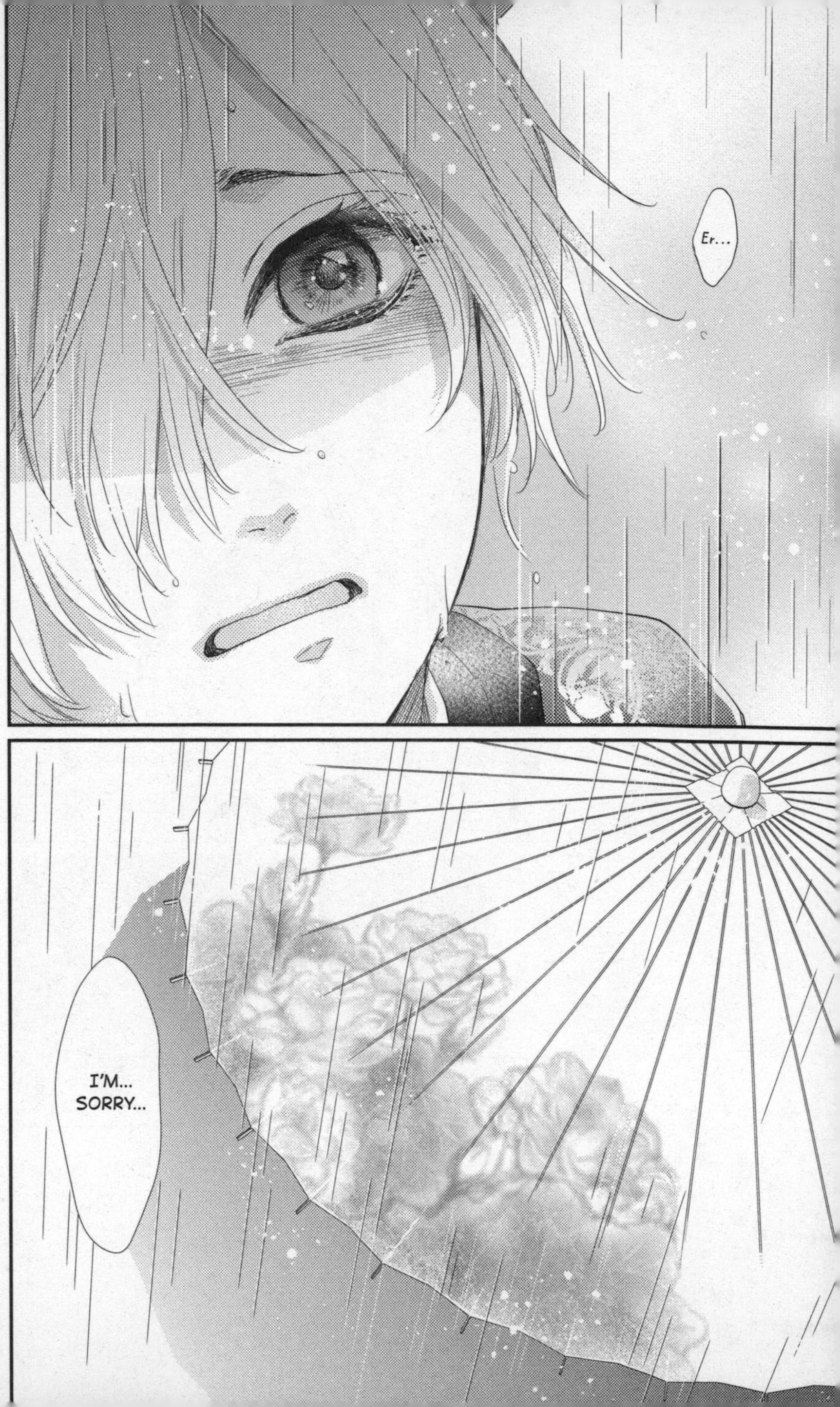
Er...
I'M... SORRY...

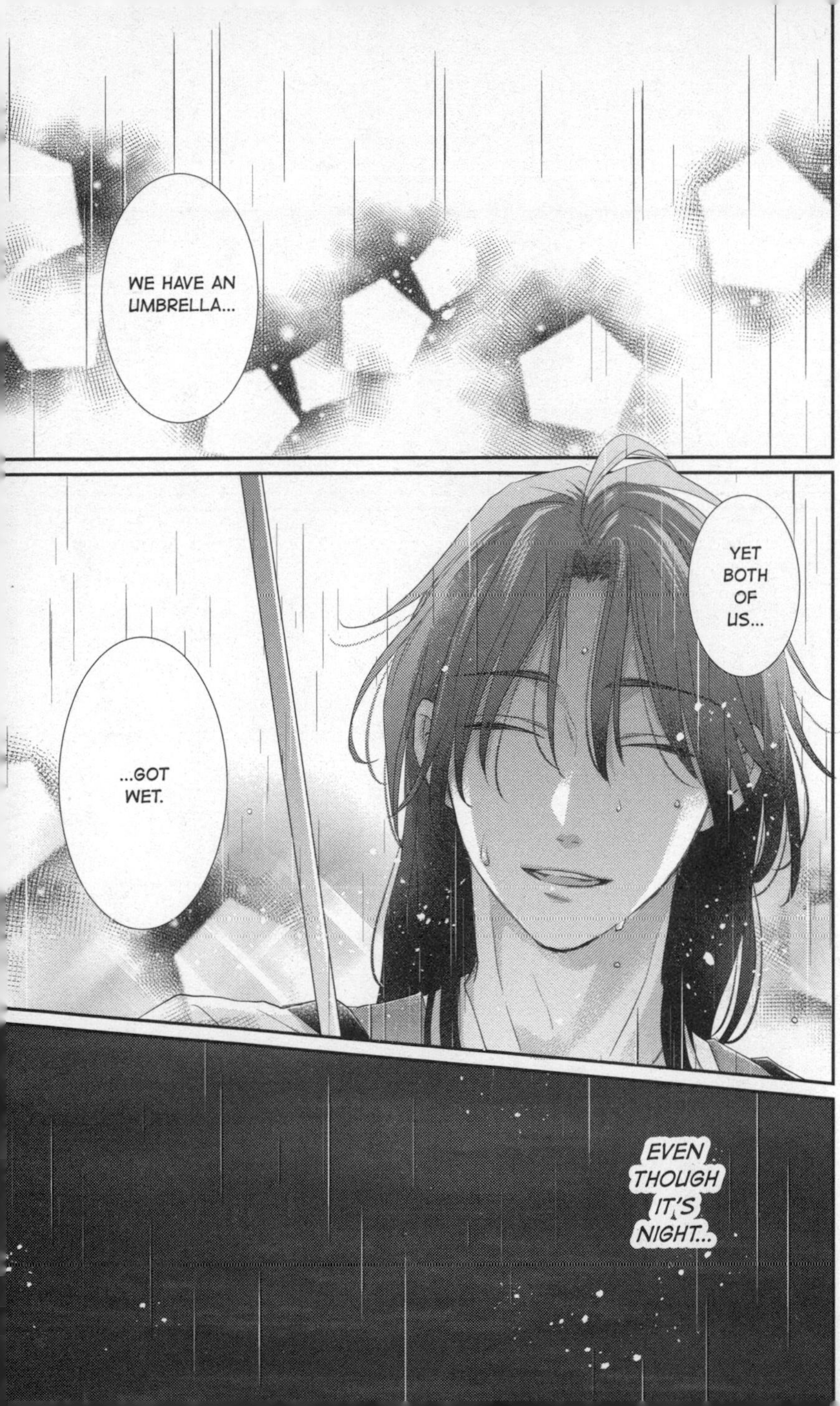
WE HAVE AN UMBRELLA...
YET BOTH OF US...
...GOT WET.
EVEN THOUGH IT'S NIGHT...

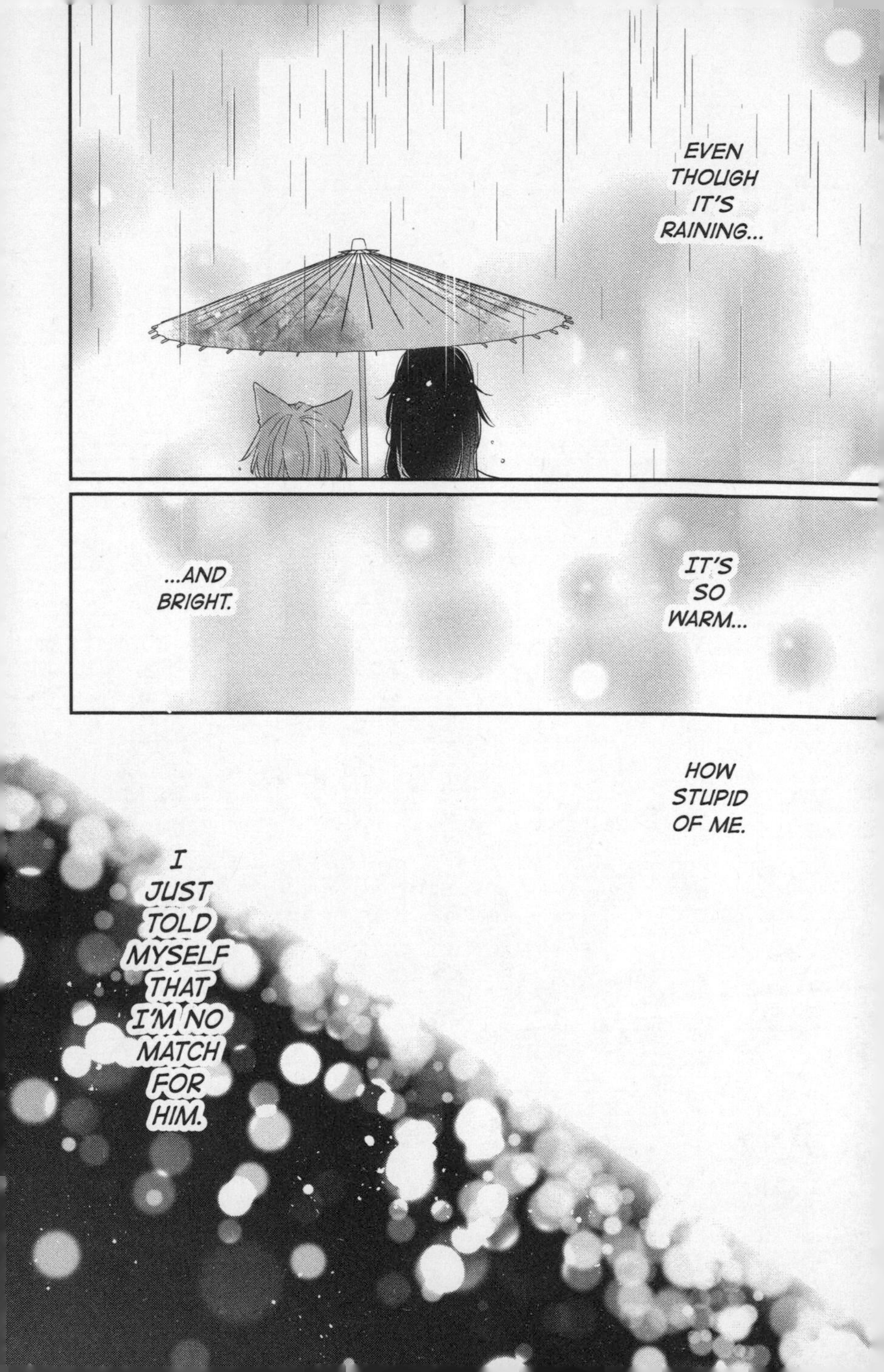
EVEN THOUGH IT'S RAINING...
IT'S SO WARM...
...AND BRIGHT.
HOW STUPID OF ME.
I JUST TOLD MYSELF THAT I'M NO MATCH FOR HIM.

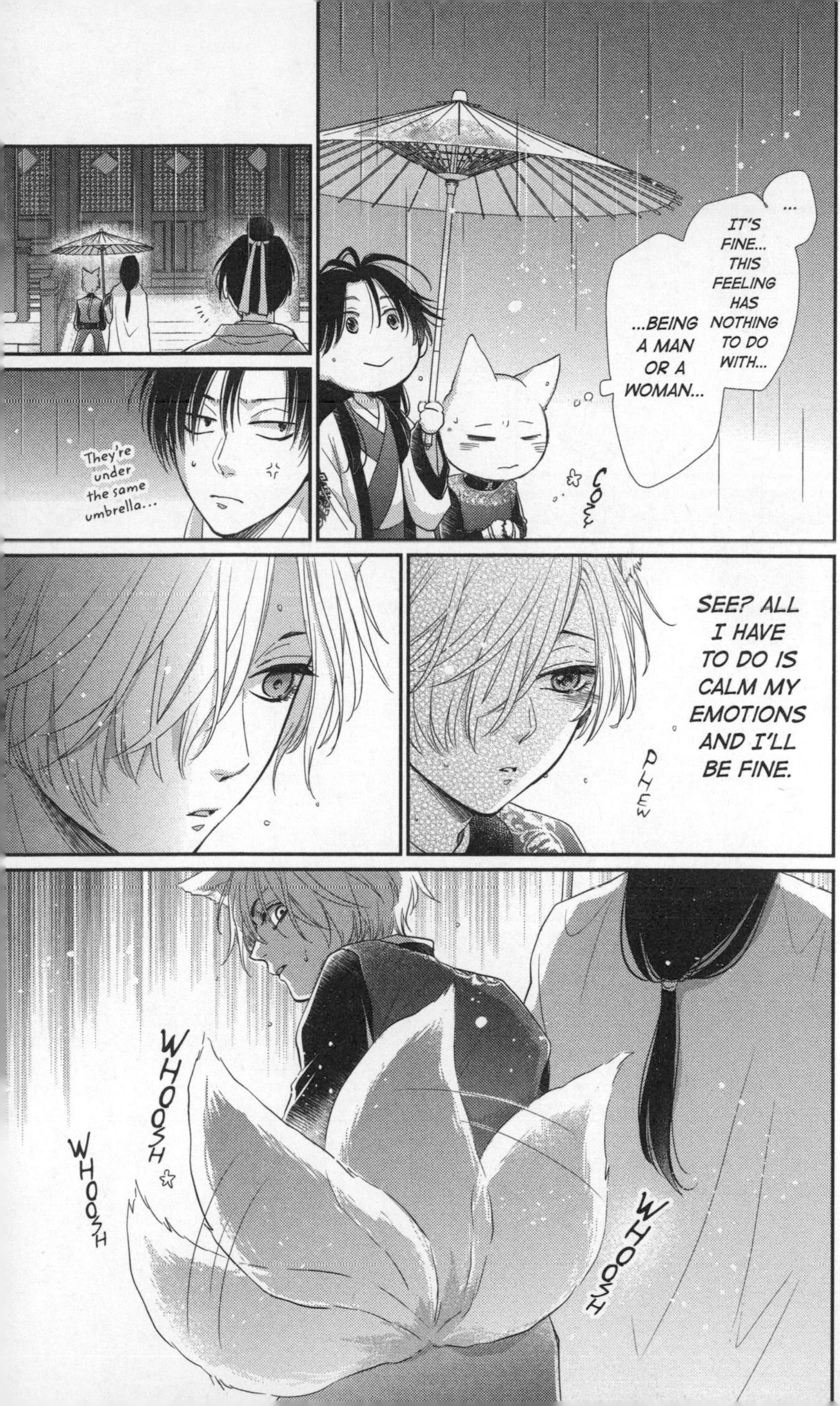
...
IT'S FINE... THIS FEELING HAS NOTHING TO DO WITH...
...BEING A MAN OR A WOMAN...
COZY
They're under the same umbrella...
SEE? ALL I HAVE TO DO IS CALM MY EMOTIONS AND I'LL BE FINE.
PHEW
WHOOSH
WHOOSH
WHOOSH

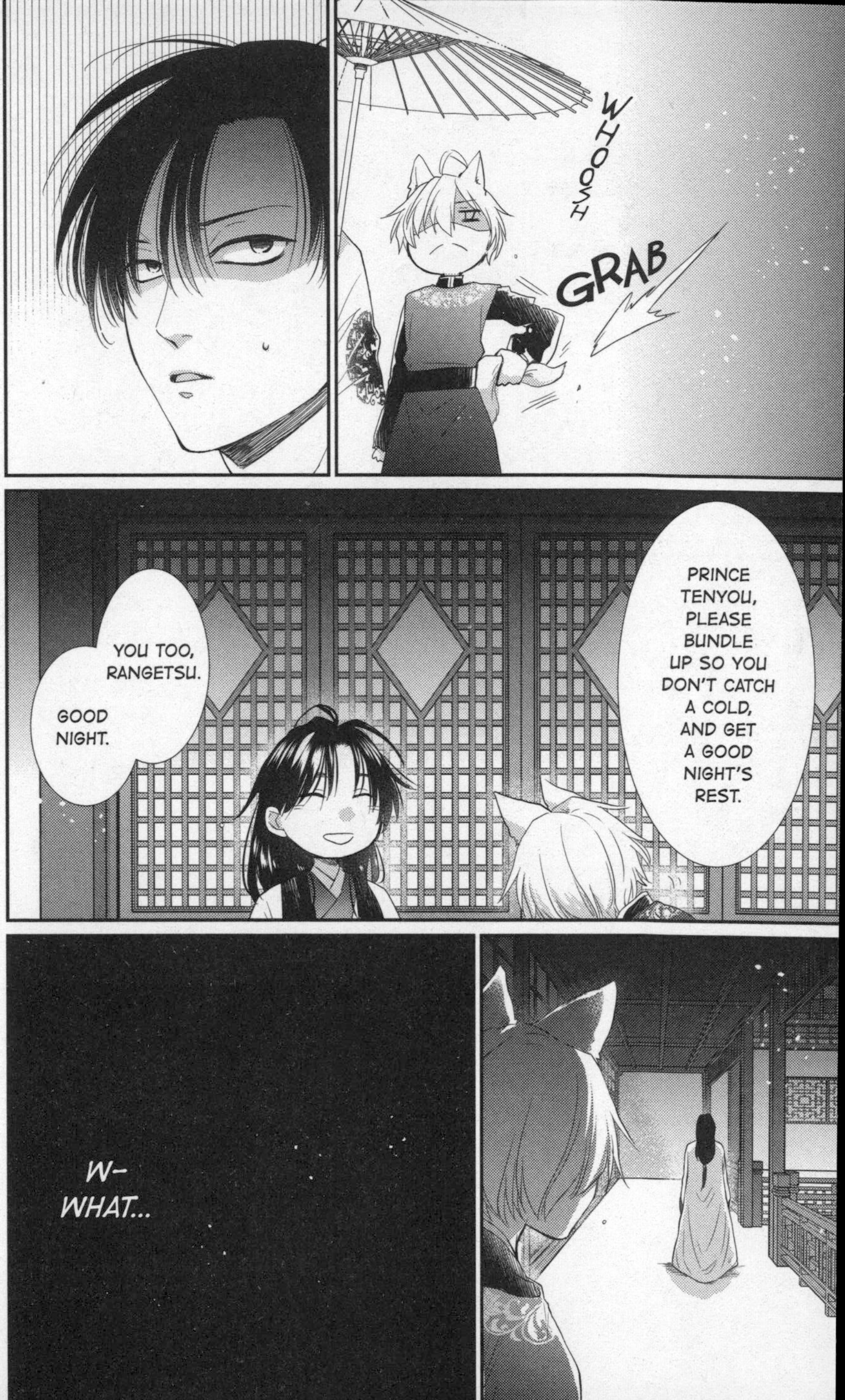
WHOOOSH
GRAB
PRINCE TENYOU, PLEASE BUNDLE UP SO YOU DON'T CATCH A COLD, AND GET A GOOD NIGHT'S REST.
YOU TOO, RANGETSU.
GOOD NIGHT.
W-WHAT...

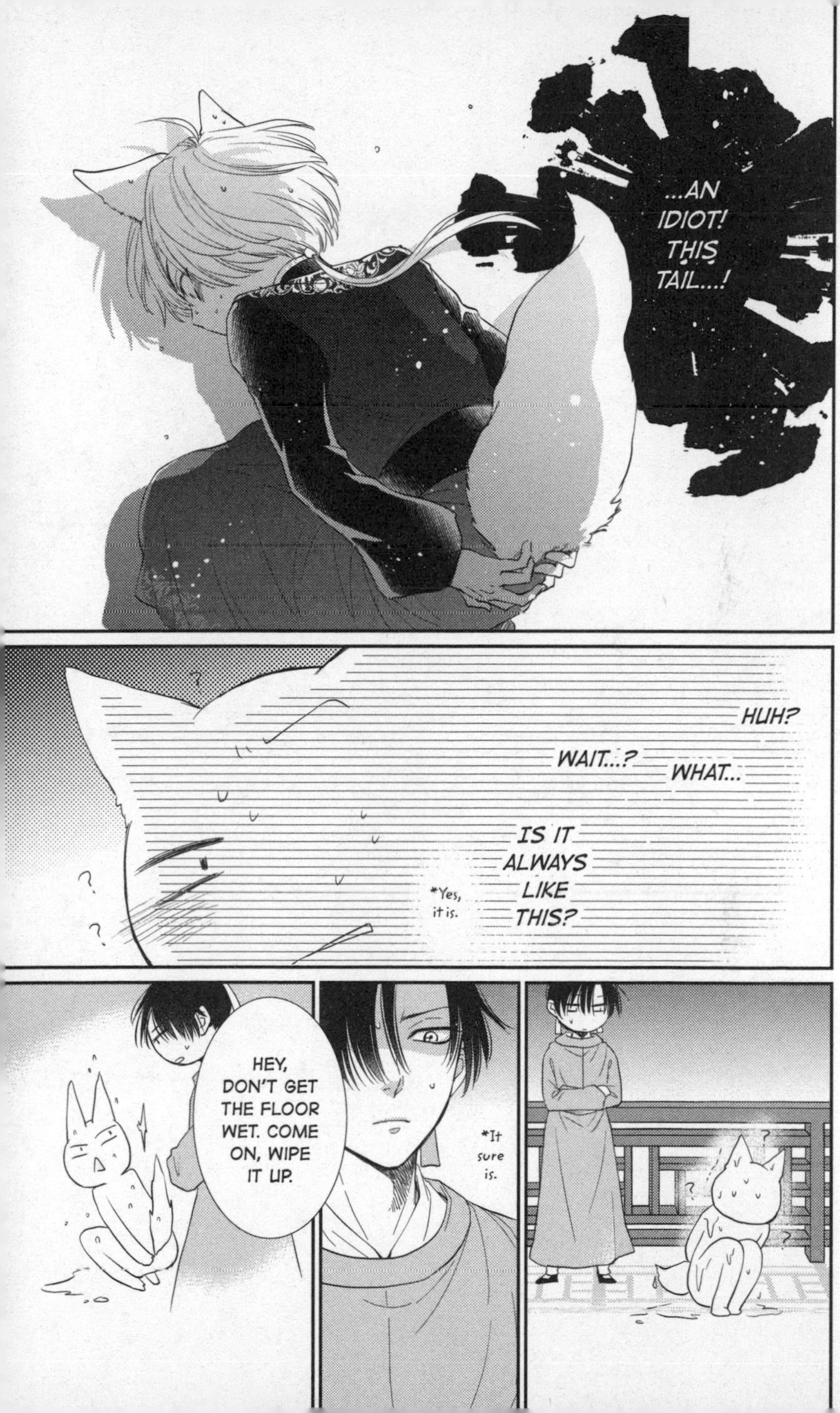
...AN IDIOT! THIS TAIL...!
HUH?
WHAT...
WAIT...?
IS IT ALWAYS LIKE THIS?
*Yes, it is.
*It sure is.
HEY, DON'T GET THE FLOOR WET. COME ON, WIPE IT UP.

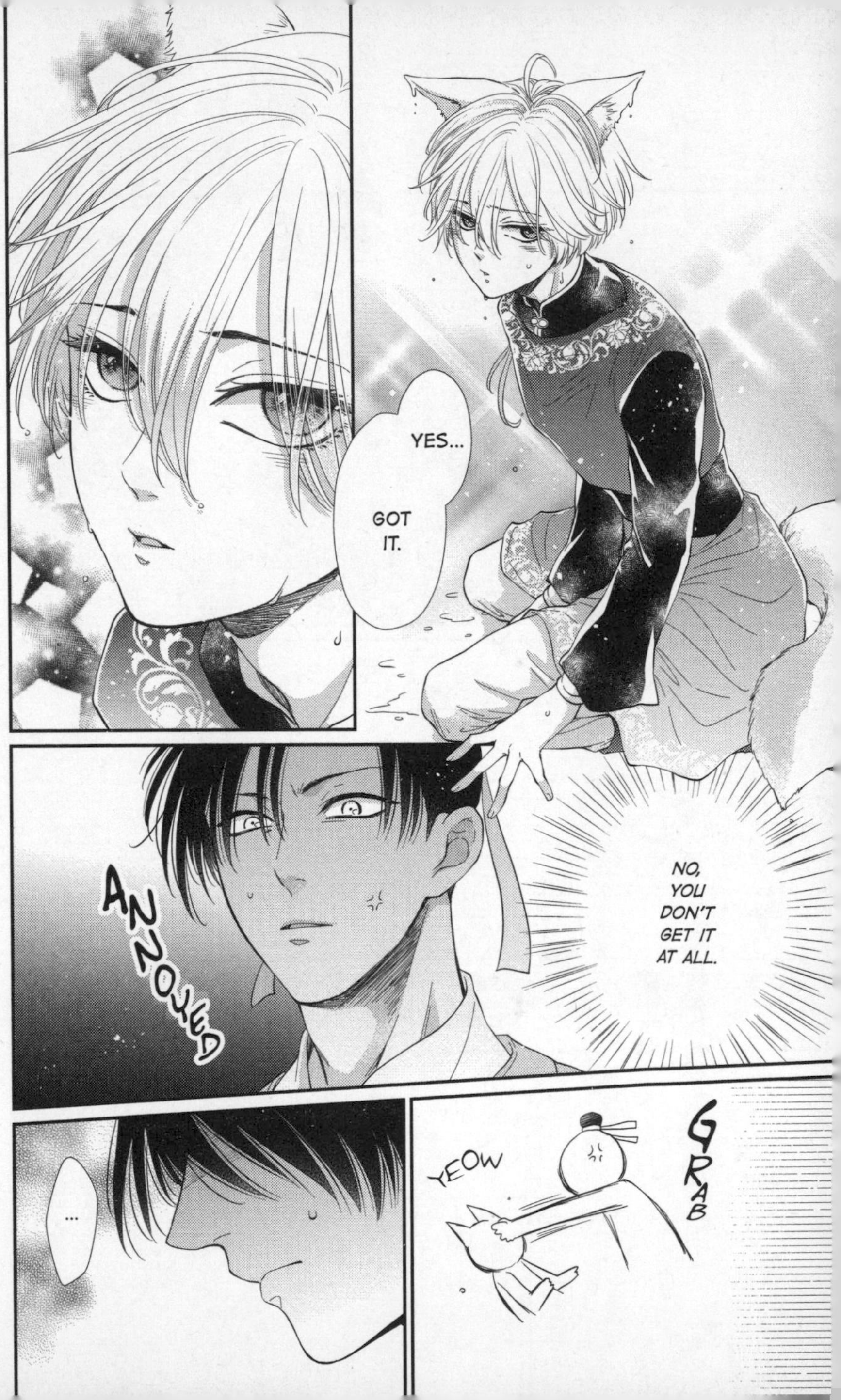
YES...
GOT IT.
NO, YOU DON'T GET IT AT ALL.
ANNOYED
GRAB
YEOW
...

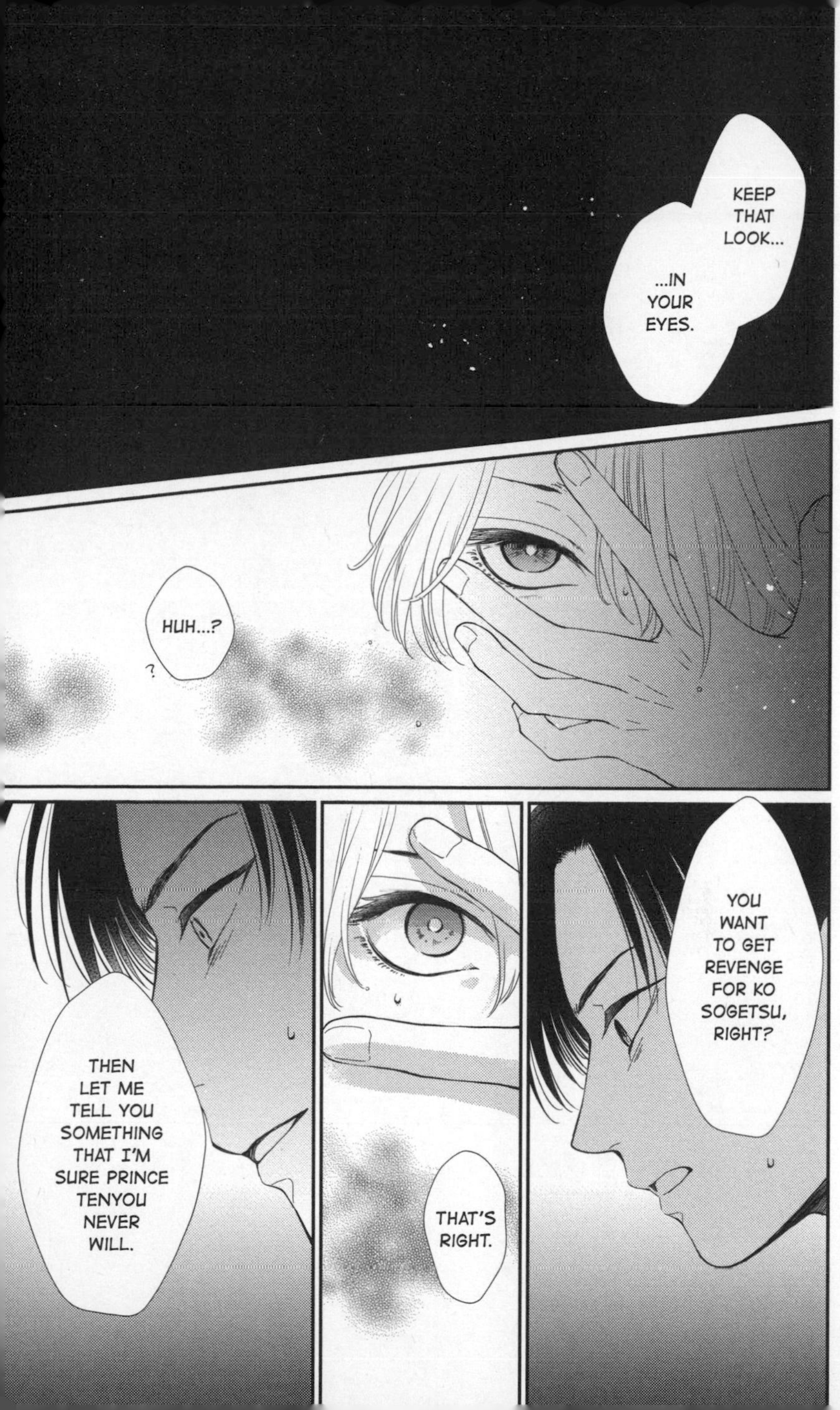
KEEP THAT LOOK...
...IN YOUR EYES.
HUH...?
?
YOU WANT TO GET REVENGE FOR KO SOGETSU, RIGHT?
THAT'S RIGHT.
THEN LET ME TELL YOU SOMETHING THAT I'M SURE PRINCE TENYOU NEVER WILL.

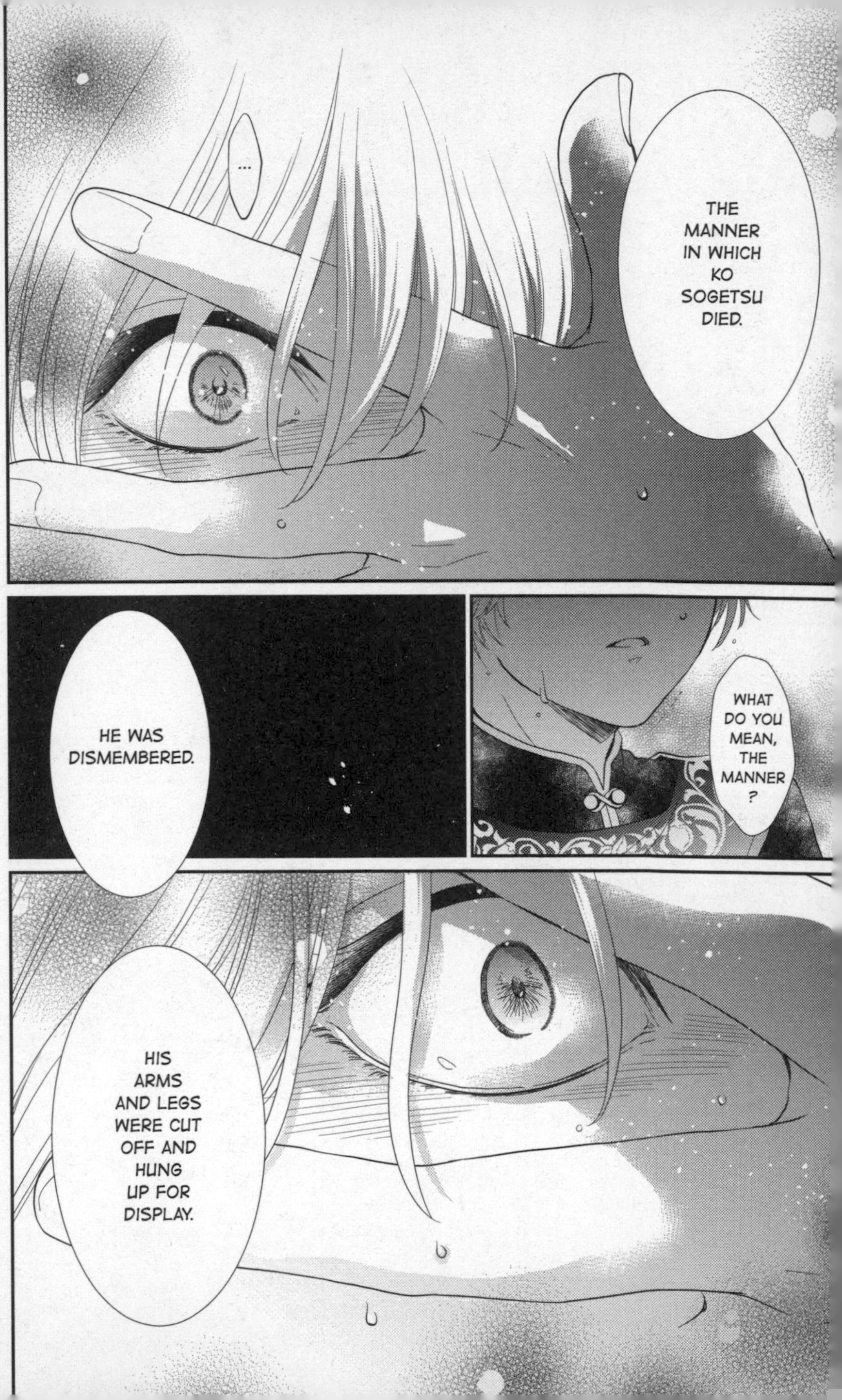
THE MANNER IN WHICH KO SOGETSU DIED.
...
WHAT DO YOU MEAN, THE MANNER?
HE WAS DISMEMBERED.
HIS ARMS AND LEGS WERE CUT OFF AND HUNG UP FOR DISPLAY.

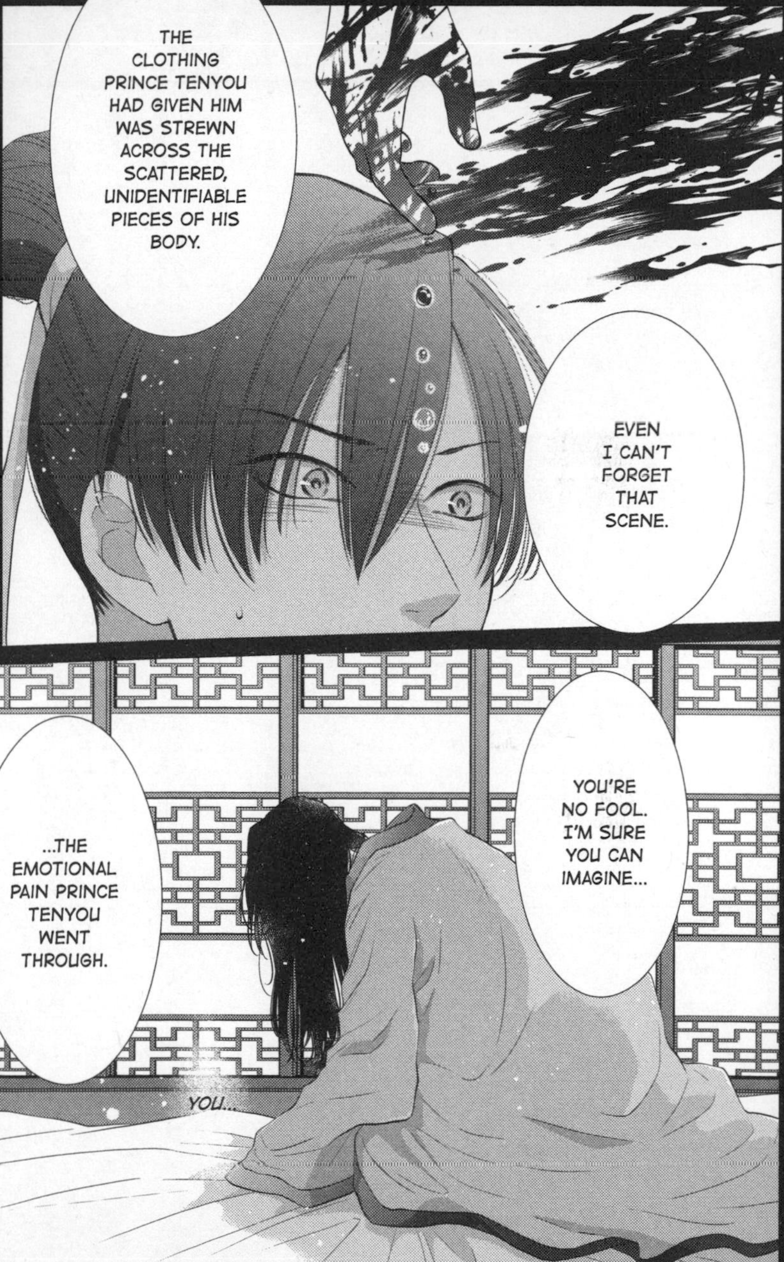
THE CLOTHING PRINCE TENYOU HAD GIVEN HIM WAS STREWN ACROSS THE SCATTERED, UNIDENTIFIABLE PIECES OF HIS BODY.
EVEN I CAN'T FORGET THAT SCENE.
YOU'RE NO FOOL. I'M SURE YOU CAN IMAGINE...
...THE EMOTIONAL PAIN PRINCE TENYOU WENT THROUGH.
YOU...

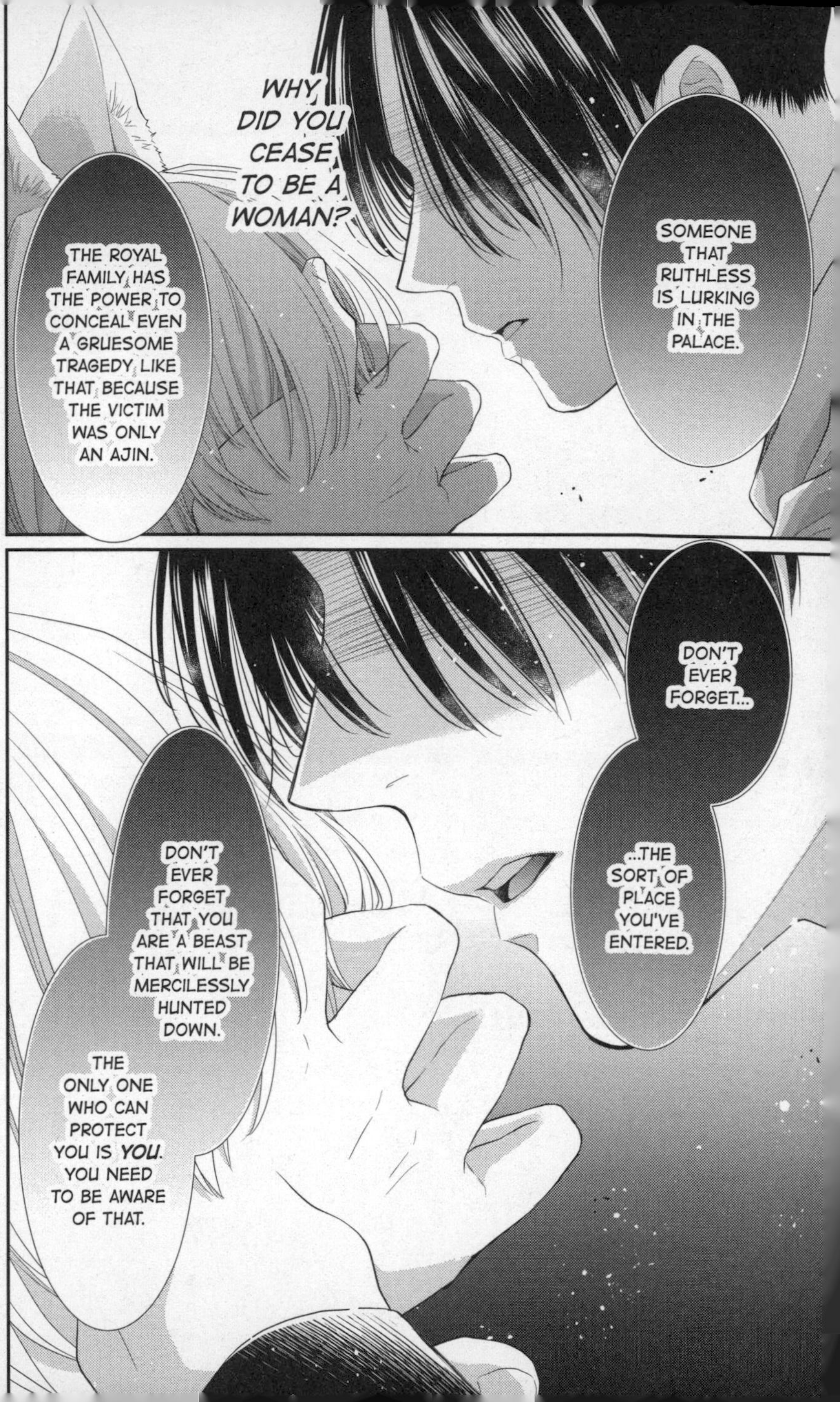
SOMEONE THAT RUTHLESS IS LURKING IN THE PALACE.
WHY DID YOU CEASE TO BE A WOMAN?
THE ROYAL FAMILY HAS THE POWER TO CONCEAL EVEN A GRUESOME TRAGEDY LIKE THAT BECAUSE THE VICTIM WAS ONLY AN AJIN.
DON'T EVER FORGET...
...THE SORT OF PLACE YOU'VE ENTERED.
DON'T EVER FORGET THAT YOU ARE A BEAST THAT WILL BE MERCILESSLY HUNTED DOWN.
THE ONLY ONE WHO CAN PROTECT YOU IS *YOU*. YOU NEED TO BE AWARE OF THAT.

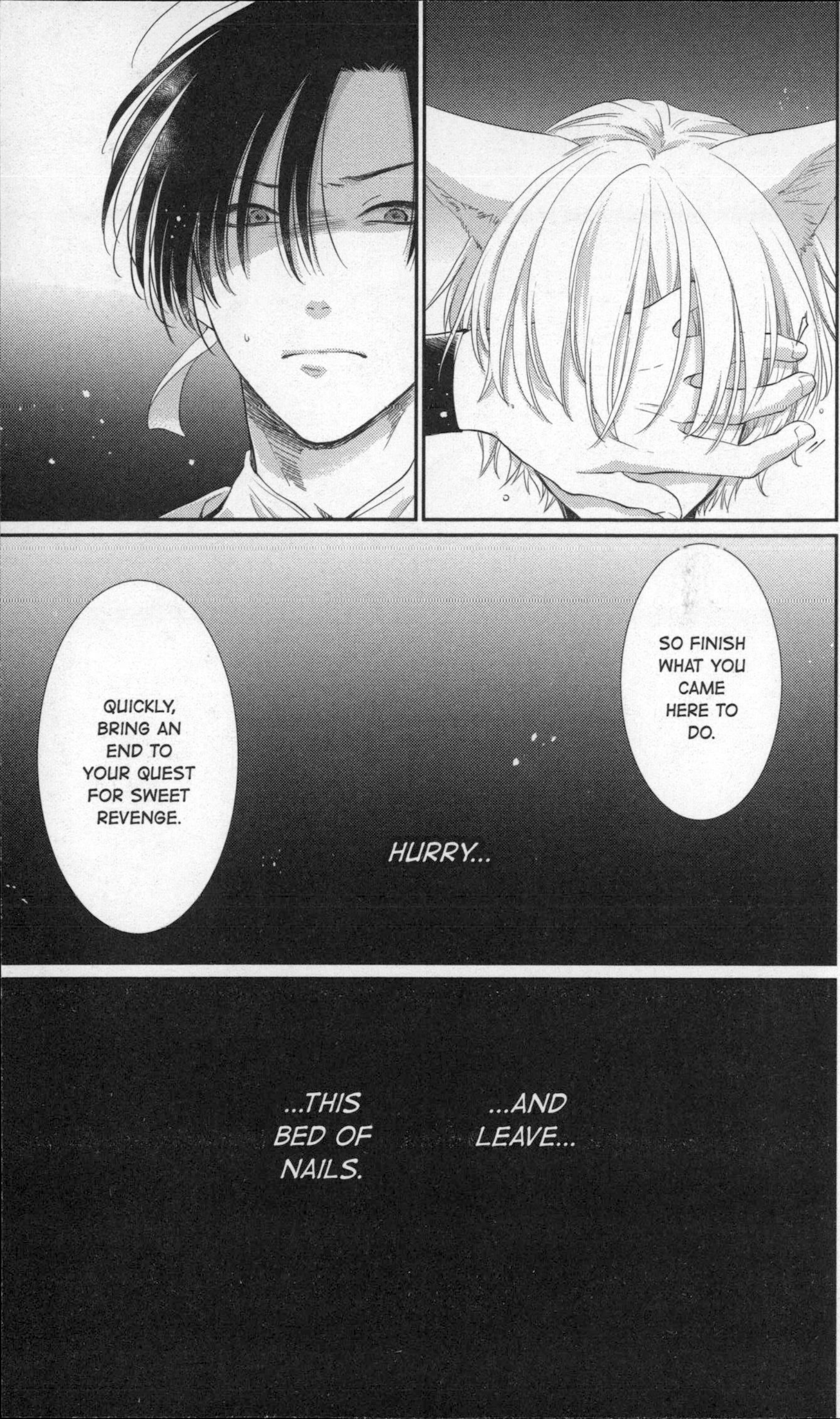
SO FINISH WHAT YOU CAME HERE TO DO.
QUICKLY, BRING AN END TO YOUR QUEST FOR SWEET REVENGE.
HURRY...
...AND LEAVE...
...THIS BED OF NAILS.

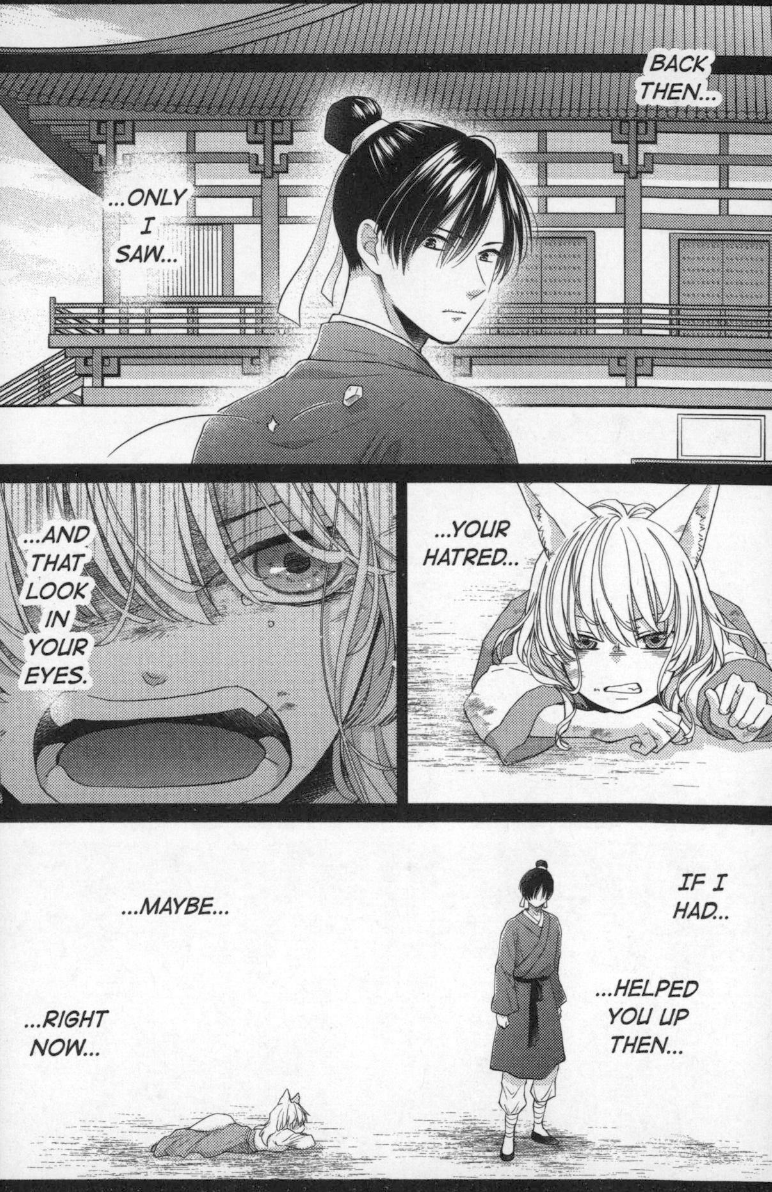
BACK THEN...
...ONLY I SAW...
...YOUR HATRED...
...AND THAT LOOK IN YOUR EYES.
IF I HAD...
...HELPED YOU UP THEN...
...MAYBE...
...RIGHT NOW...

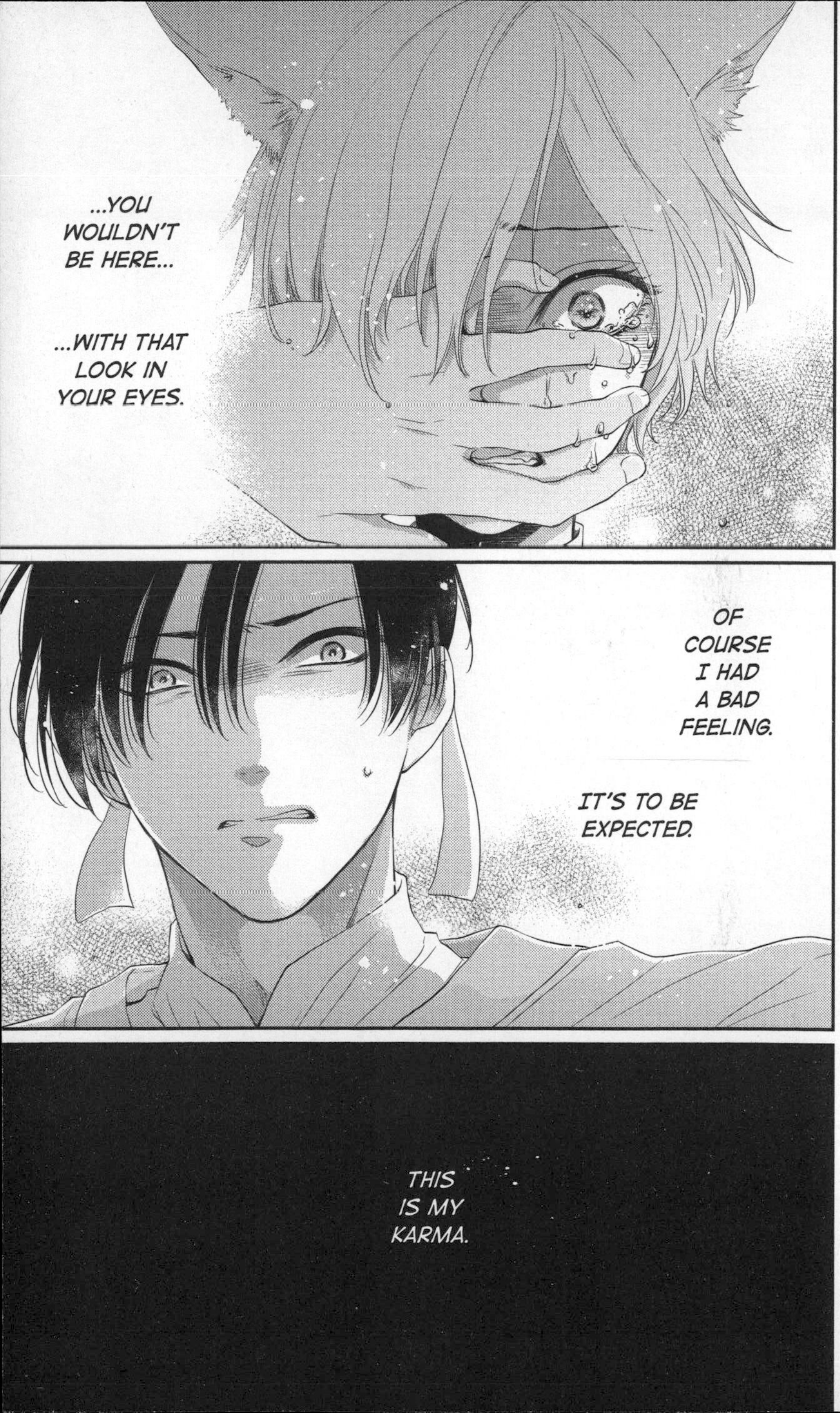
...YOU WOULDN'T BE HERE...
...WITH THAT LOOK IN YOUR EYES.
OF COURSE I HAD A BAD FEELING.
IT'S TO BE EXPECTED.
THIS IS MY KARMA.

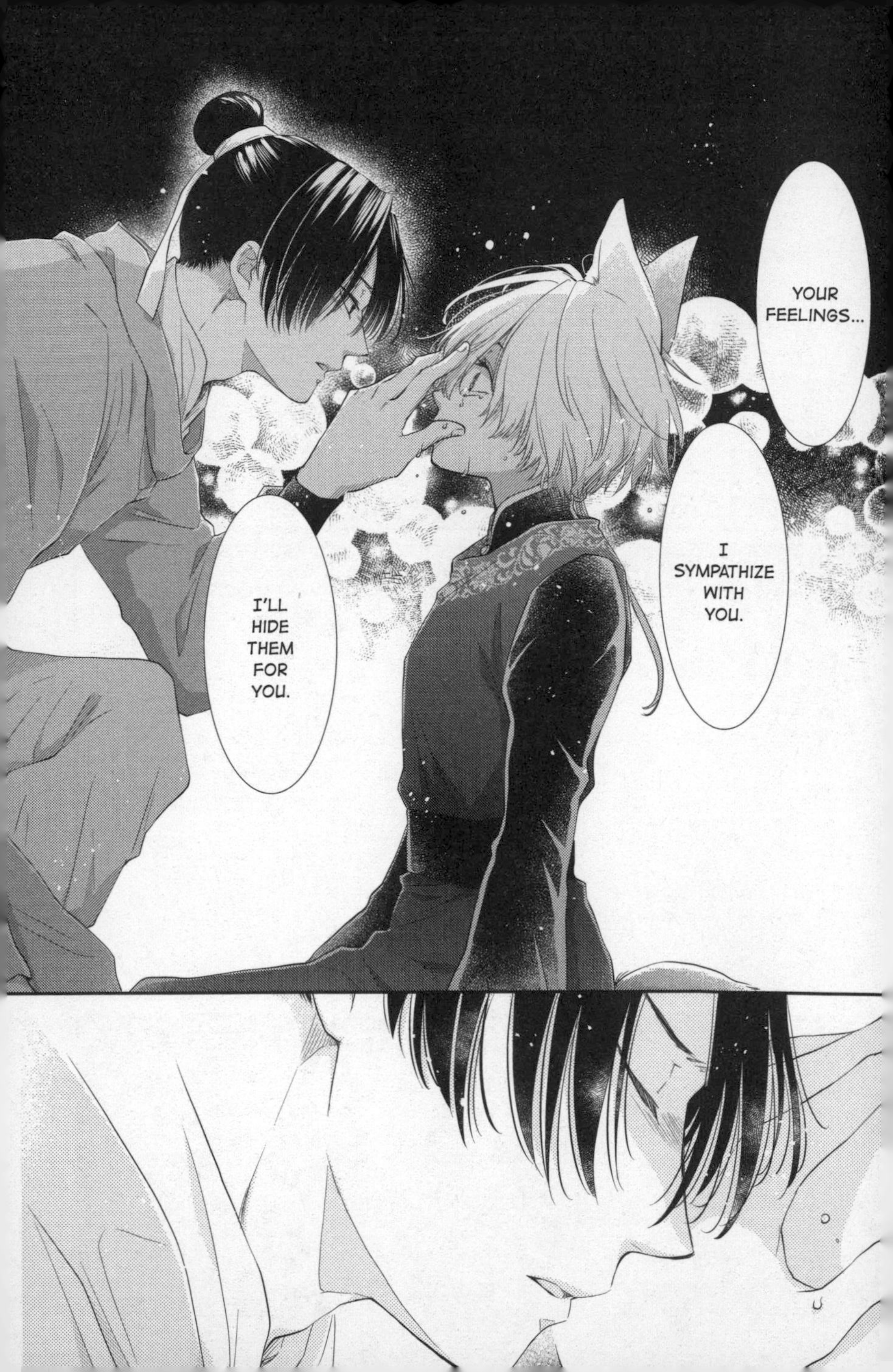
YOUR FEELINGS...
I SYMPATHIZE WITH YOU.
I'LL HIDE THEM FOR YOU.

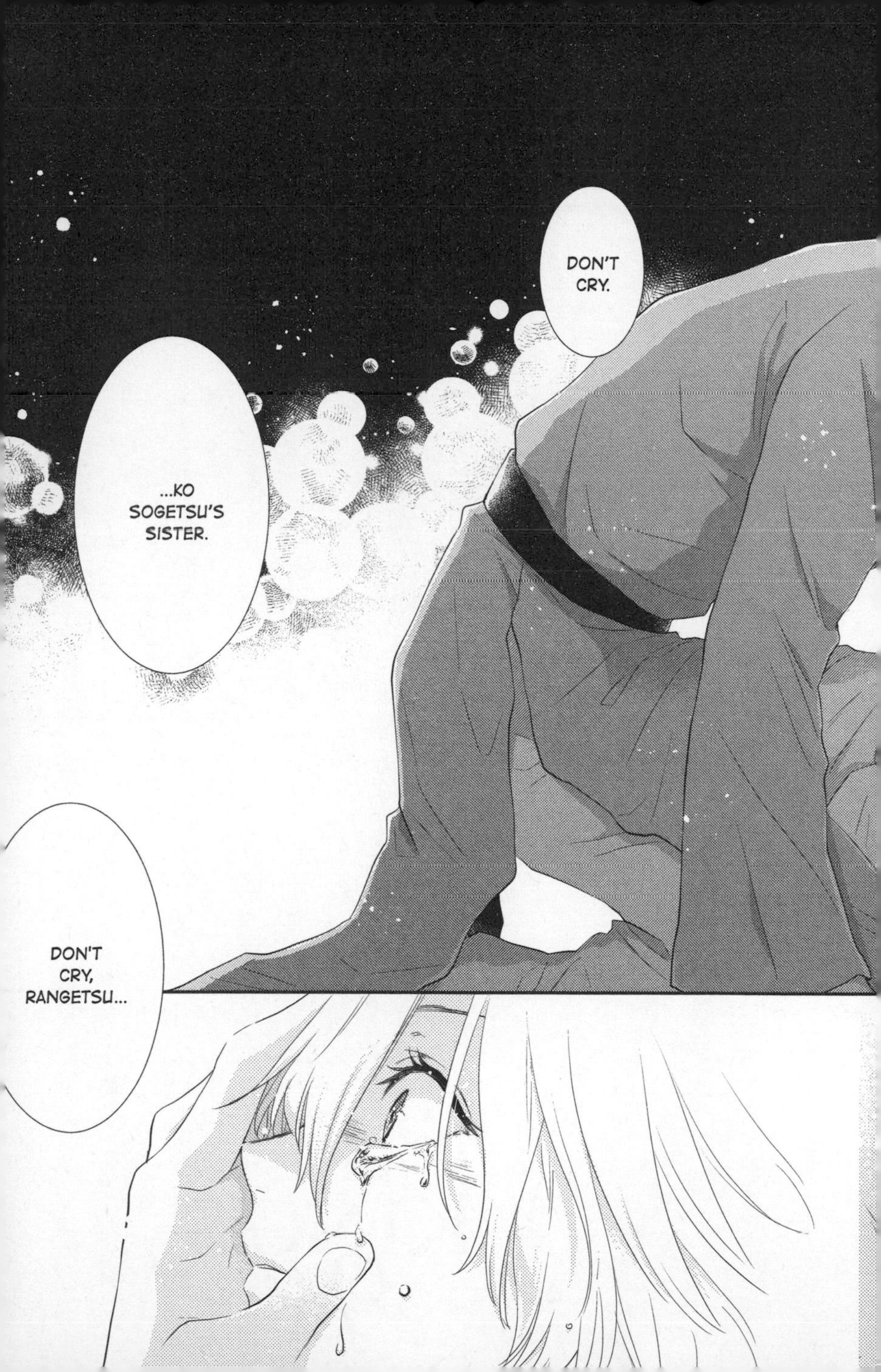
DON'T CRY.
...KO SOGETSU'S SISTER.
DON'T CRY, RANGETSU...

THE KING'S *Beast*

麗

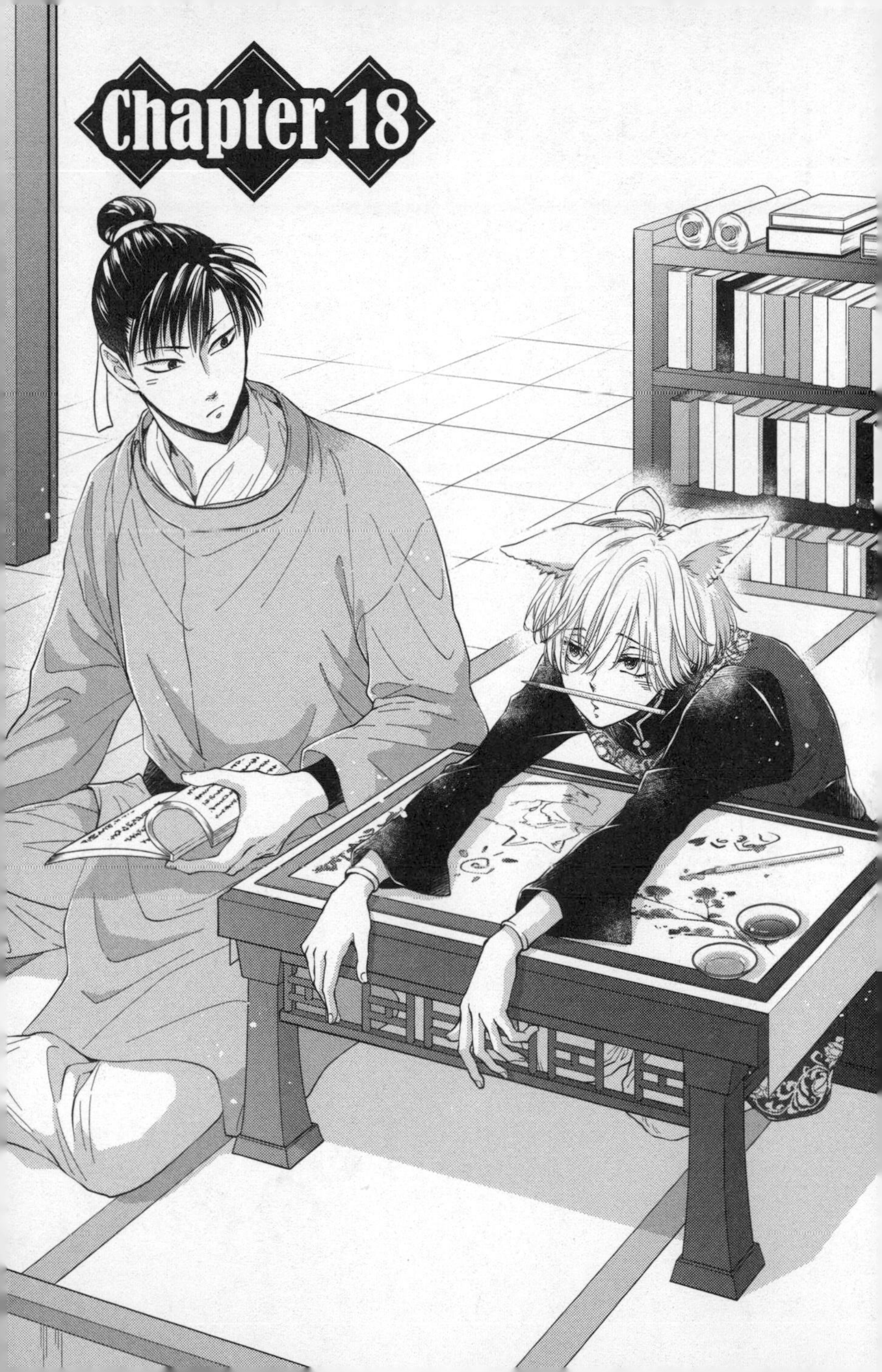
Chapter 18

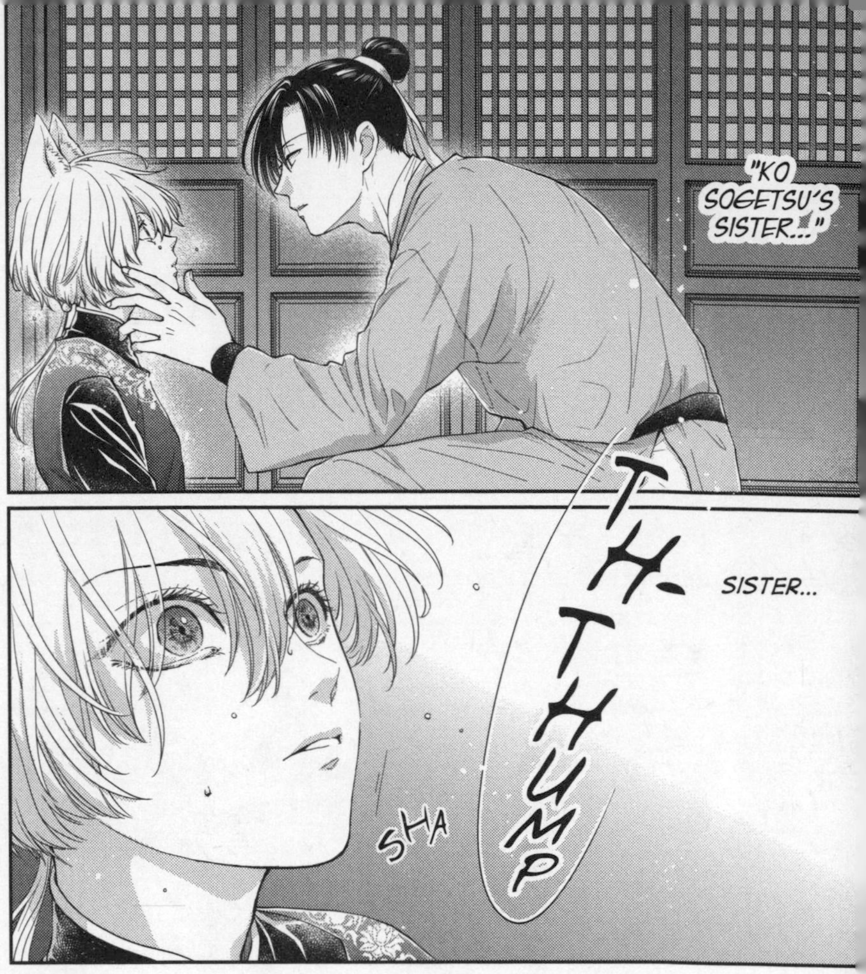
"KO SOGETSU'S SISTER..."
SISTER...
TH-THUMP
SHA

THE KING'S Beast 麗

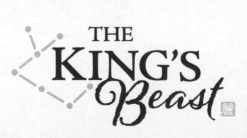

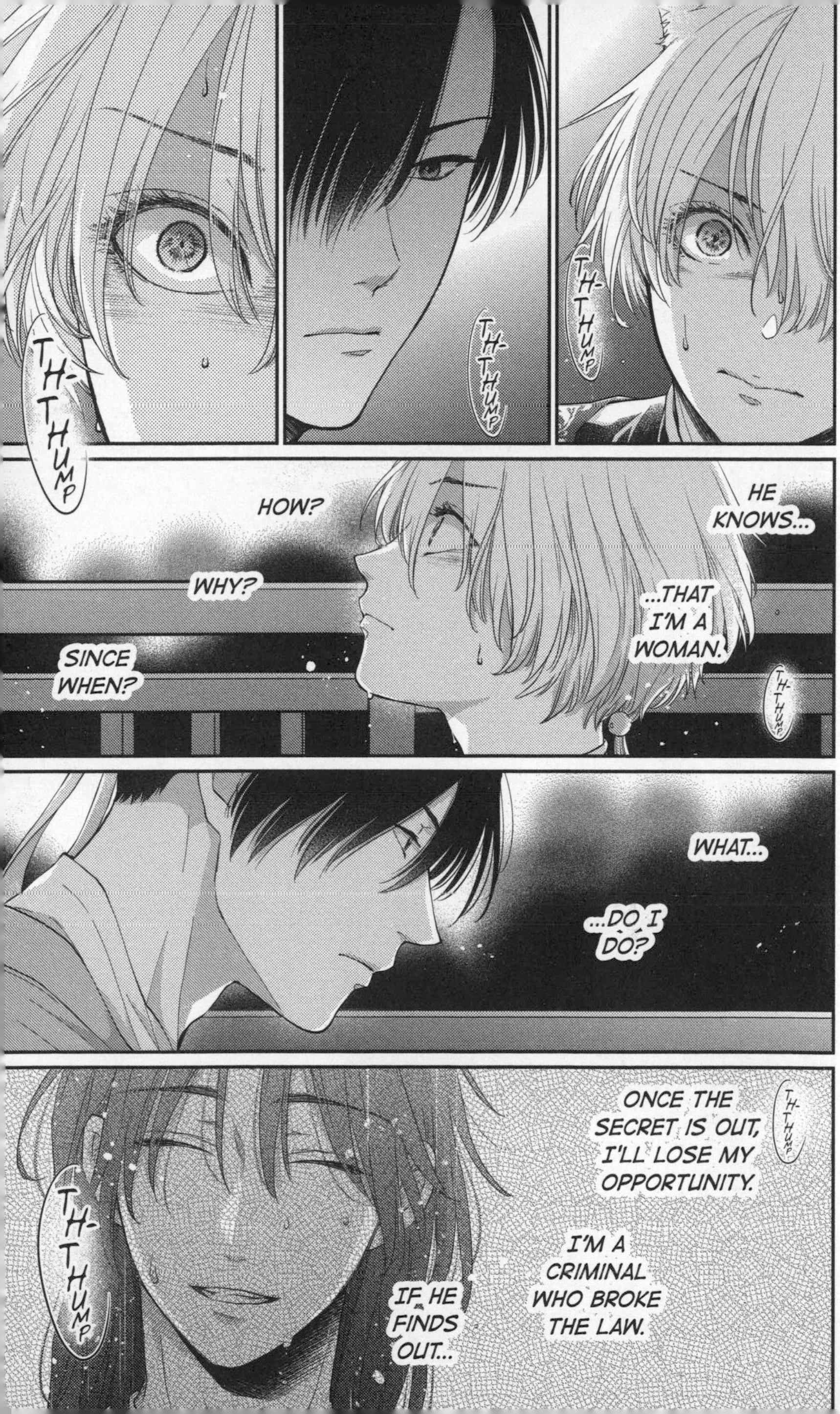
TH-THUMP
TH-THUMP
TH-THUMP
HE KNOWS...
...THAT I'M A WOMAN.
HOW?
WHY?
TH-THUMP
SINCE WHEN?
WHAT...
...DO I DO?
TH-THUMP
ONCE THE SECRET IS OUT, I'LL LOSE MY OPPORTUNITY.
I'M A CRIMINAL WHO BROKE THE LAW.
IF HE FINDS OUT...
TH-THUMP

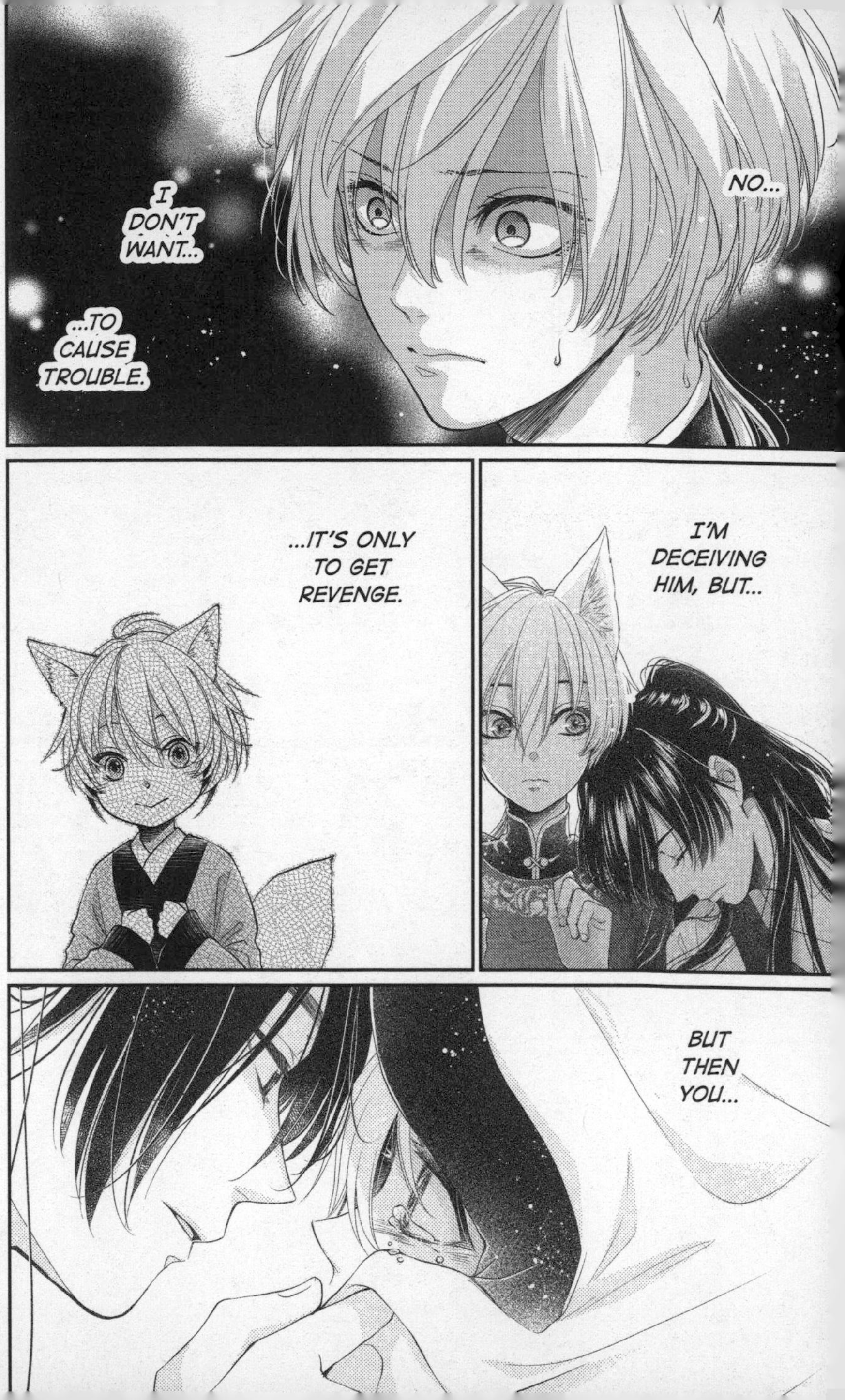
NO...
I DON'T WANT...
...TO CAUSE TROUBLE.
I'M DECEIVING HIM, BUT...
...IT'S ONLY TO GET REVENGE.
BUT THEN YOU...

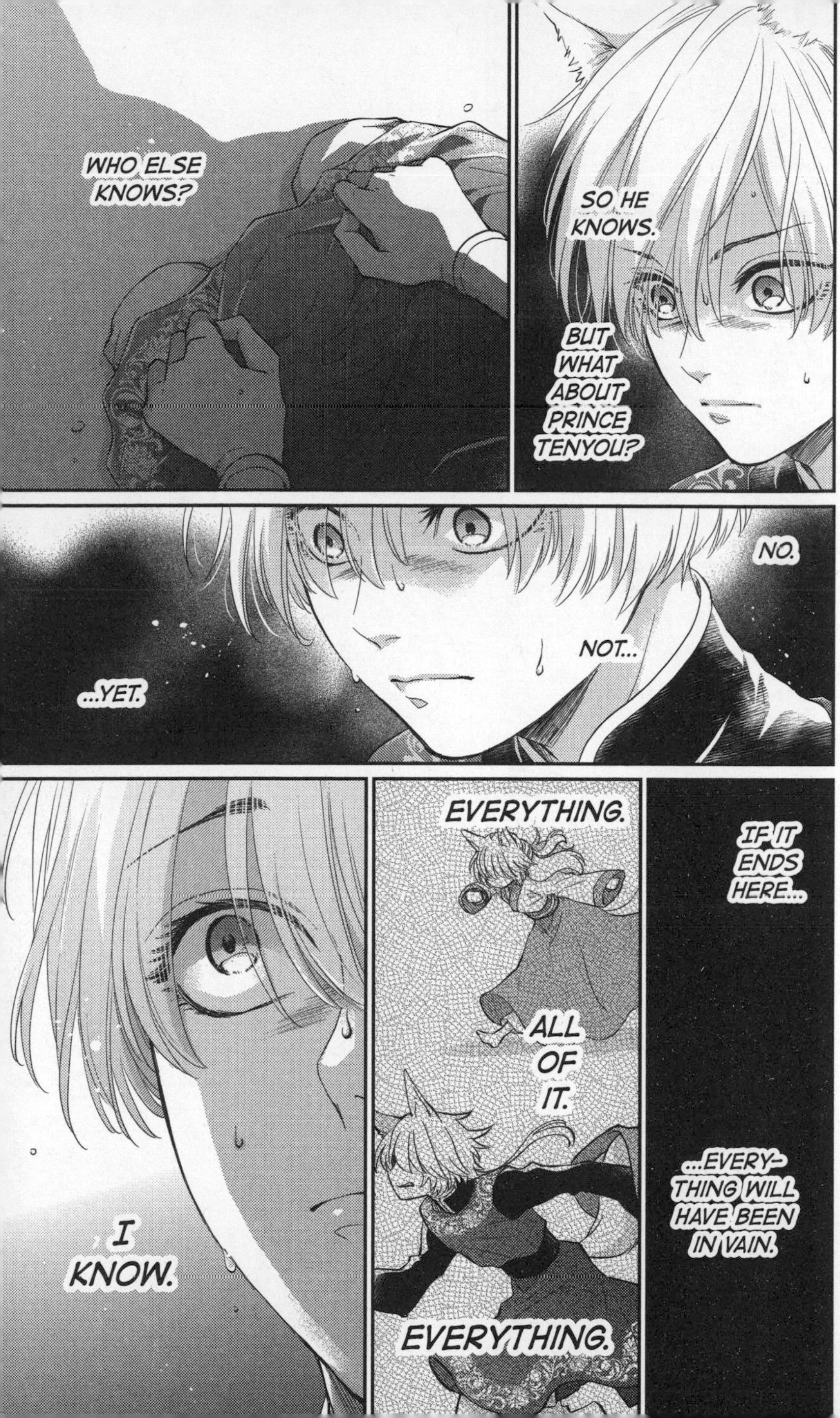
SO HE KNOWS.
BUT WHAT ABOUT PRINCE TENYOU?
WHO ELSE KNOWS?
NO.
NOT...
...YET.
IF IT ENDS HERE...
...EVERY-THING WILL HAVE BEEN IN VAIN.
EVERYTHING.
ALL OF IT.
EVERYTHING.
I KNOW.

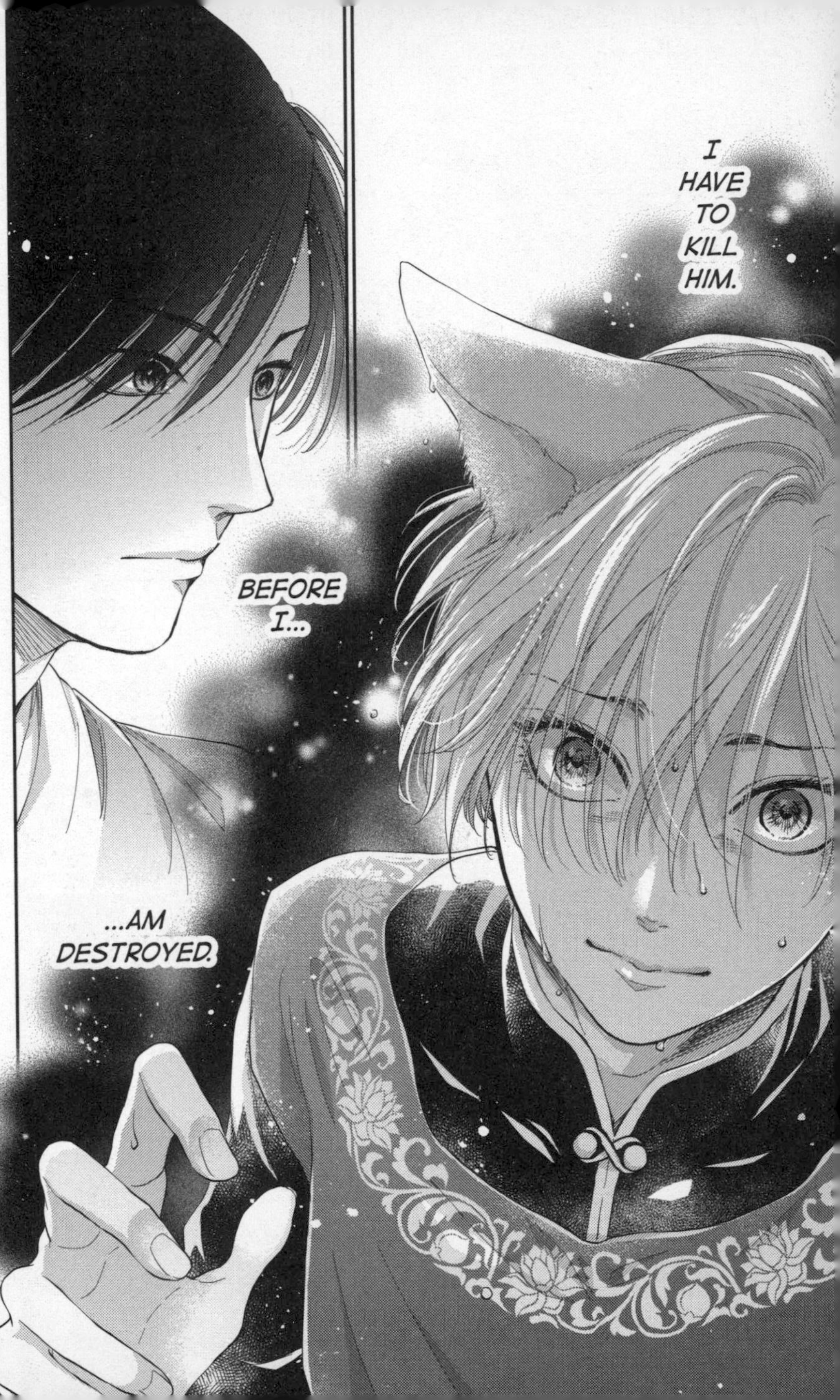
I HAVE TO KILL HIM.
BEFORE I...
...AM DESTROYED.

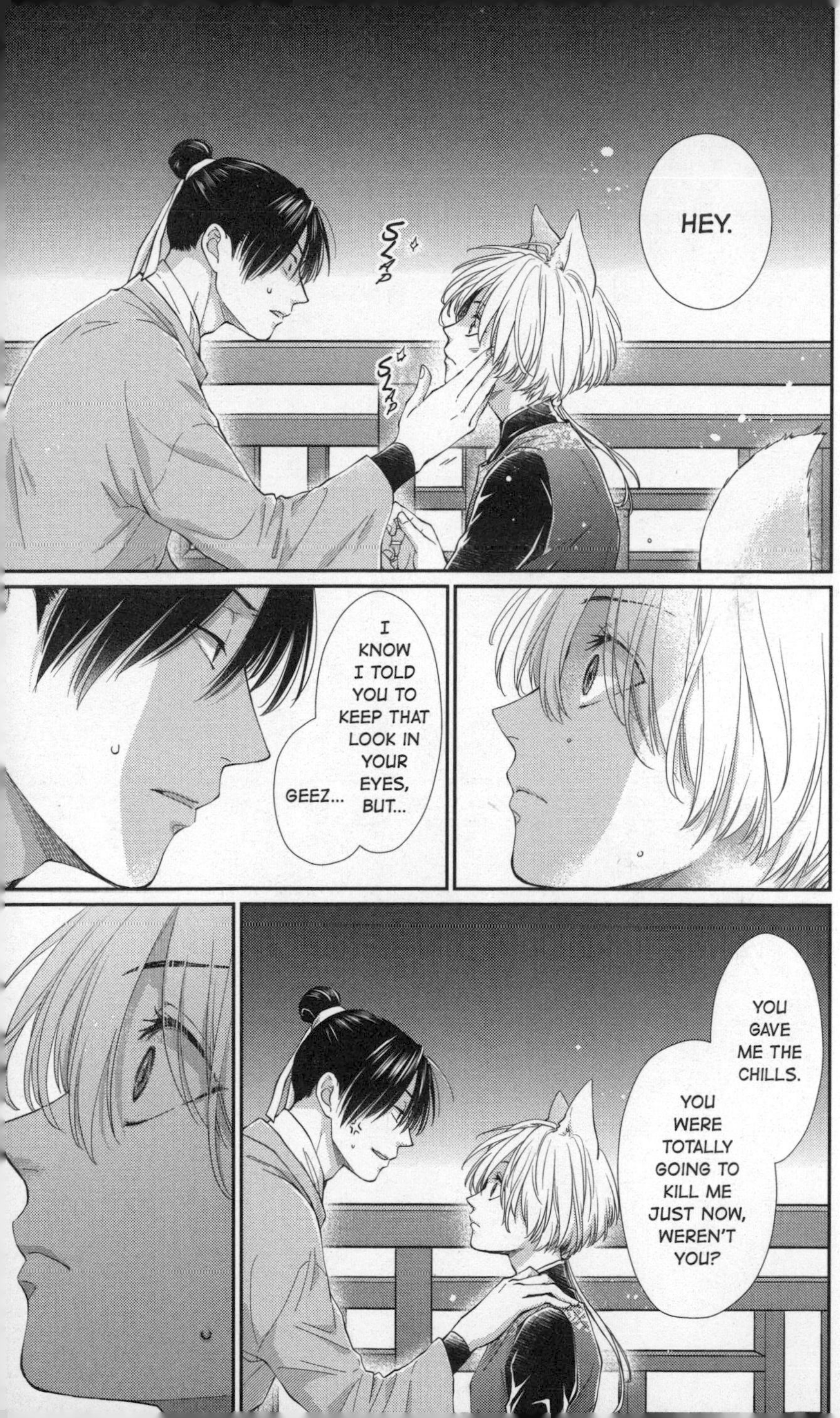
HEY.
SLAP
SLAP
I KNOW I TOLD YOU TO KEEP THAT LOOK IN YOUR EYES, BUT...
GEEZ...
YOU GAVE ME THE CHILLS.
YOU WERE TOTALLY GOING TO KILL ME JUST NOW, WEREN'T YOU?

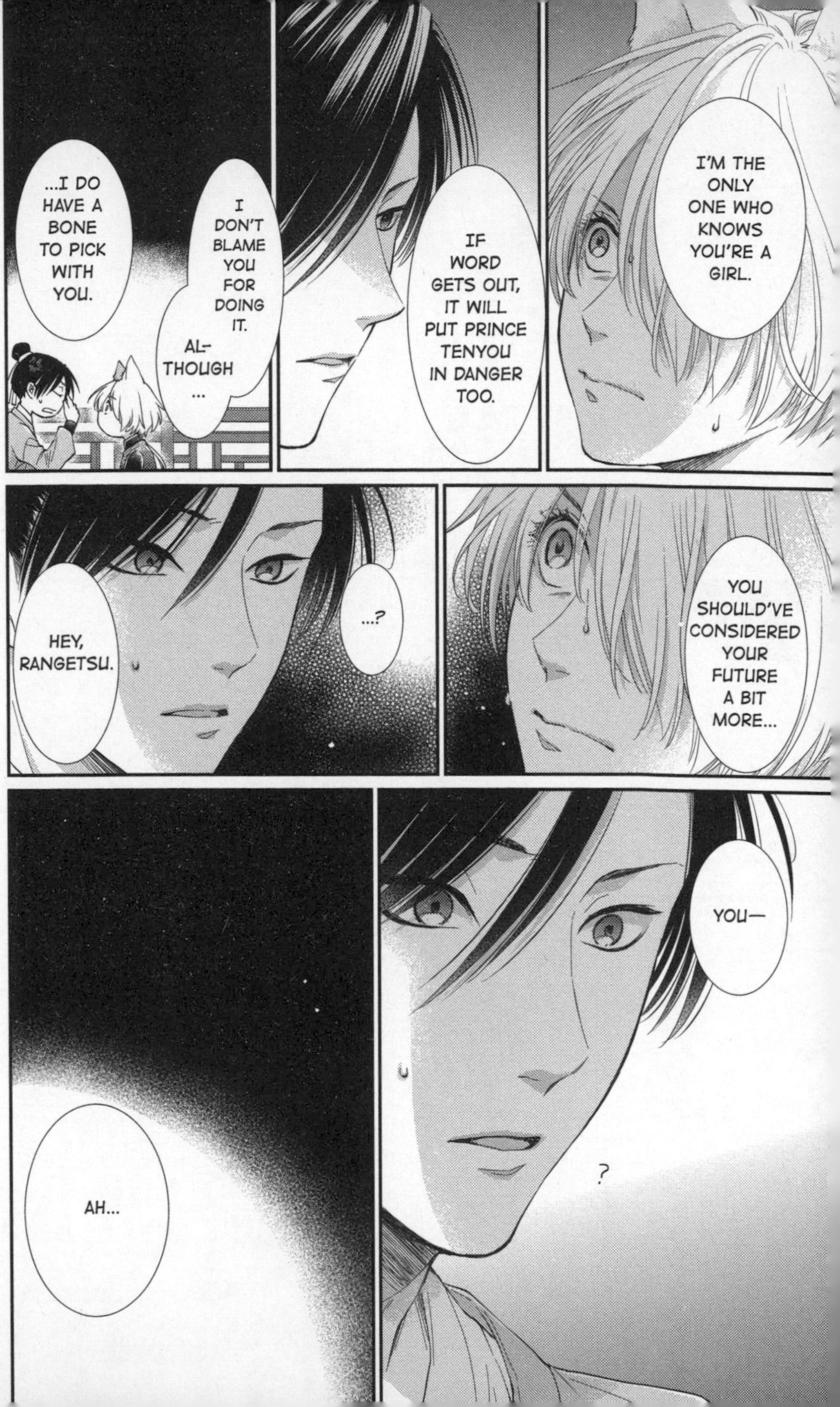
I'M THE ONLY ONE WHO KNOWS YOU'RE A GIRL.
IF WORD GETS OUT, IT WILL PUT PRINCE TENYOU IN DANGER TOO.
I DON'T BLAME YOU FOR DOING IT.
AL-THOUGH ...
...I DO HAVE A BONE TO PICK WITH YOU.
YOU SHOULD'VE CONSIDERED YOUR FUTURE A BIT MORE...
...?
HEY, RANGETSU.
YOU—
?
AH...

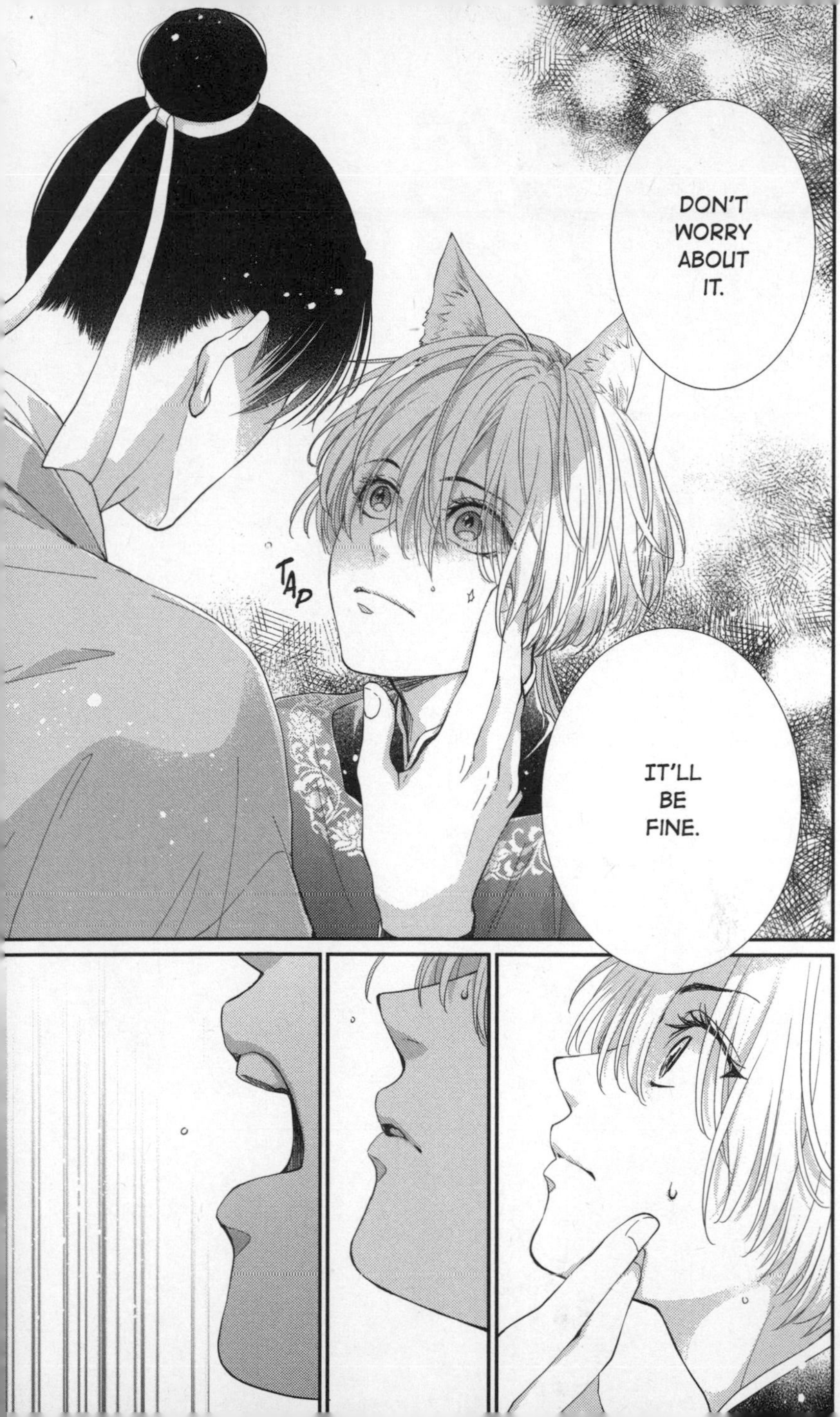
DON'T WORRY ABOUT IT.
TAP
IT'LL BE FINE.

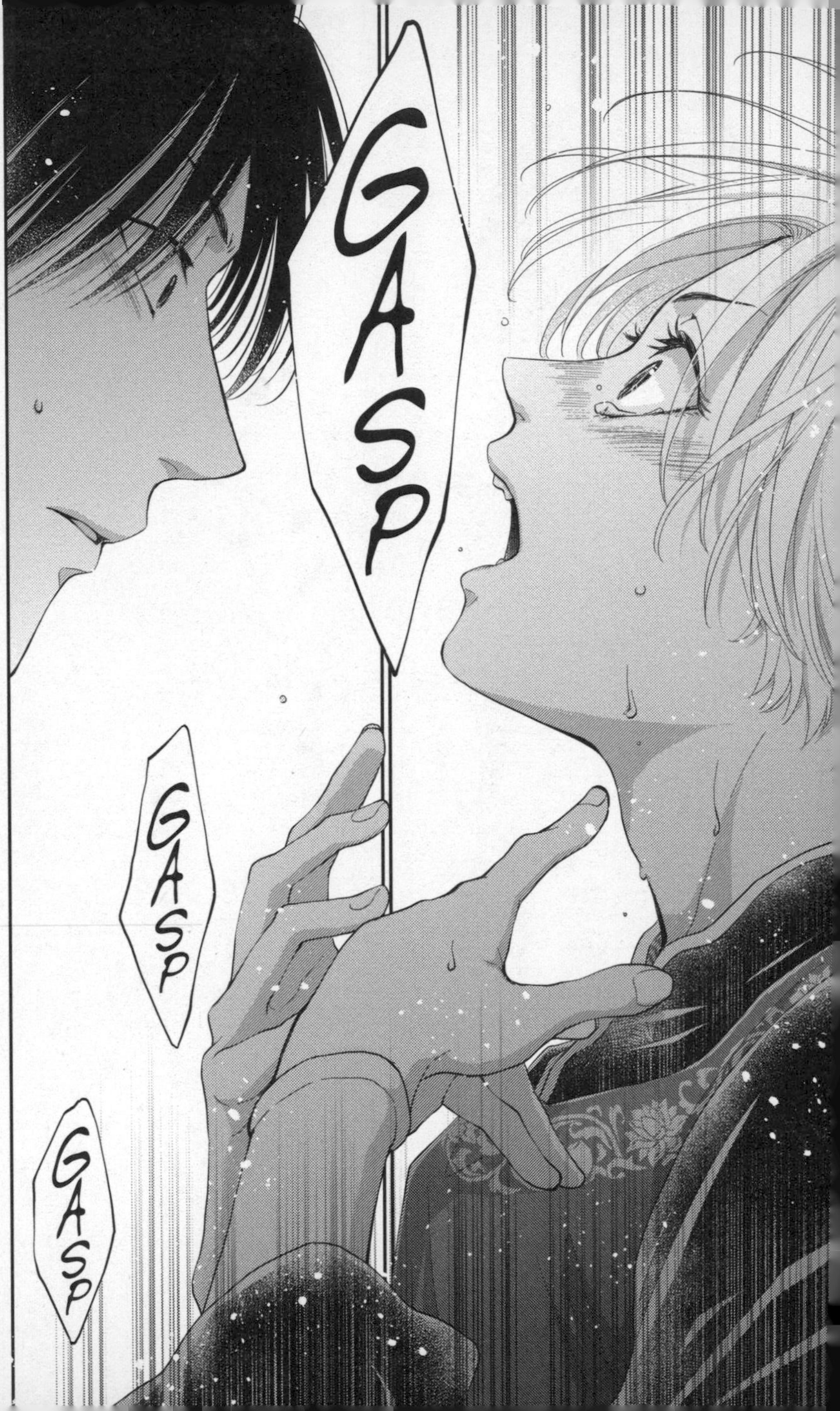
GASP
GASP
GASP

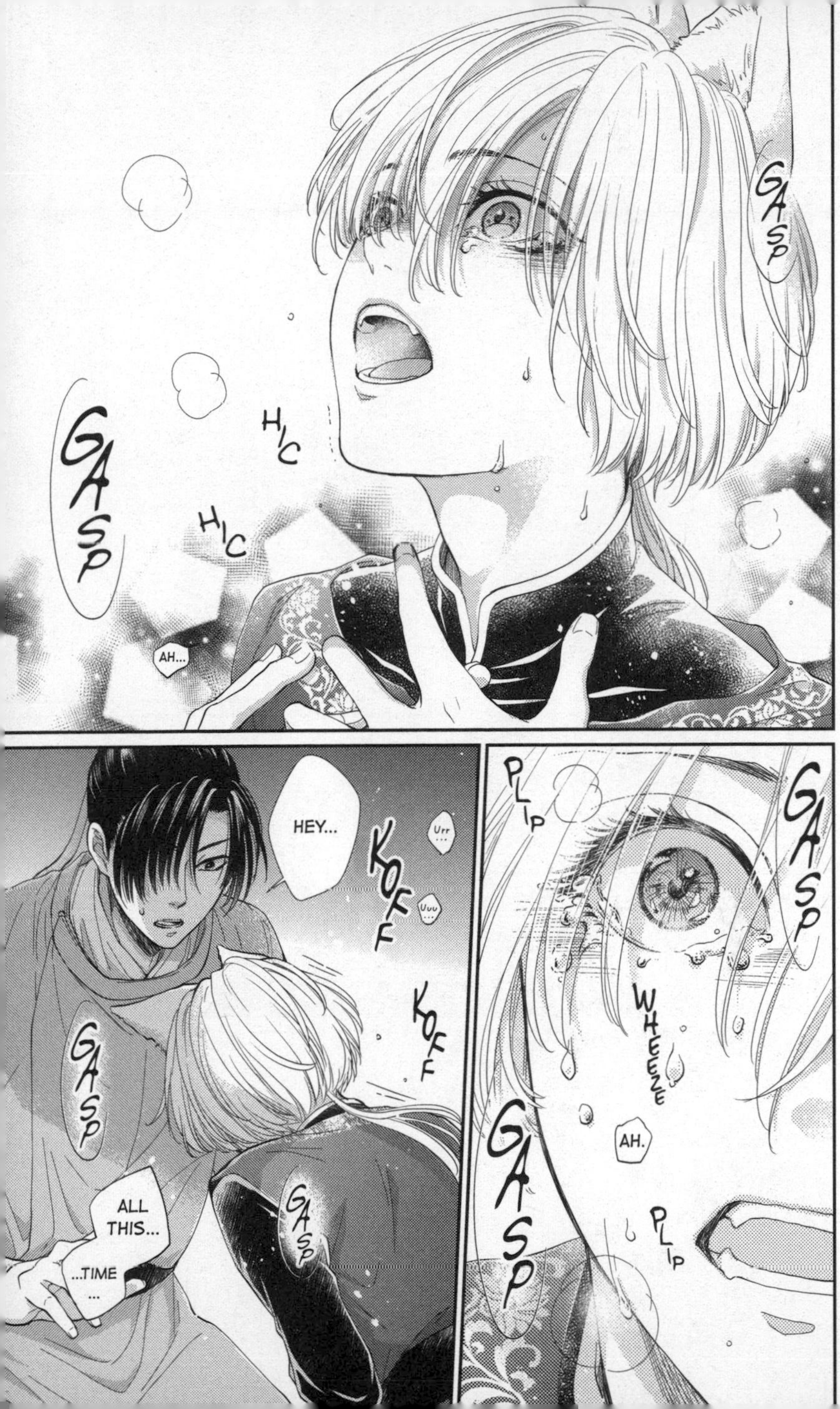
GASP
HIC
GASP
HIC
AH...
PLIP
GASP
WHEEZE
AH.
GASP
PLIP
Urr...
KOFF
HEY...
Uuu...
KOFF
GASP
GASP
ALL THIS...
...TIME ...

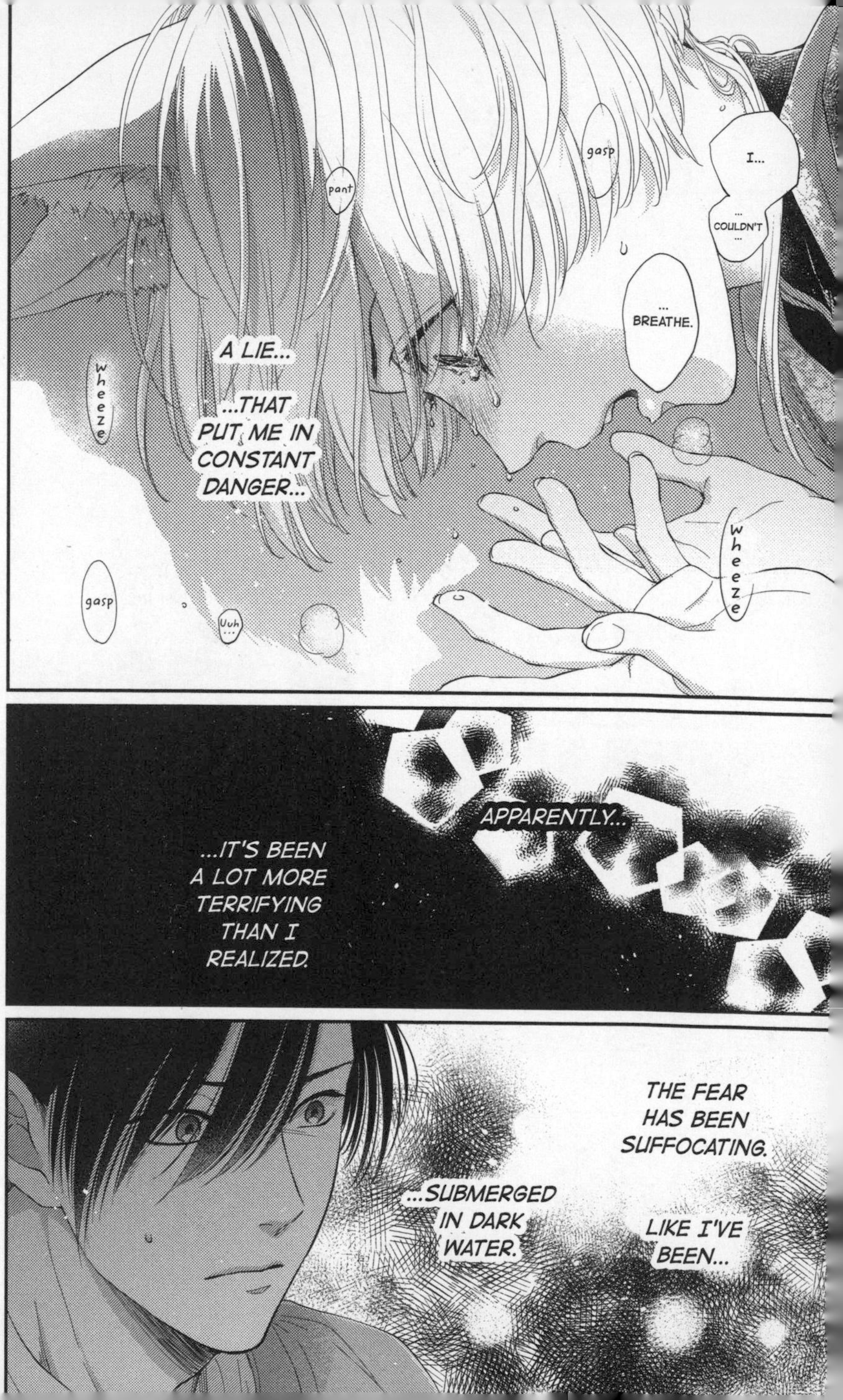
I...
...COULDN'T...
...BREATHE.
gasp
pant
A LIE...
...THAT PUT ME IN CONSTANT DANGER...
wheeze
wheeze
gasp
Uuh...
APPARENTLY...
...IT'S BEEN A LOT MORE TERRIFYING THAN I REALIZED.
THE FEAR HAS BEEN SUFFOCATING.
LIKE I'VE BEEN...
...SUBMERGED IN DARK WATER.

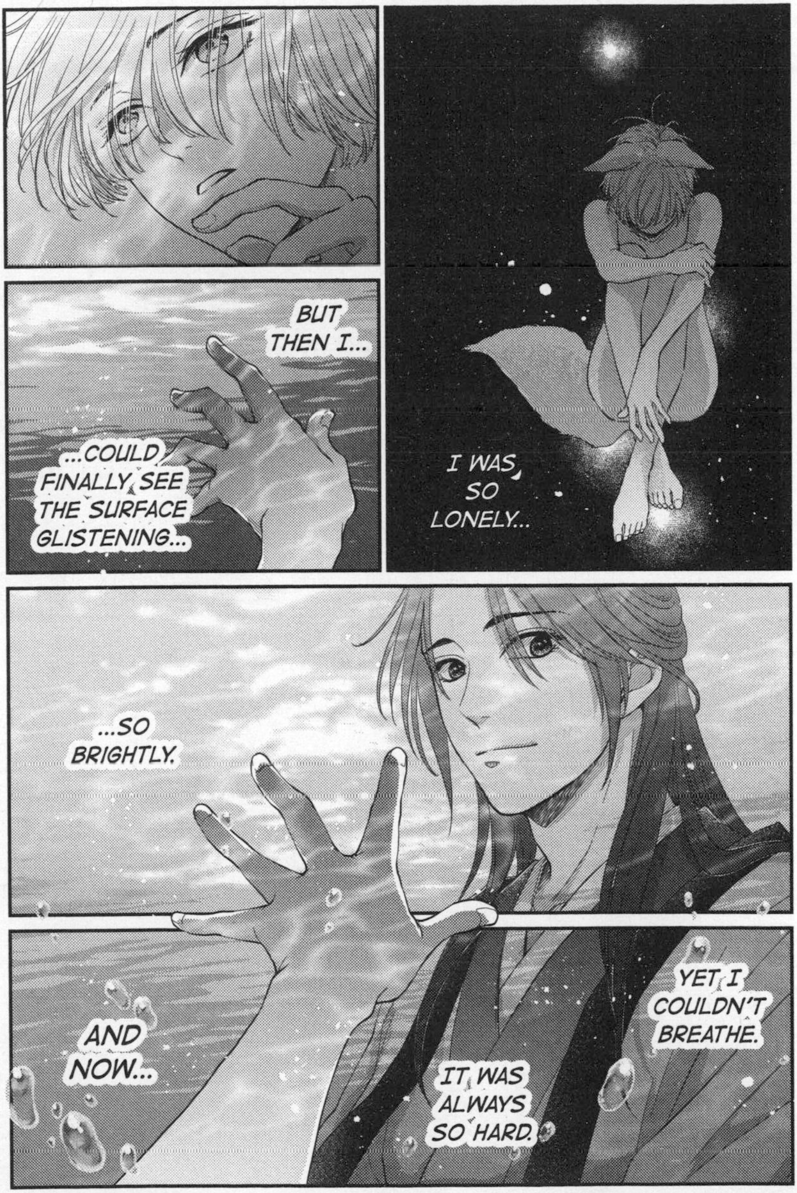
I WAS SO LONELY...
BUT THEN I...
...COULD FINALLY SEE THE SURFACE GLISTENING...
...SO BRIGHTLY.
YET I COULDN'T BREATHE.
IT WAS ALWAYS SO HARD.
AND NOW...

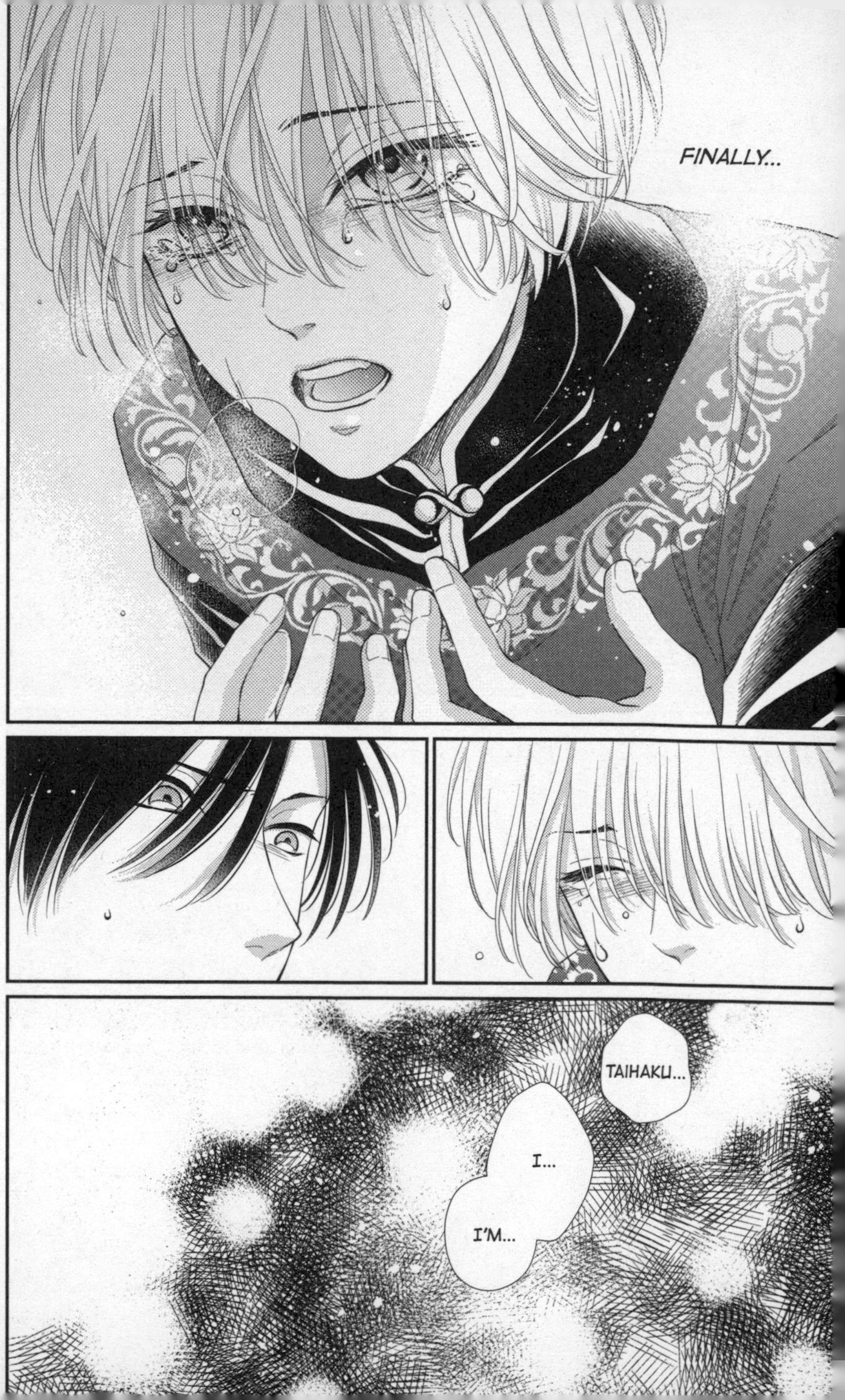
FINALLY...
TAIHAKU...
I...
I'M...

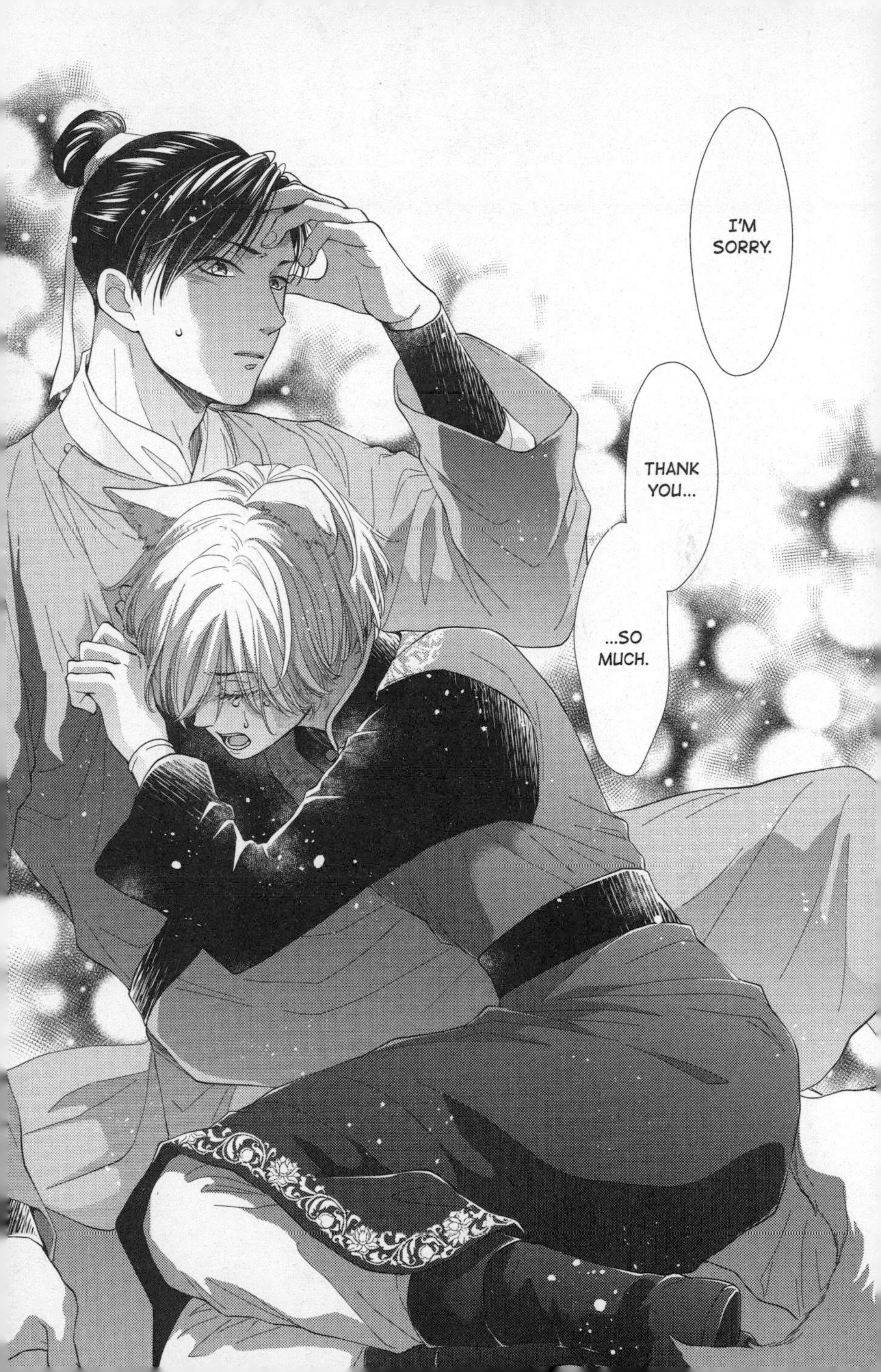
I'M SORRY.
THANK YOU...
...SO MUCH.

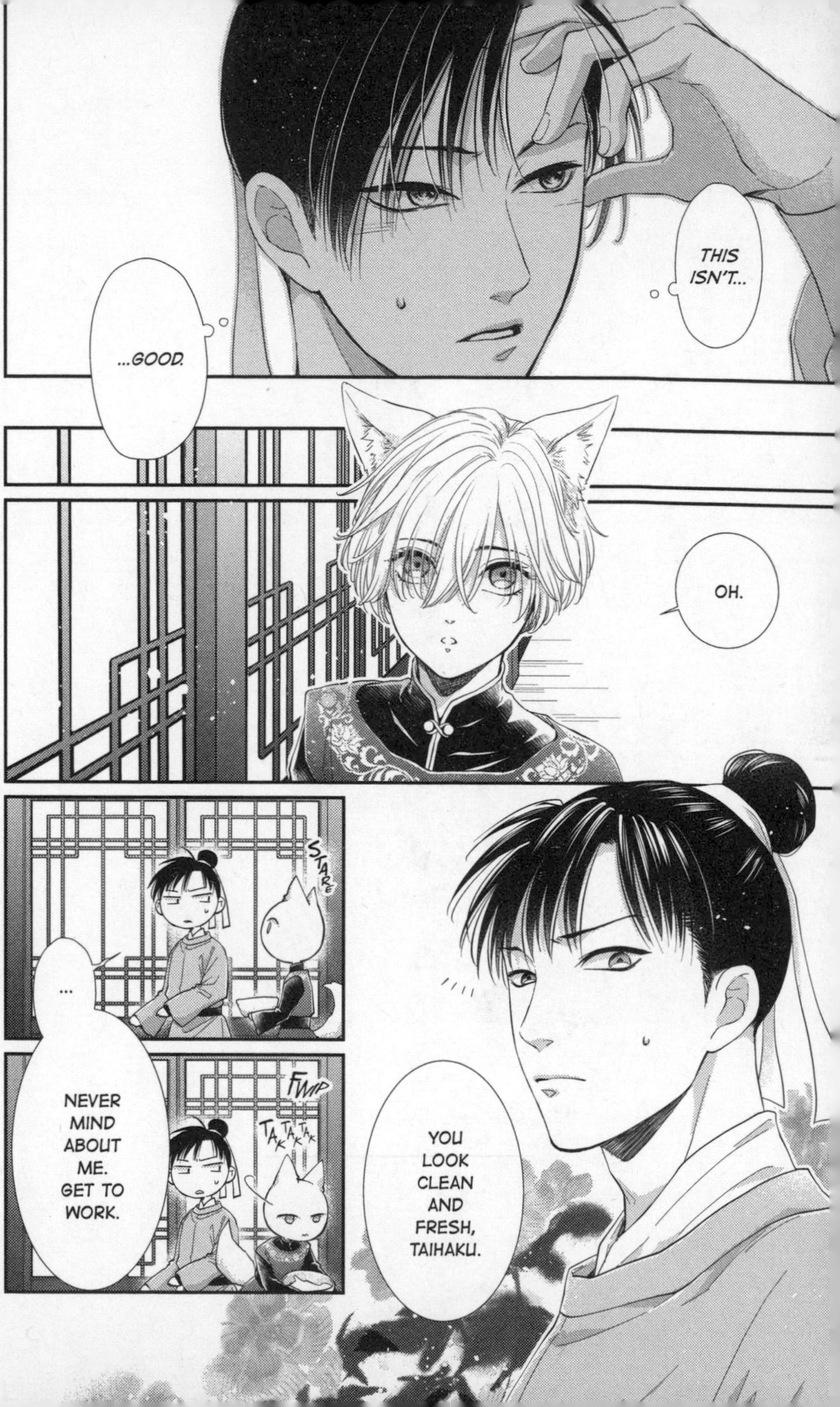
THIS ISN'T...
...GOOD.
OH.
YOU LOOK CLEAN AND FRESH, TAIHAKU.
STARE
...
FWIP
TAK TAK TAK
NEVER MIND ABOUT ME. GET TO WORK.

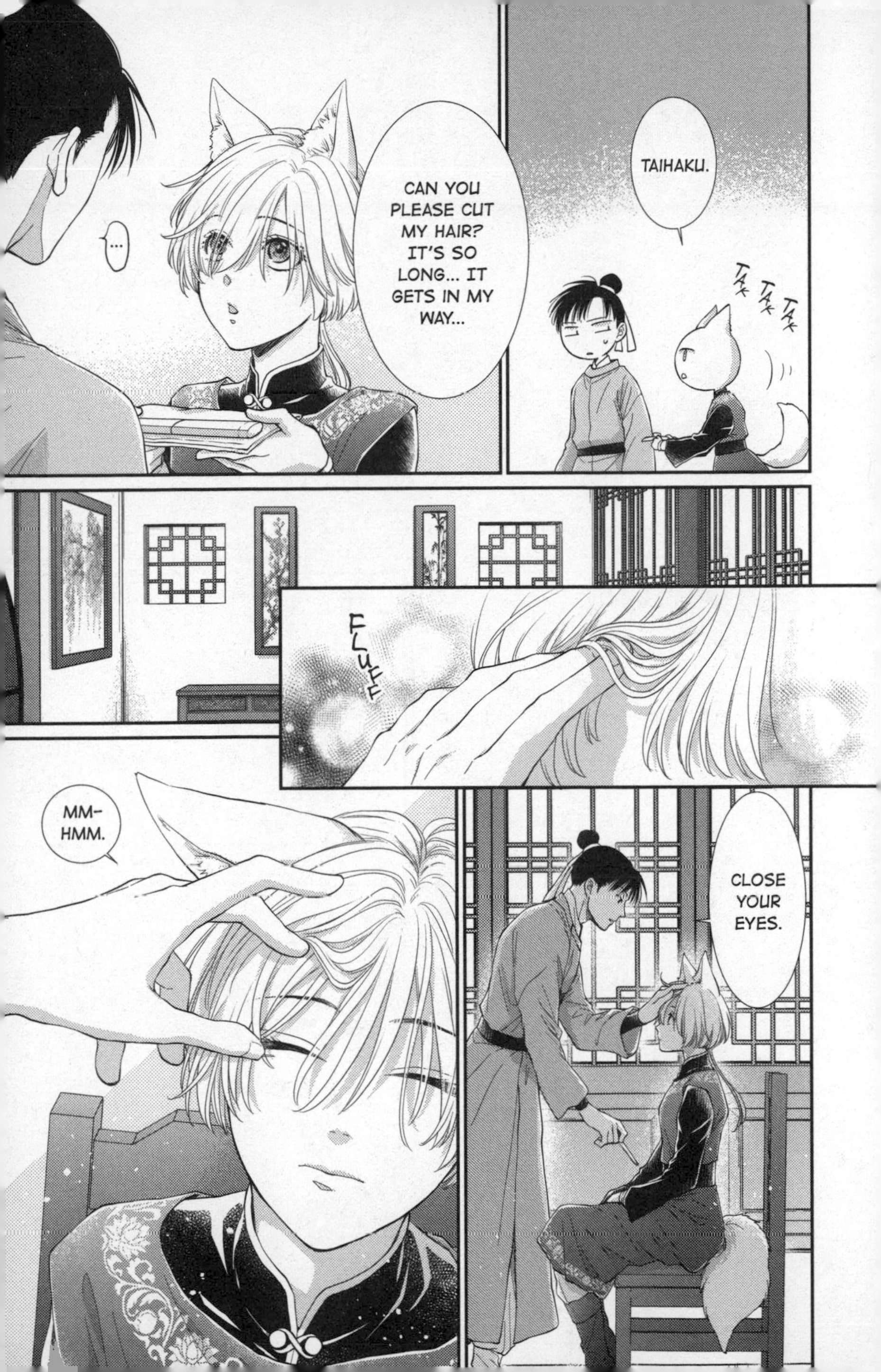
TAIHAKU.
TAK TAK TAK
CAN YOU PLEASE CUT MY HAIR? IT'S SO LONG... IT GETS IN MY WAY...
...
FLUFF
CLOSE YOUR EYES.
MM-HMM.

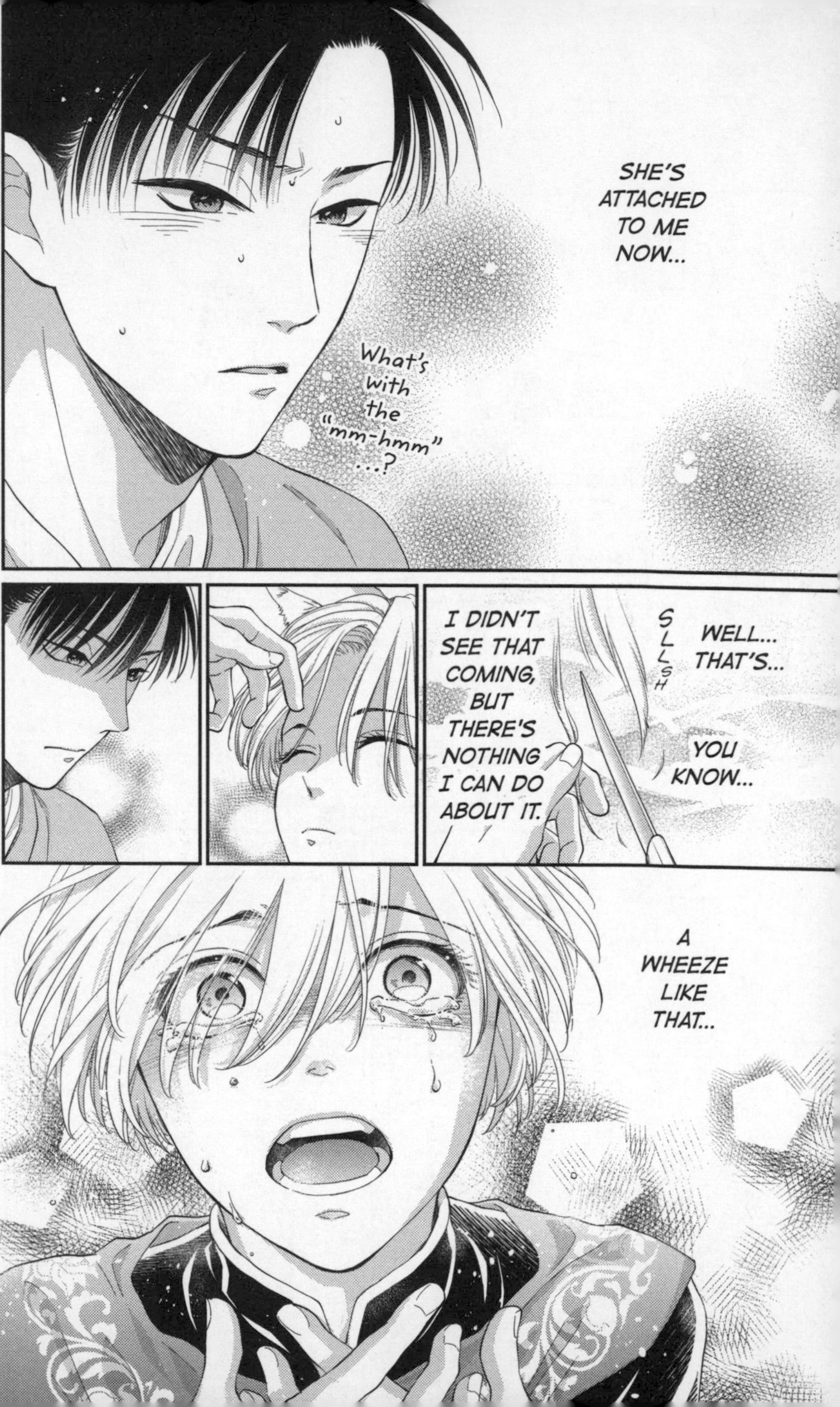
SHE'S ATTACHED TO ME NOW...
What's with the "mm-hmm"...?
WELL... THAT'S...
YOU KNOW...
SLLSH
I DIDN'T SEE THAT COMING, BUT THERE'S NOTHING I CAN DO ABOUT IT.
A WHEEZE LIKE THAT...

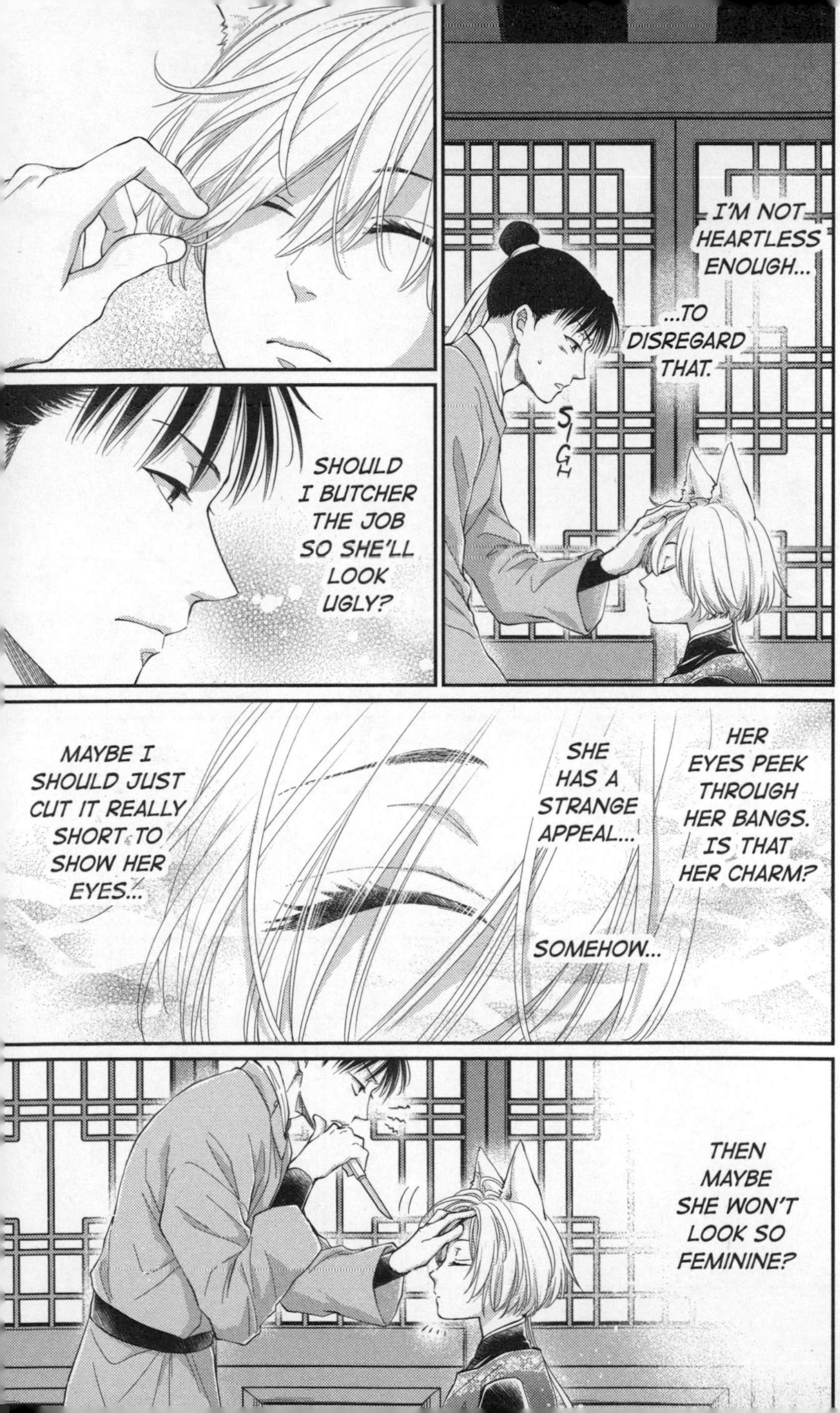
I'M NOT HEARTLESS ENOUGH...
...TO DISREGARD THAT.
SIGH
SHOULD I BUTCHER THE JOB SO SHE'LL LOOK UGLY?
HER EYES PEEK THROUGH HER BANGS. IS THAT HER CHARM?
SHE HAS A STRANGE APPEAL...
SOMEHOW...
MAYBE I SHOULD JUST CUT IT REALLY SHORT TO SHOW HER EYES...
THEN MAYBE SHE WON'T LOOK SO FEMININE?

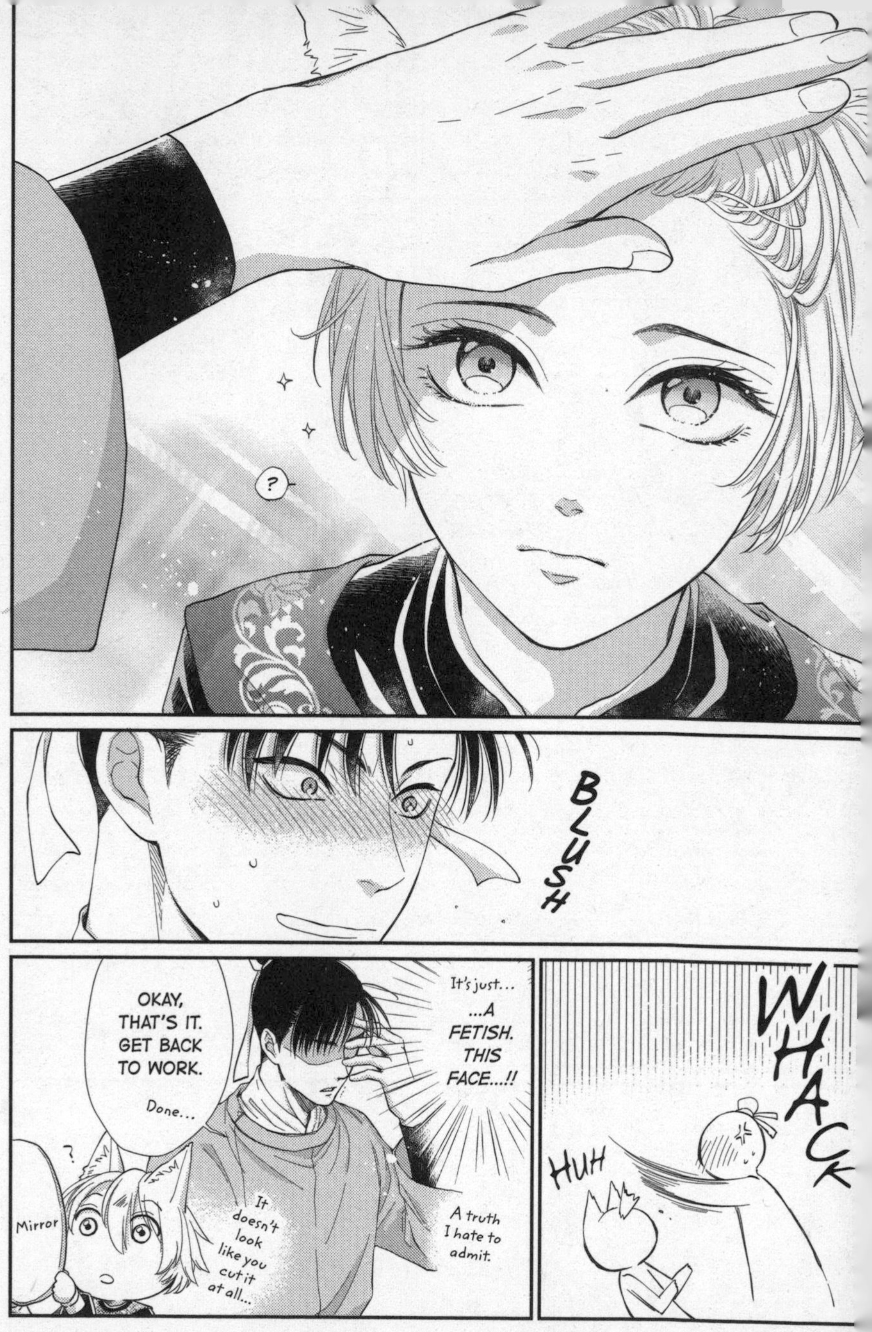
?
BLUSH
WHACK
HUH
It's just...
...A FETISH. THIS FACE...!!
A truth I hate to admit.
OKAY, THAT'S IT. GET BACK TO WORK.
Done...
?
Mirror
It doesn't look like you cut it at all...

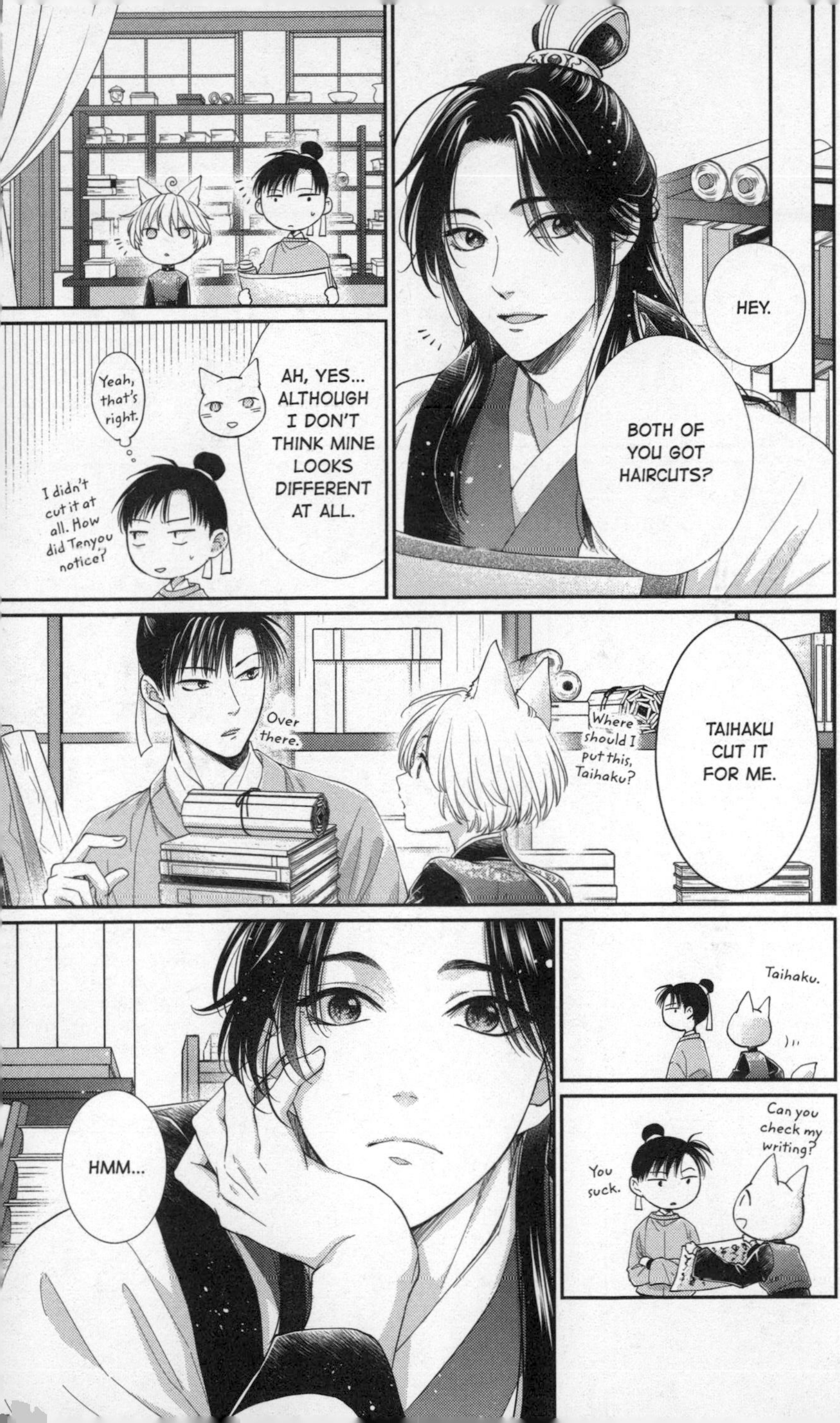
HEY.
BOTH OF YOU GOT HAIRCUTS?
AH, YES... ALTHOUGH I DON'T THINK MINE LOOKS DIFFERENT AT ALL.
Yeah, that's right.
I didn't cut it at all. How did Tenyou notice?
TAIHAKU CUT IT FOR ME.
Where should I put this, Taihaku?
Over there.
Taihaku.
Can you check my writing?
You suck.
HMM...

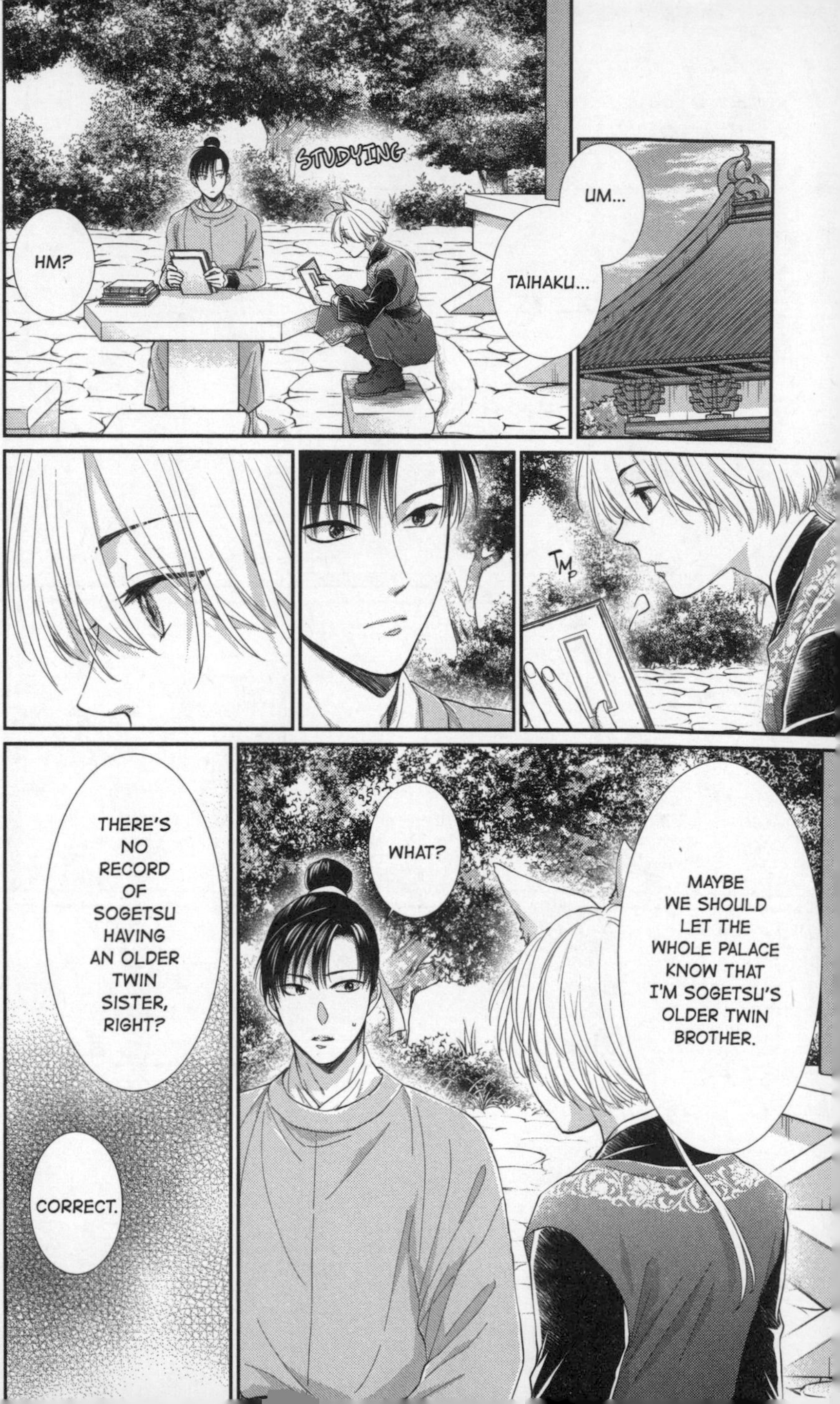
UM...
TAIHAKU...
STUDYING
HM?
TMP
MAYBE WE SHOULD LET THE WHOLE PALACE KNOW THAT I'M SOGETSU'S OLDER TWIN BROTHER.
WHAT?
THERE'S NO RECORD OF SOGETSU HAVING AN OLDER TWIN SISTER, RIGHT?
CORRECT.

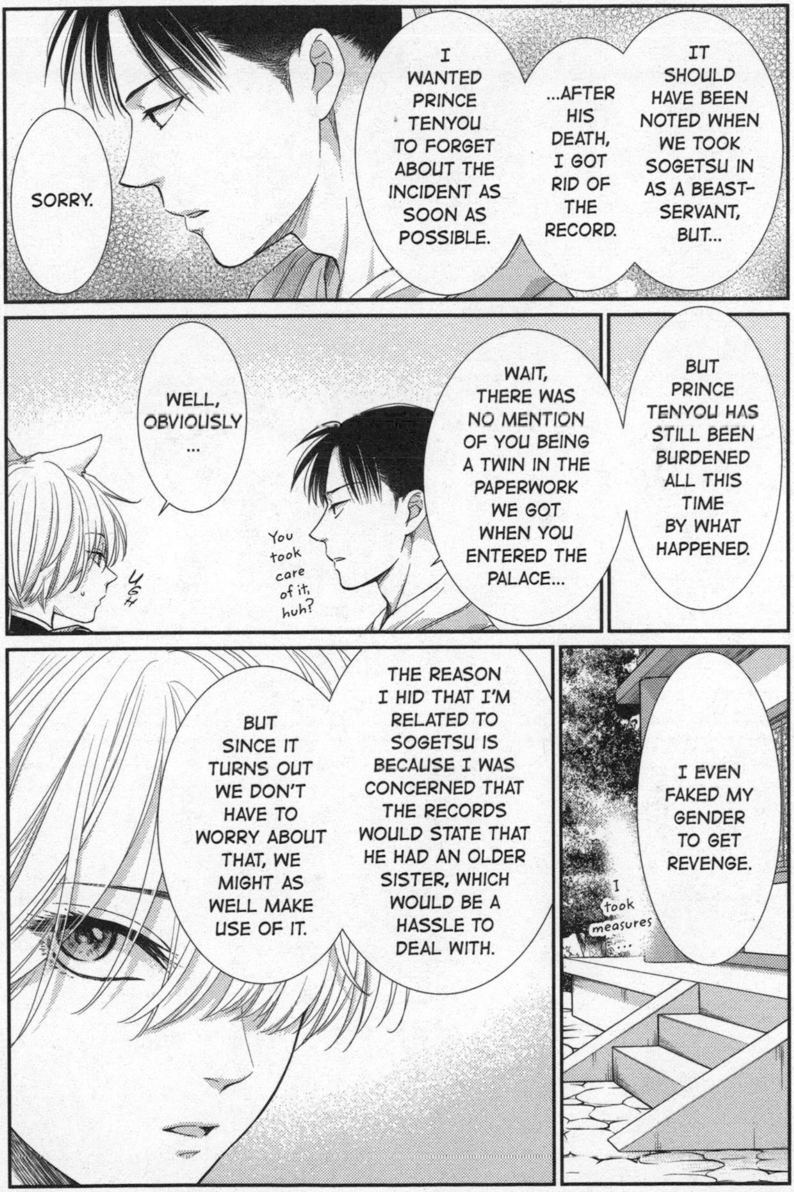
IT SHOULD HAVE BEEN NOTED WHEN WE TOOK SOGETSU IN AS A BEAST-SERVANT, BUT...
...AFTER HIS DEATH, I GOT RID OF THE RECORD.
I WANTED PRINCE TENYOU TO FORGET ABOUT THE INCIDENT AS SOON AS POSSIBLE.
SORRY.
BUT PRINCE TENYOU HAS STILL BEEN BURDENED ALL THIS TIME BY WHAT HAPPENED.
WAIT, THERE WAS NO MENTION OF YOU BEING A TWIN IN THE PAPERWORK WE GOT WHEN YOU ENTERED THE PALACE...
You took care of it, huh?
WELL, OBVIOUSLY...
UGH
I EVEN FAKED MY GENDER TO GET REVENGE.
I took measures...
THE REASON I HID THAT I'M RELATED TO SOGETSU IS BECAUSE I WAS CONCERNED THAT THE RECORDS WOULD STATE THAT HE HAD AN OLDER SISTER, WHICH WOULD BE A HASSLE TO DEAL WITH.
BUT SINCE IT TURNS OUT WE DON'T HAVE TO WORRY ABOUT THAT, WE MIGHT AS WELL MAKE USE OF IT.

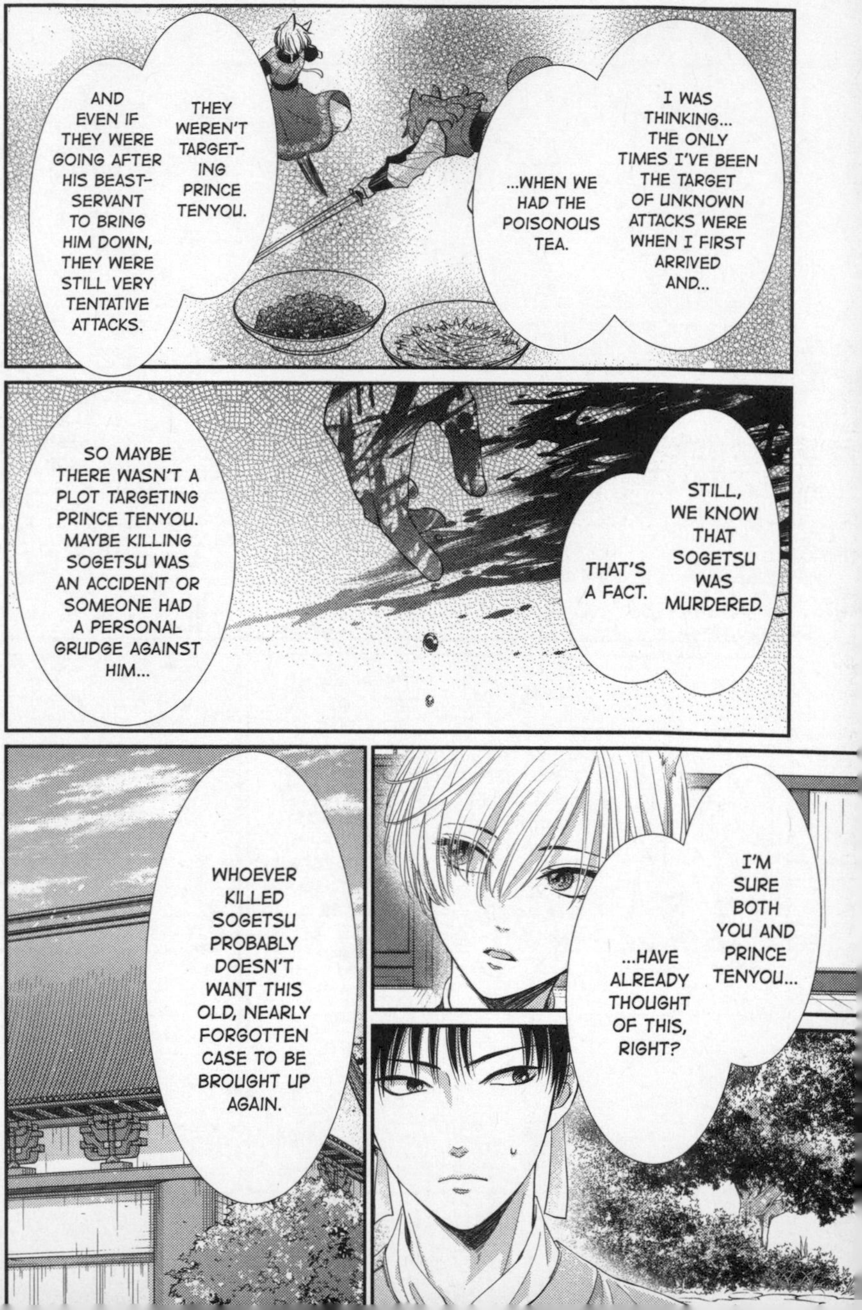
I WAS THINKING... THE ONLY TIMES I'VE BEEN THE TARGET OF UNKNOWN ATTACKS WERE WHEN I FIRST ARRIVED AND...
...WHEN WE HAD THE POISONOUS TEA.
THEY WEREN'T TARGET-ING PRINCE TENYOU.
AND EVEN IF THEY WERE GOING AFTER HIS BEAST-SERVANT TO BRING HIM DOWN, THEY WERE STILL VERY TENTATIVE ATTACKS.
STILL, WE KNOW THAT SOGETSU WAS MURDERED.
THAT'S A FACT.
SO MAYBE THERE WASN'T A PLOT TARGETING PRINCE TENYOU. MAYBE KILLING SOGETSU WAS AN ACCIDENT OR SOMEONE HAD A PERSONAL GRUDGE AGAINST HIM...
I'M SURE BOTH YOU AND PRINCE TENYOU...
...HAVE ALREADY THOUGHT OF THIS, RIGHT?
WHOEVER KILLED SOGETSU PROBABLY DOESN'T WANT THIS OLD, NEARLY FORGOTTEN CASE TO BE BROUGHT UP AGAIN.

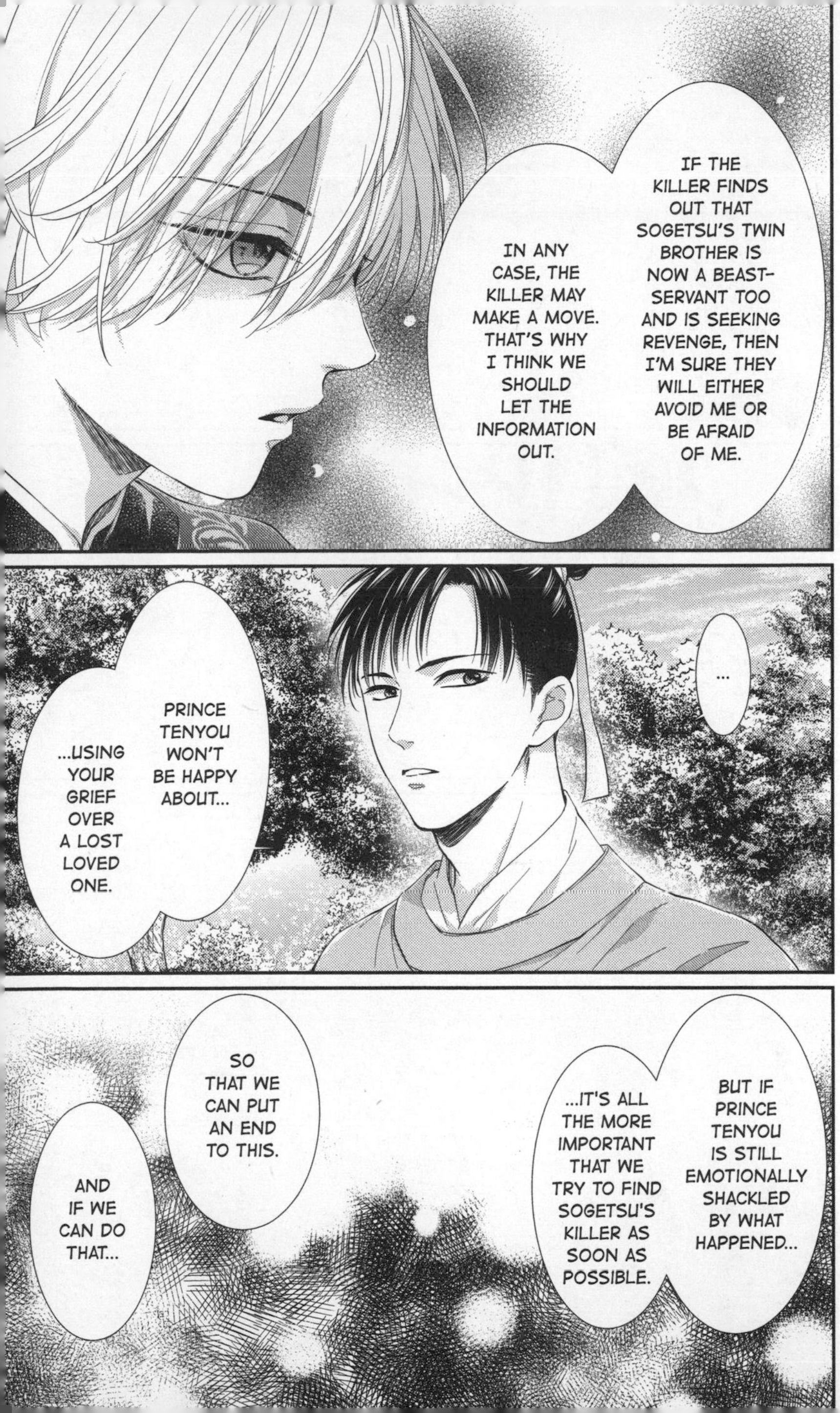
IF THE KILLER FINDS OUT THAT SOGETSU'S TWIN BROTHER IS NOW A BEAST-SERVANT TOO AND IS SEEKING REVENGE, THEN I'M SURE THEY WILL EITHER AVOID ME OR BE AFRAID OF ME.
IN ANY CASE, THE KILLER MAY MAKE A MOVE. THAT'S WHY I THINK WE SHOULD LET THE INFORMATION OUT.
...
PRINCE TENYOU WON'T BE HAPPY ABOUT...
...USING YOUR GRIEF OVER A LOST LOVED ONE.
BUT IF PRINCE TENYOU IS STILL EMOTIONALLY SHACKLED BY WHAT HAPPENED...
...IT'S ALL THE MORE IMPORTANT THAT WE TRY TO FIND SOGETSU'S KILLER AS SOON AS POSSIBLE.
SO THAT WE CAN PUT AN END TO THIS.
AND IF WE CAN DO THAT...

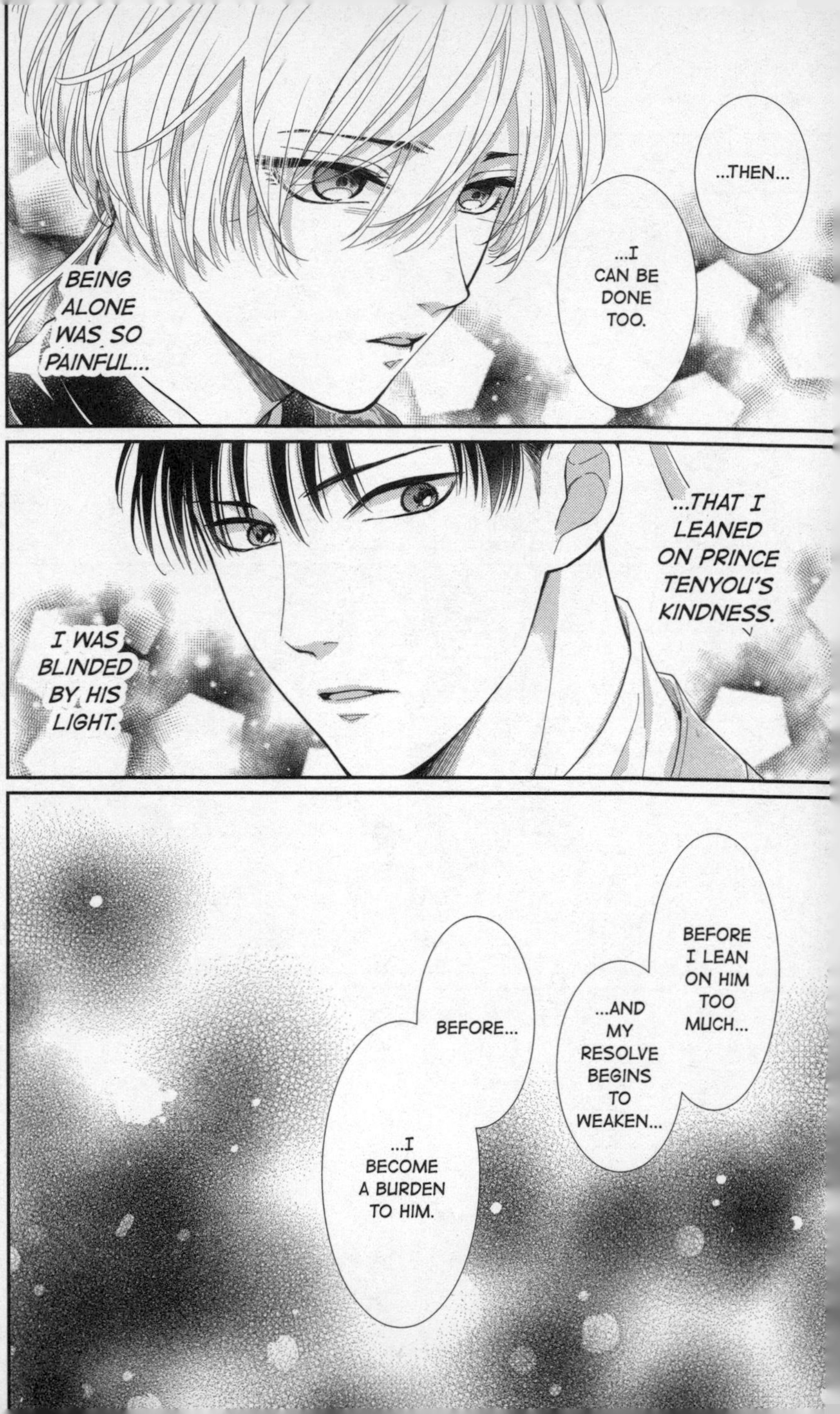
...THEN...
...I CAN BE DONE TOO.
BEING ALONE WAS SO PAINFUL...
...THAT I LEANED ON PRINCE TENYOU'S KINDNESS.
I WAS BLINDED BY HIS LIGHT.
BEFORE I LEAN ON HIM TOO MUCH...
...AND MY RESOLVE BEGINS TO WEAKEN...
BEFORE...
...I BECOME A BURDEN TO HIM.

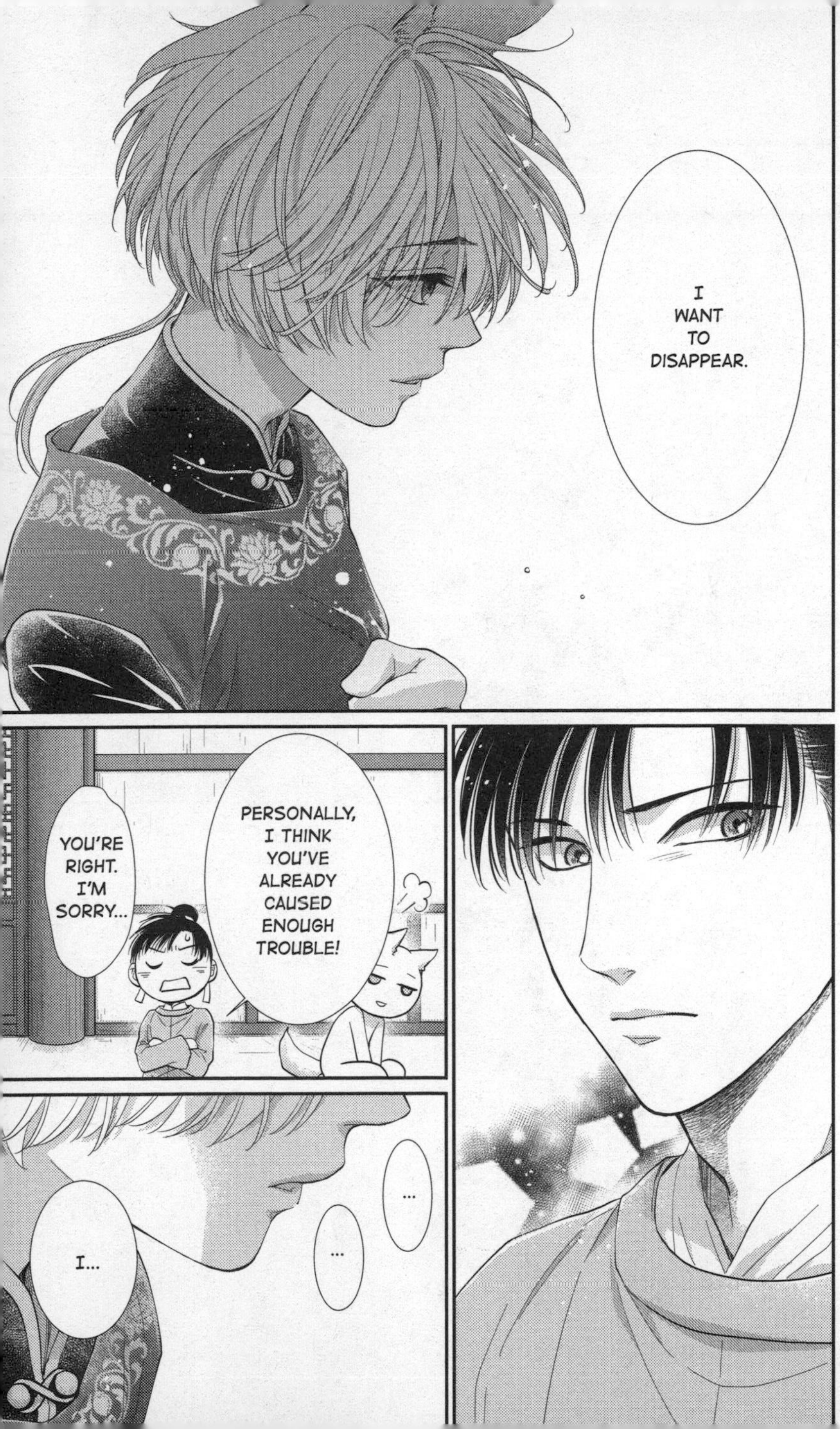
I WANT TO DISAPPEAR.
PERSONALLY, I THINK YOU'VE ALREADY CAUSED ENOUGH TROUBLE!
YOU'RE RIGHT. I'M SORRY...
...
...
I...

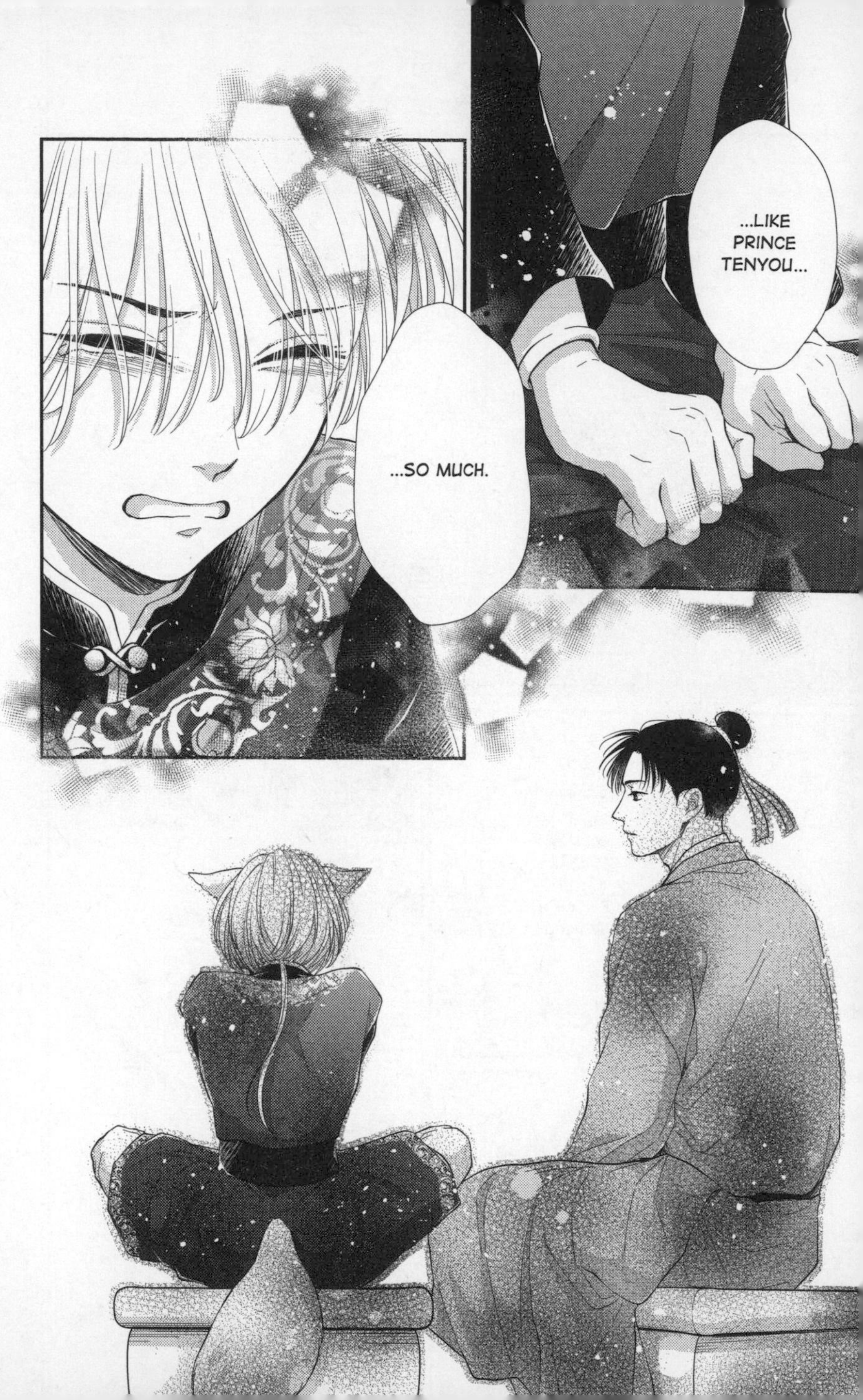
...LIKE PRINCE TENYOU...
...SO MUCH.

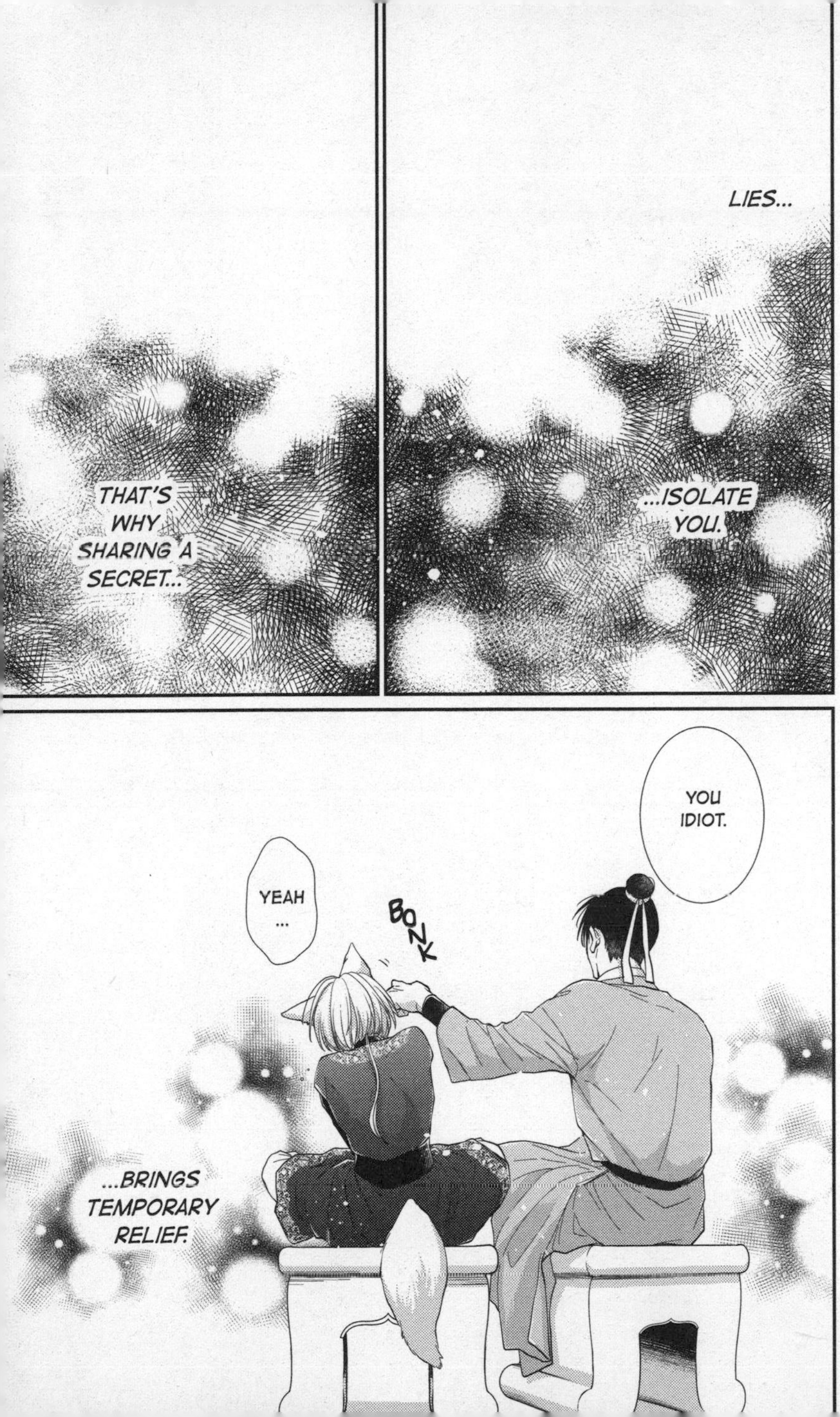
LIES...
...ISOLATE YOU.
THAT'S WHY SHARING A SECRET...
YOU IDIOT.
BONK
YEAH ...
...BRINGS TEMPORARY RELIEF.

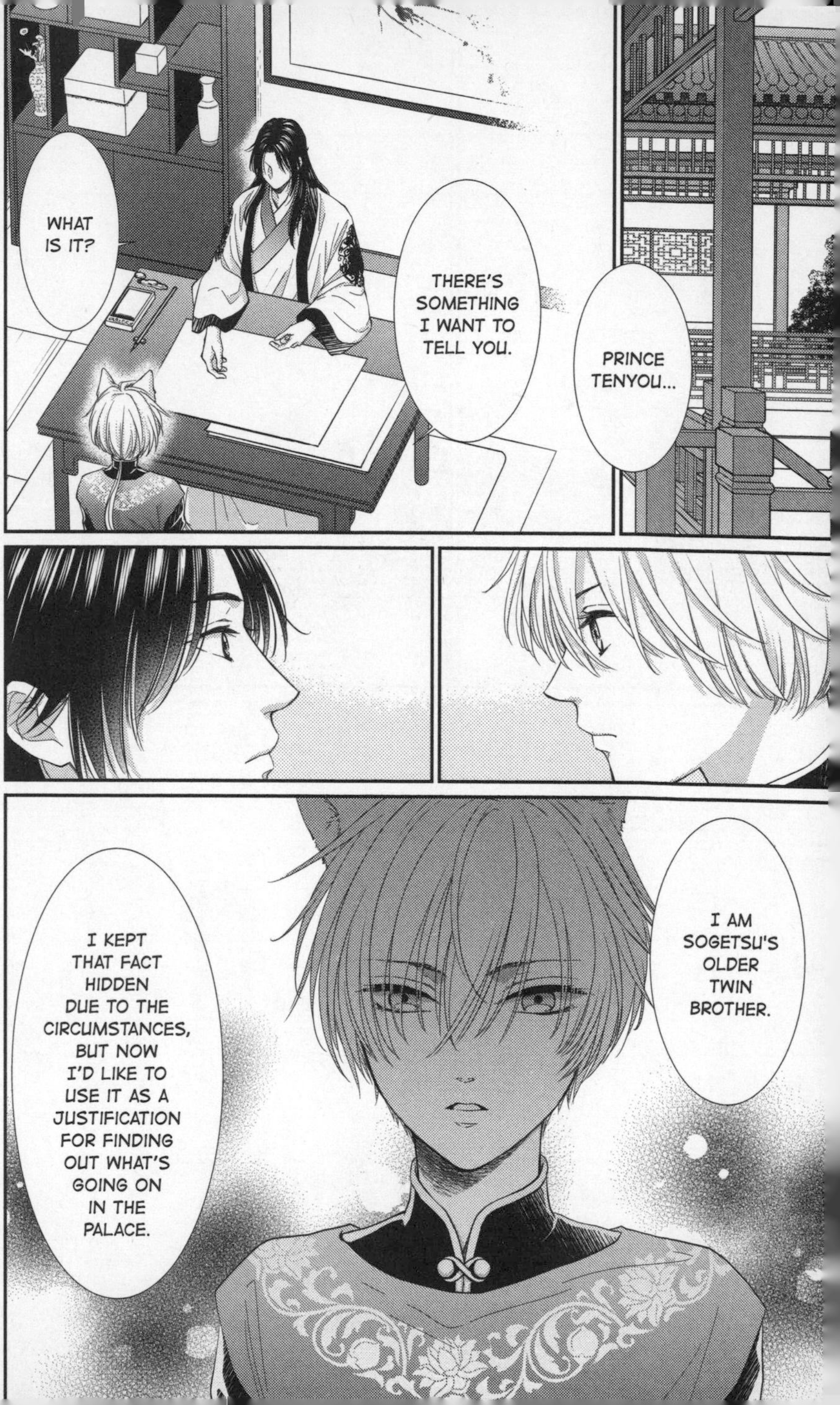
PRINCE TENYOU...
THERE'S SOMETHING I WANT TO TELL YOU.
WHAT IS IT?
I AM SOGETSU'S OLDER TWIN BROTHER.
I KEPT THAT FACT HIDDEN DUE TO THE CIRCUMSTANCES, BUT NOW I'D LIKE TO USE IT AS A JUSTIFICATION FOR FINDING OUT WHAT'S GOING ON IN THE PALACE.

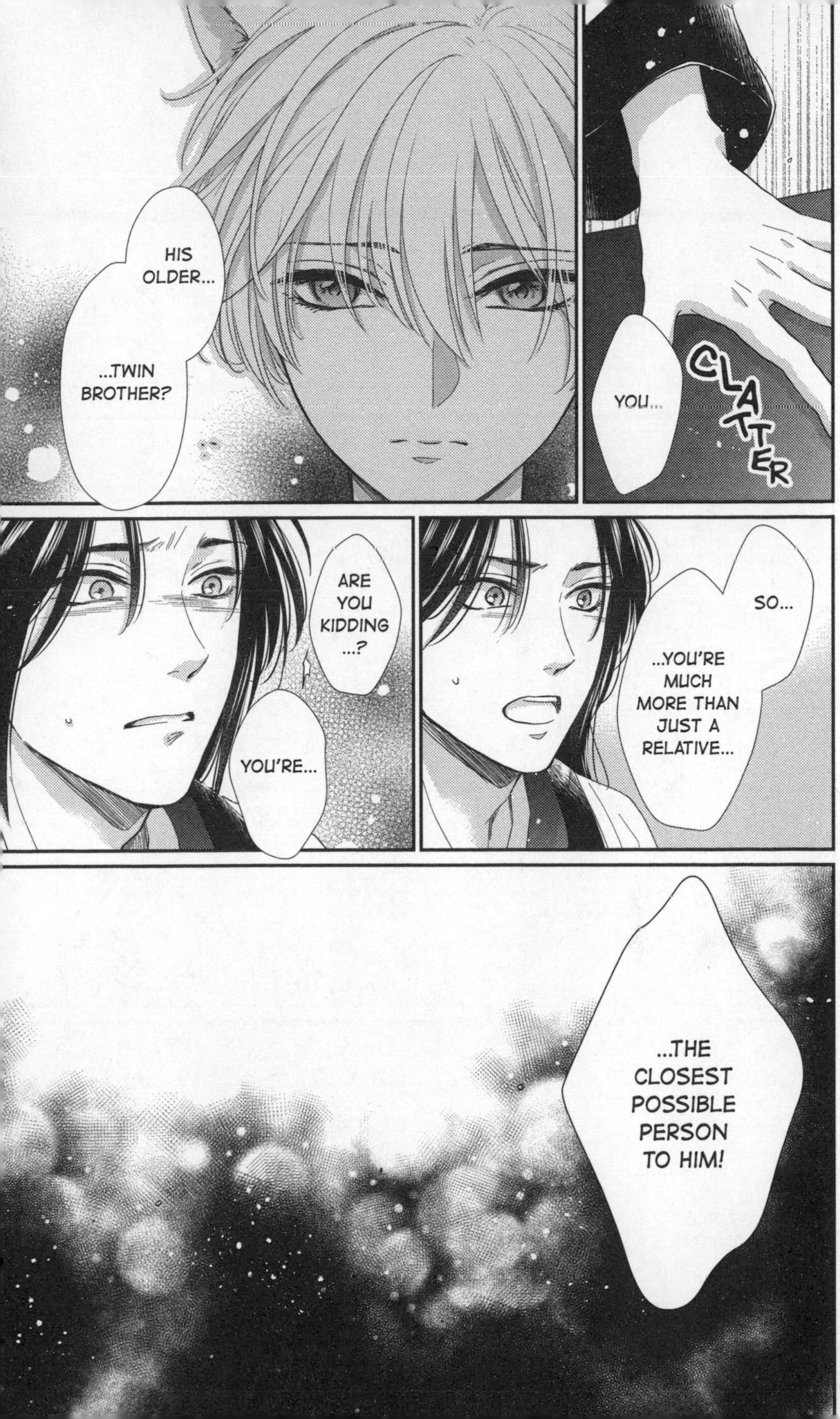
YOU...
CLATTER
HIS OLDER...
...TWIN BROTHER?
SO...
...YOU'RE MUCH MORE THAN JUST A RELATIVE...
ARE YOU KIDDING ...?
YOU'RE...
...THE CLOSEST POSSIBLE PERSON TO HIM!

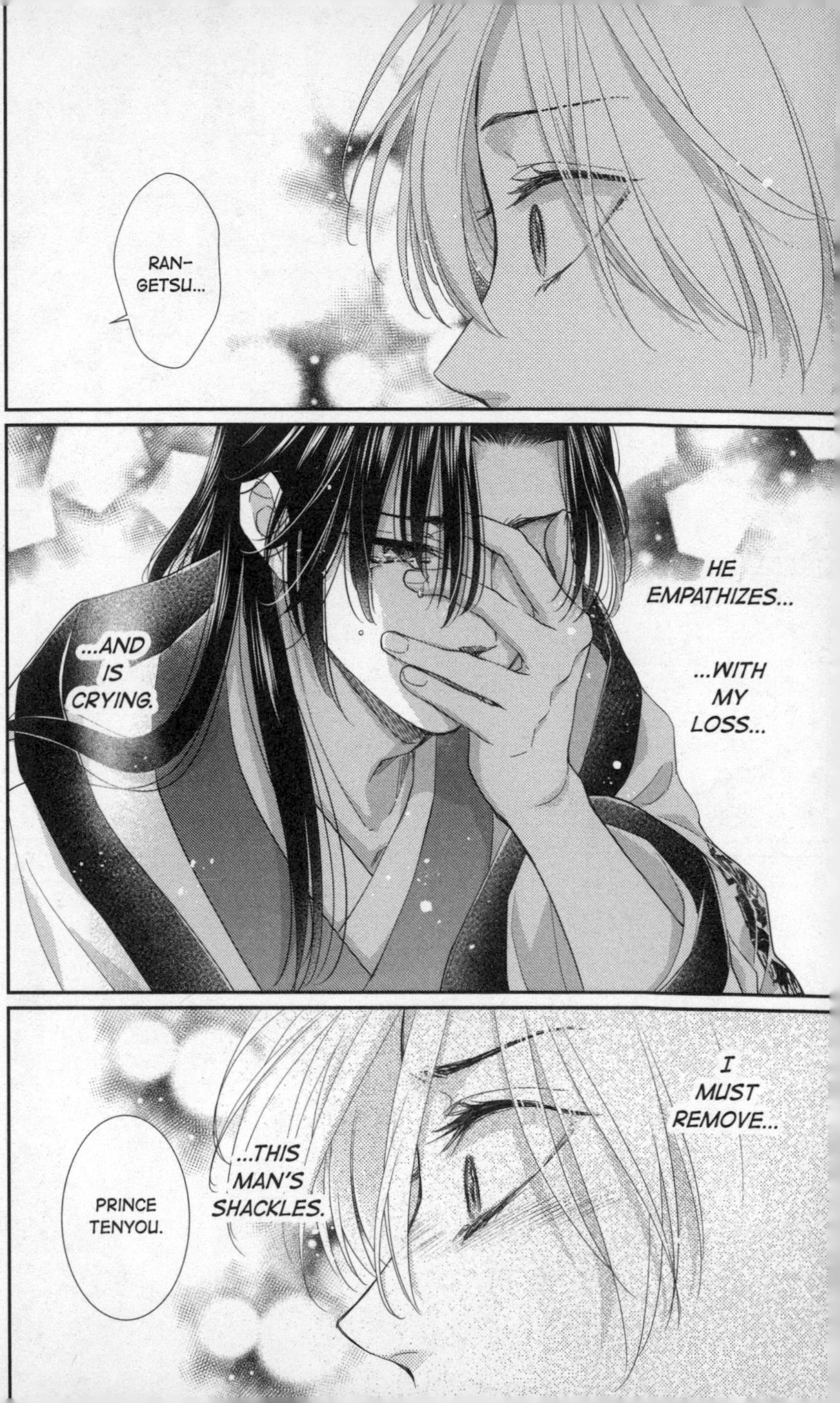
RAN-
GETSU...
HE EMPATHIZES...
...WITH MY LOSS...
...AND IS CRYING.
I MUST REMOVE...
...THIS MAN'S SHACKLES.
PRINCE TENYOU.

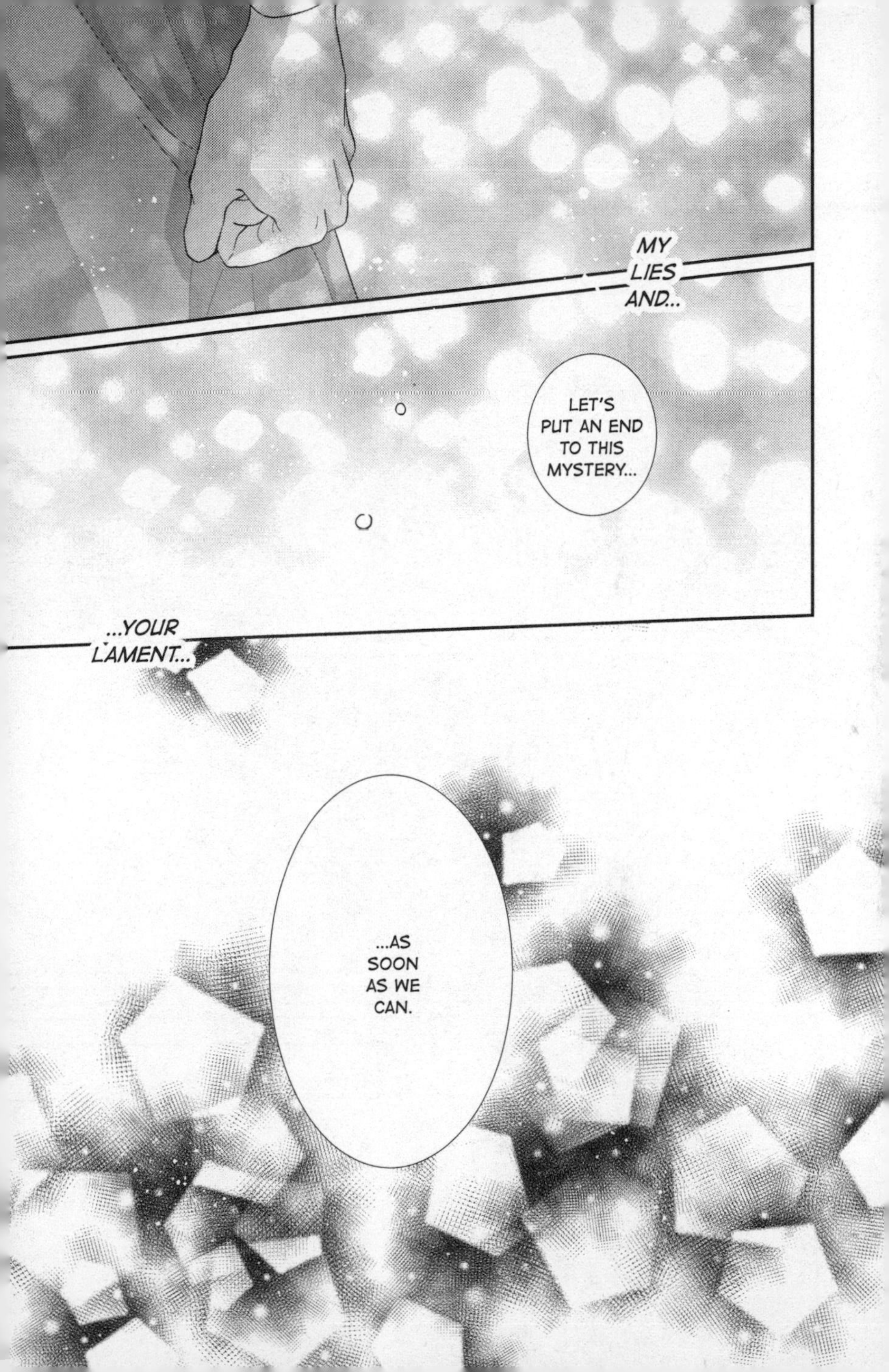
MY LIES AND...
LET'S PUT AN END TO THIS MYSTERY...
...YOUR LAMENT...
...AS SOON AS WE CAN.

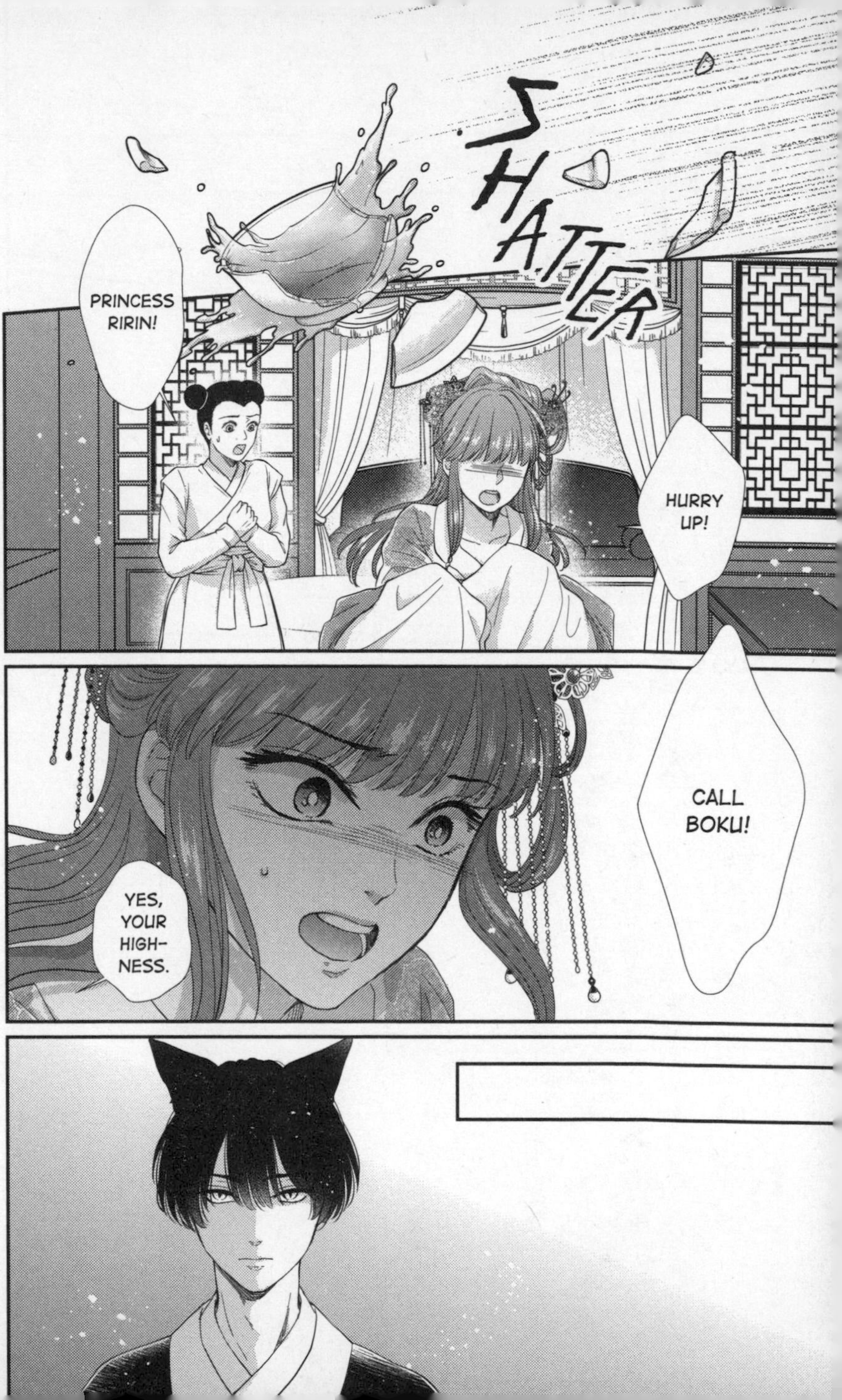
SHATTER
PRINCESS RIRIN!
HURRY UP!
CALL BOKU!
YES, YOUR HIGH-NESS.

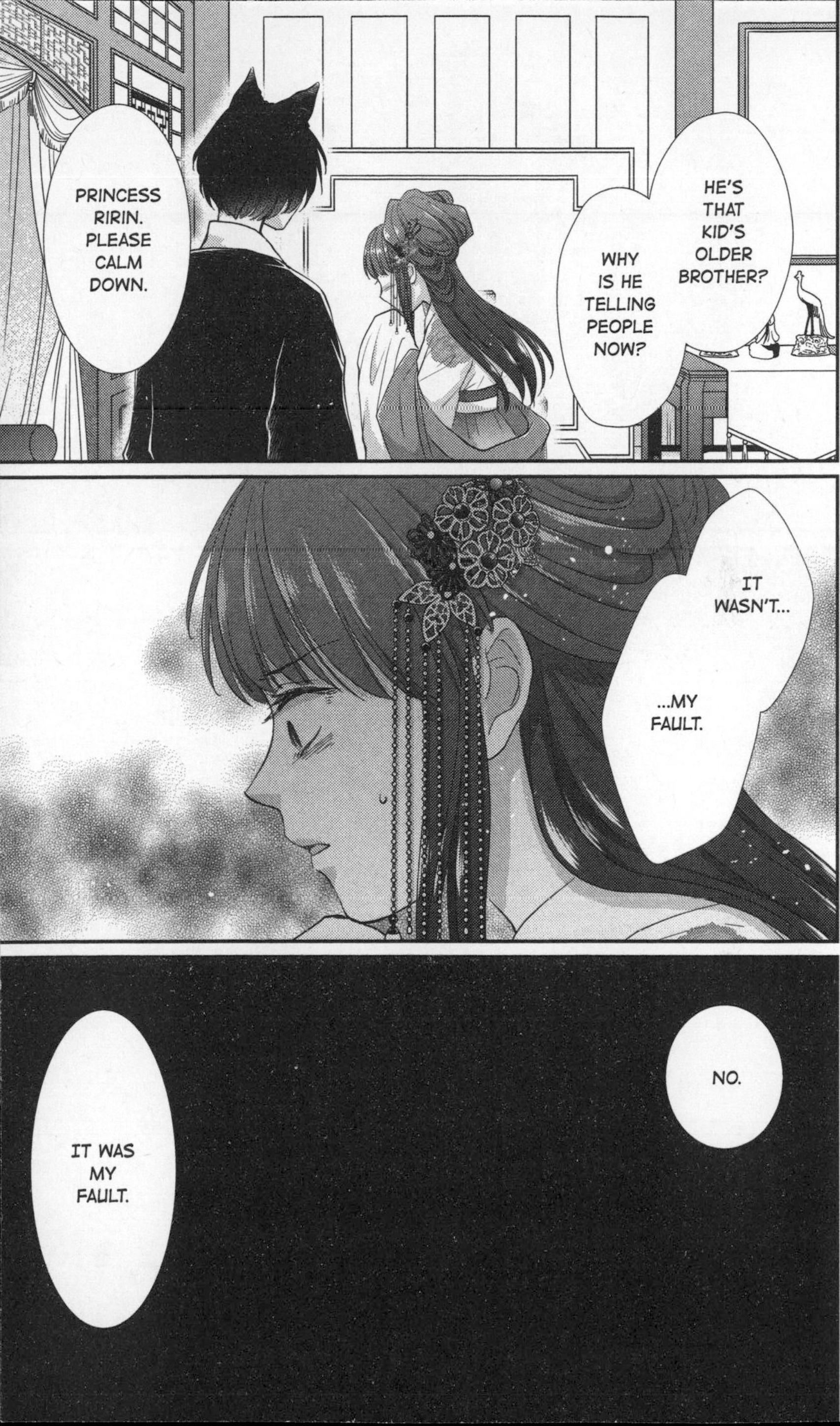
HE'S THAT KID'S OLDER BROTHER?
WHY IS HE TELLING PEOPLE NOW?
PRINCESS RIRIN. PLEASE CALM DOWN.
IT WASN'T...
...MY FAULT.
NO.
IT WAS MY FAULT.

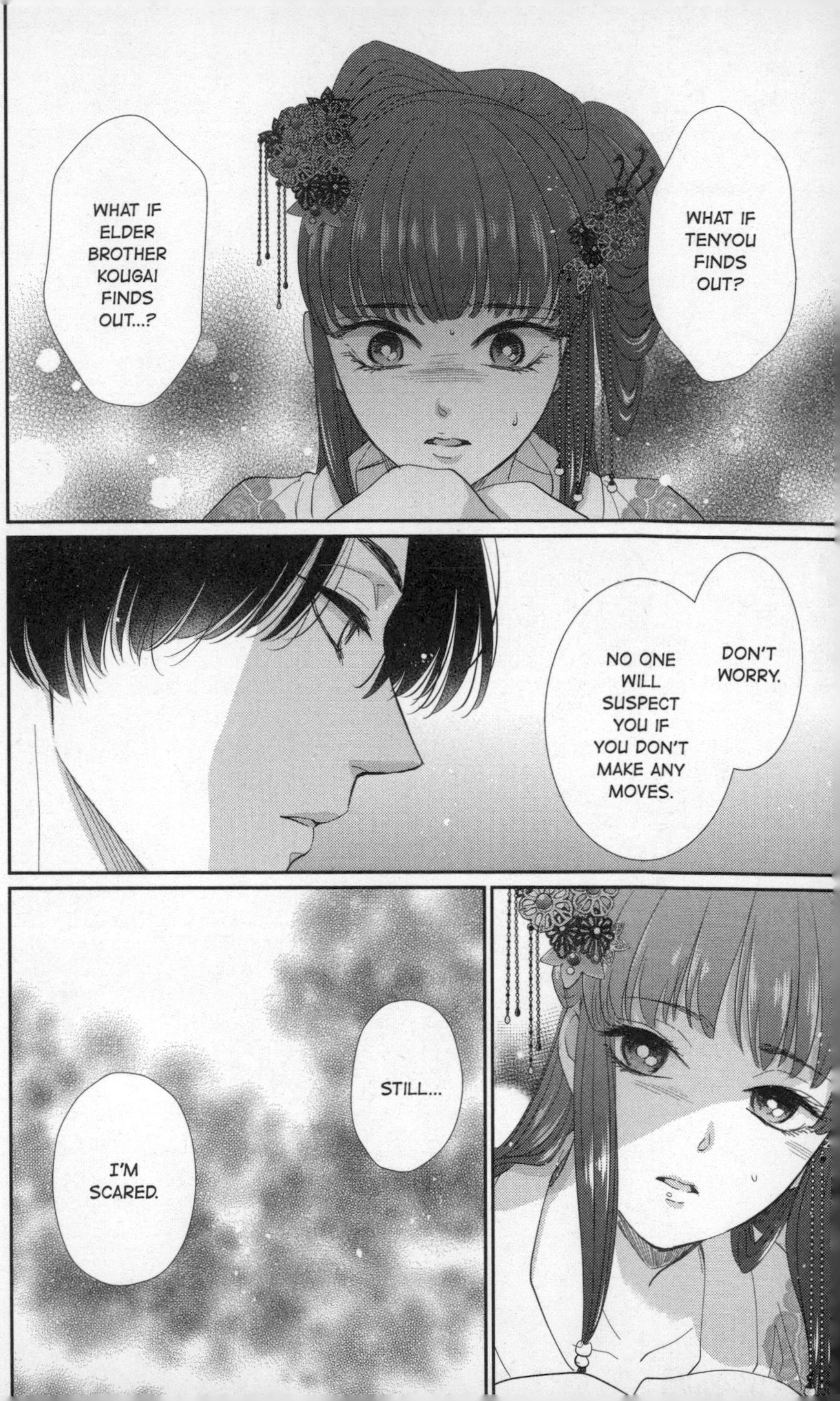
WHAT IF TENYOU FINDS OUT?
WHAT IF ELDER BROTHER KOUGAI FINDS OUT...?
DON'T WORRY.
NO ONE WILL SUSPECT YOU IF YOU DON'T MAKE ANY MOVES.
STILL...
I'M SCARED.

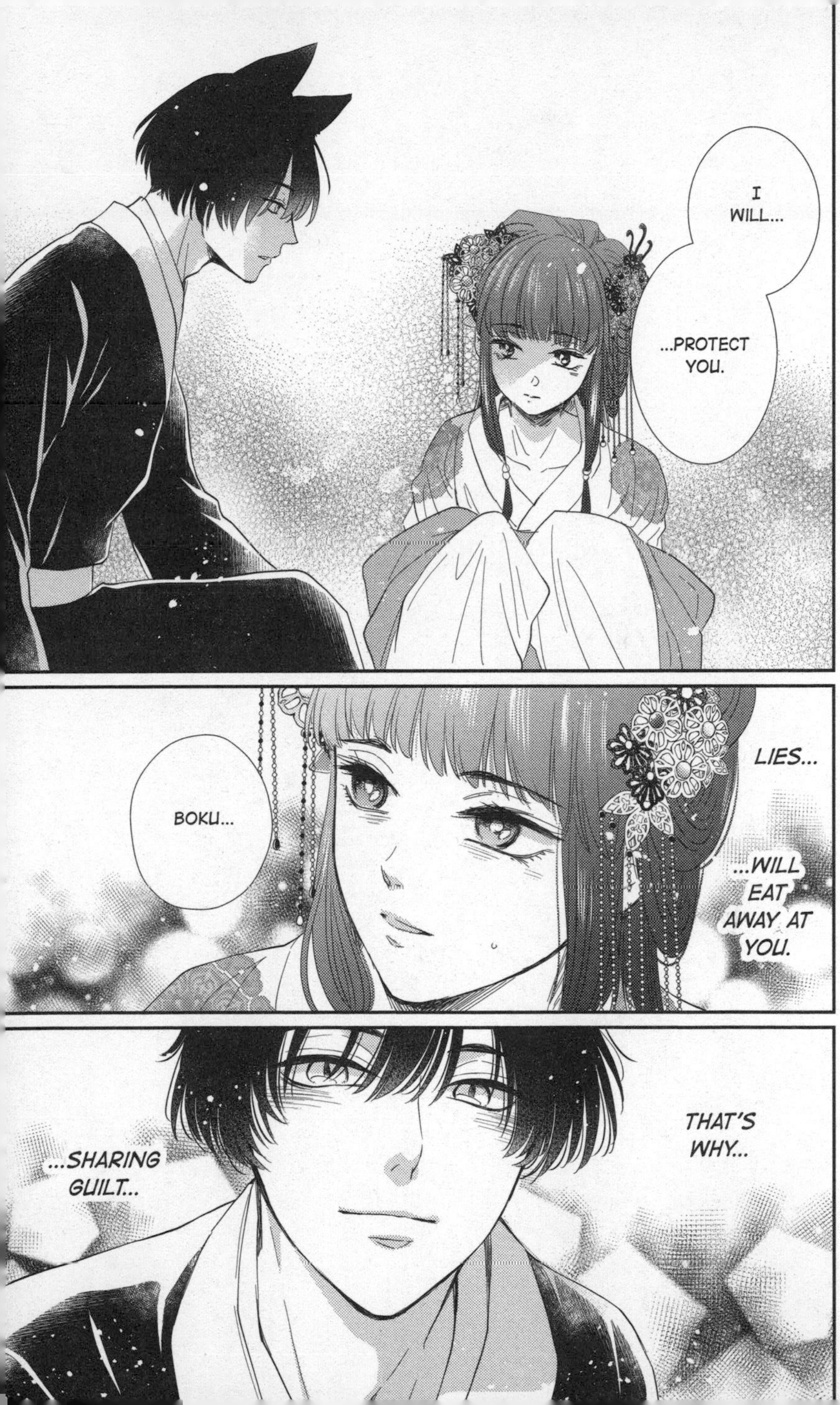
I WILL...
...PROTECT YOU.
LIES...
...WILL EAT AWAY AT YOU.
BOKU...
THAT'S WHY...
...SHARING GUILT...

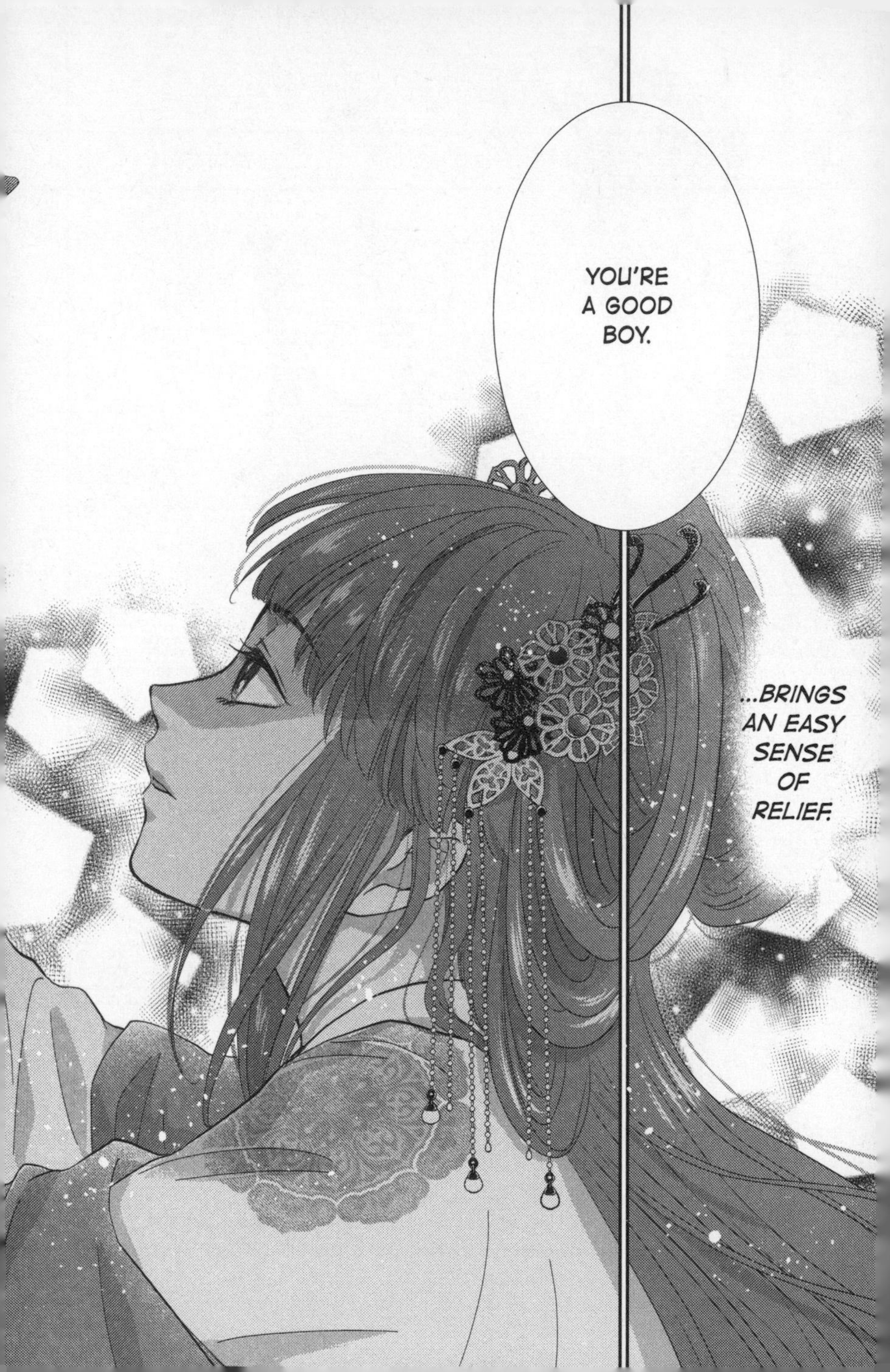
YOU'RE A GOOD BOY.
...BRINGS AN EASY SENSE OF RELIEF.

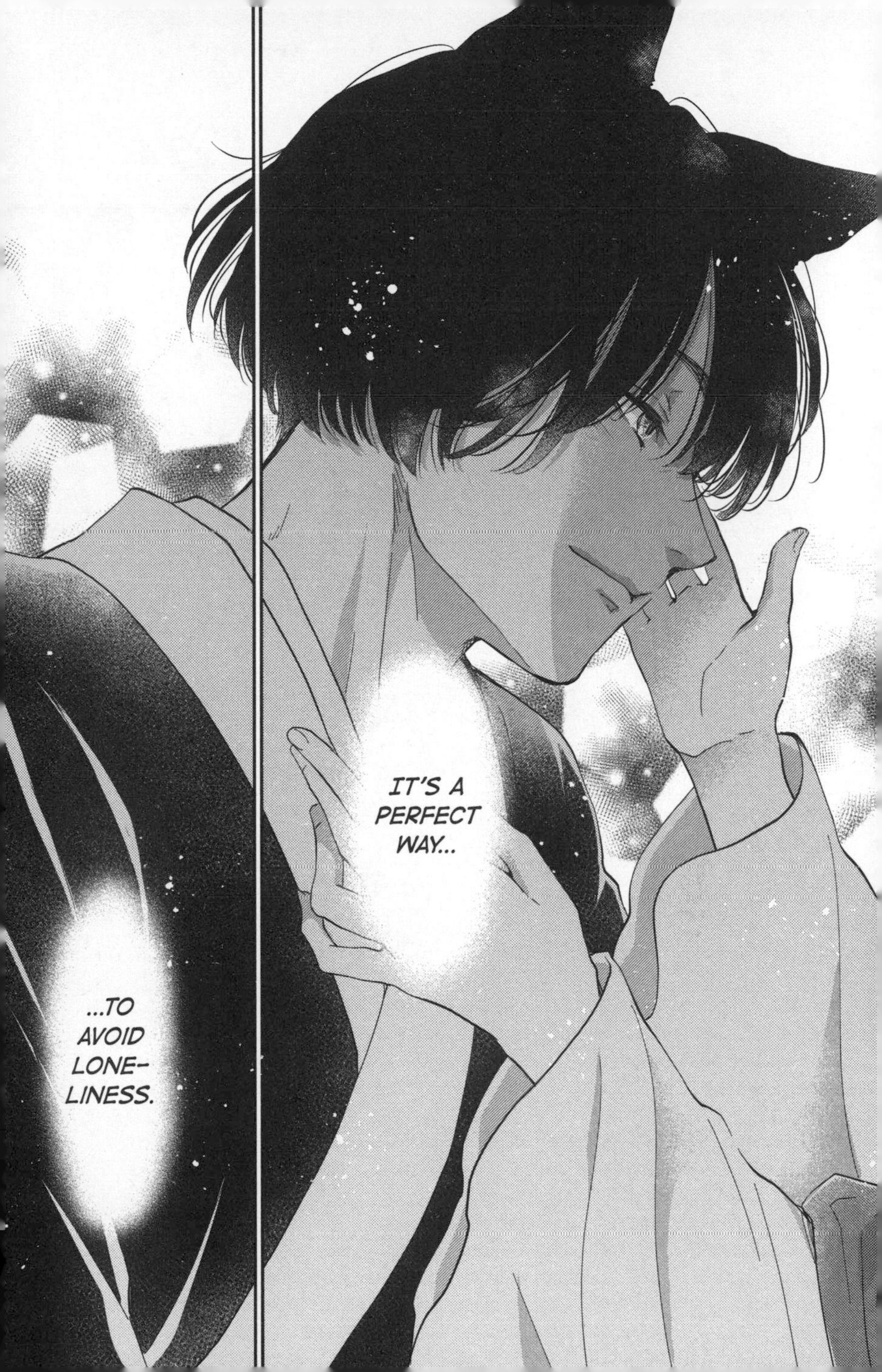
IT'S A PERFECT WAY...
...TO AVOID LONE-LINESS.

THE KING'S *Beast*

麗

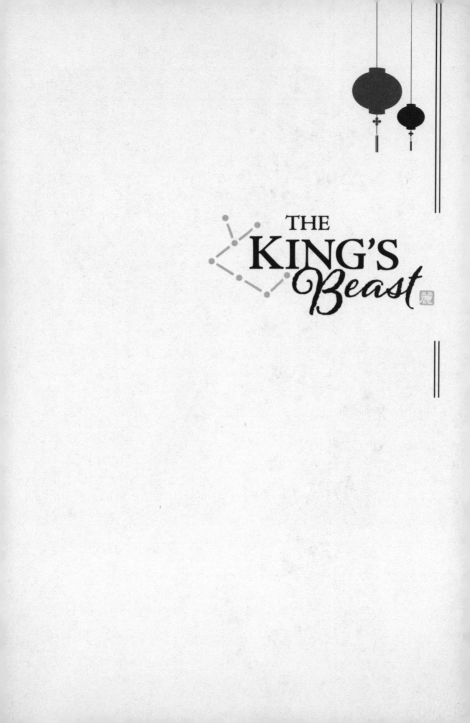

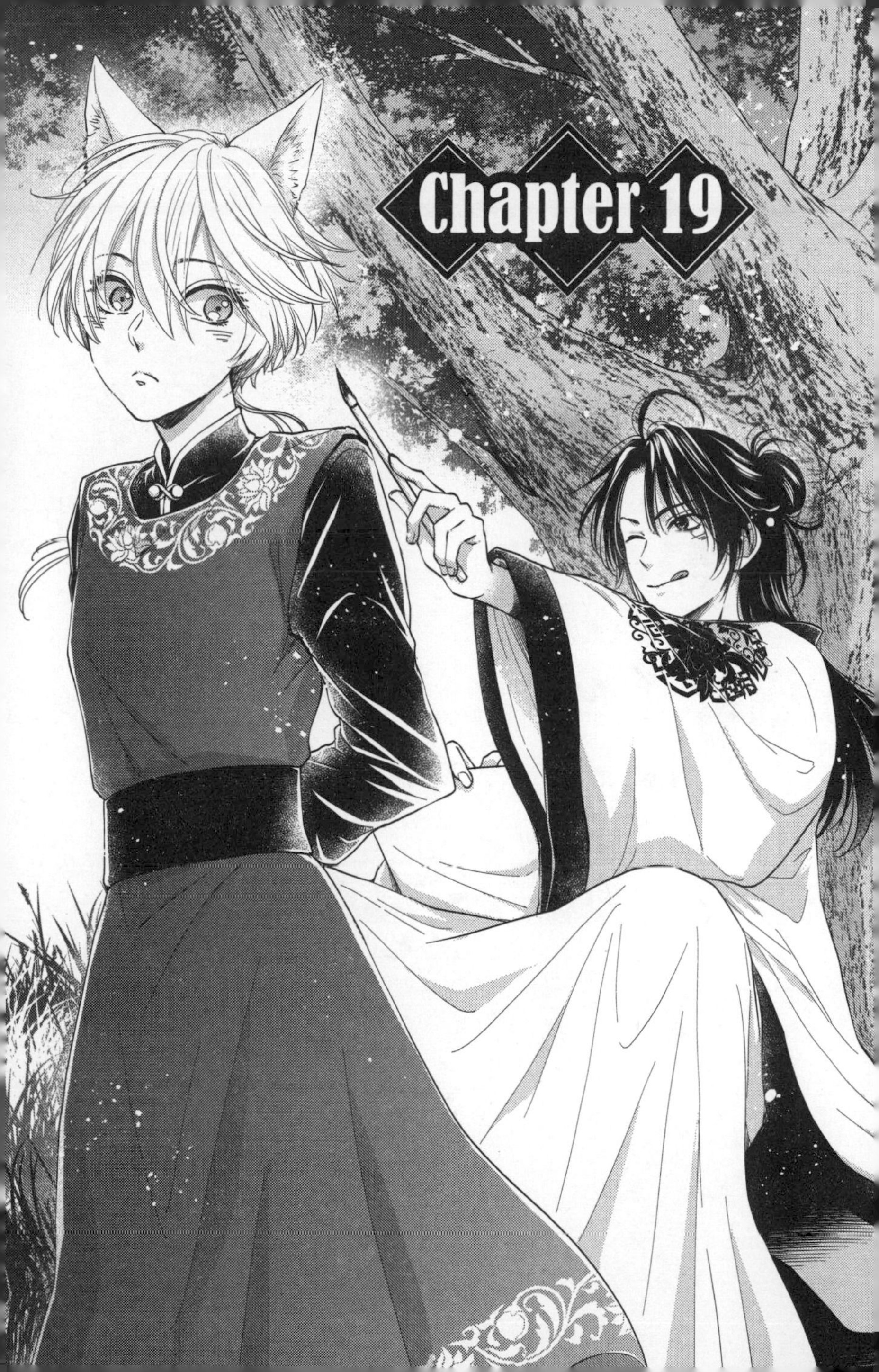
Chapter 19

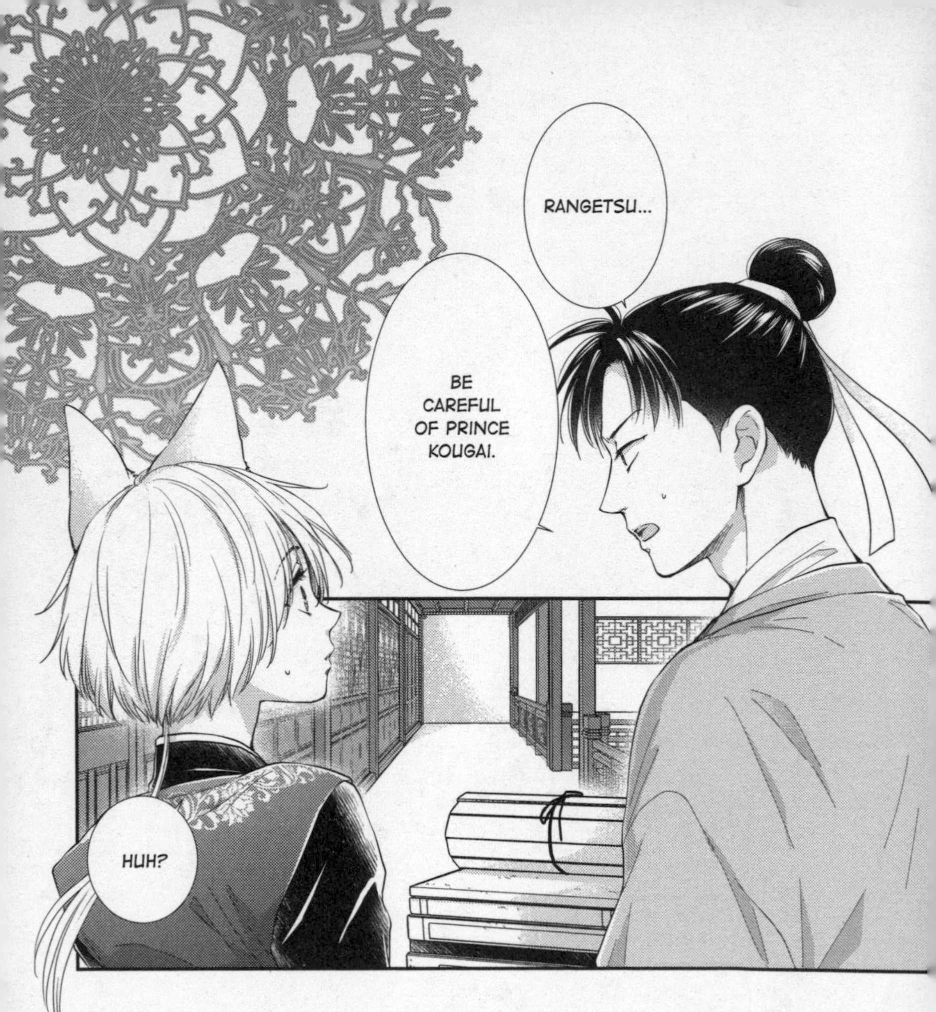
RANGETSU...
BE CAREFUL OF PRINCE KOUGAI.
HUH?

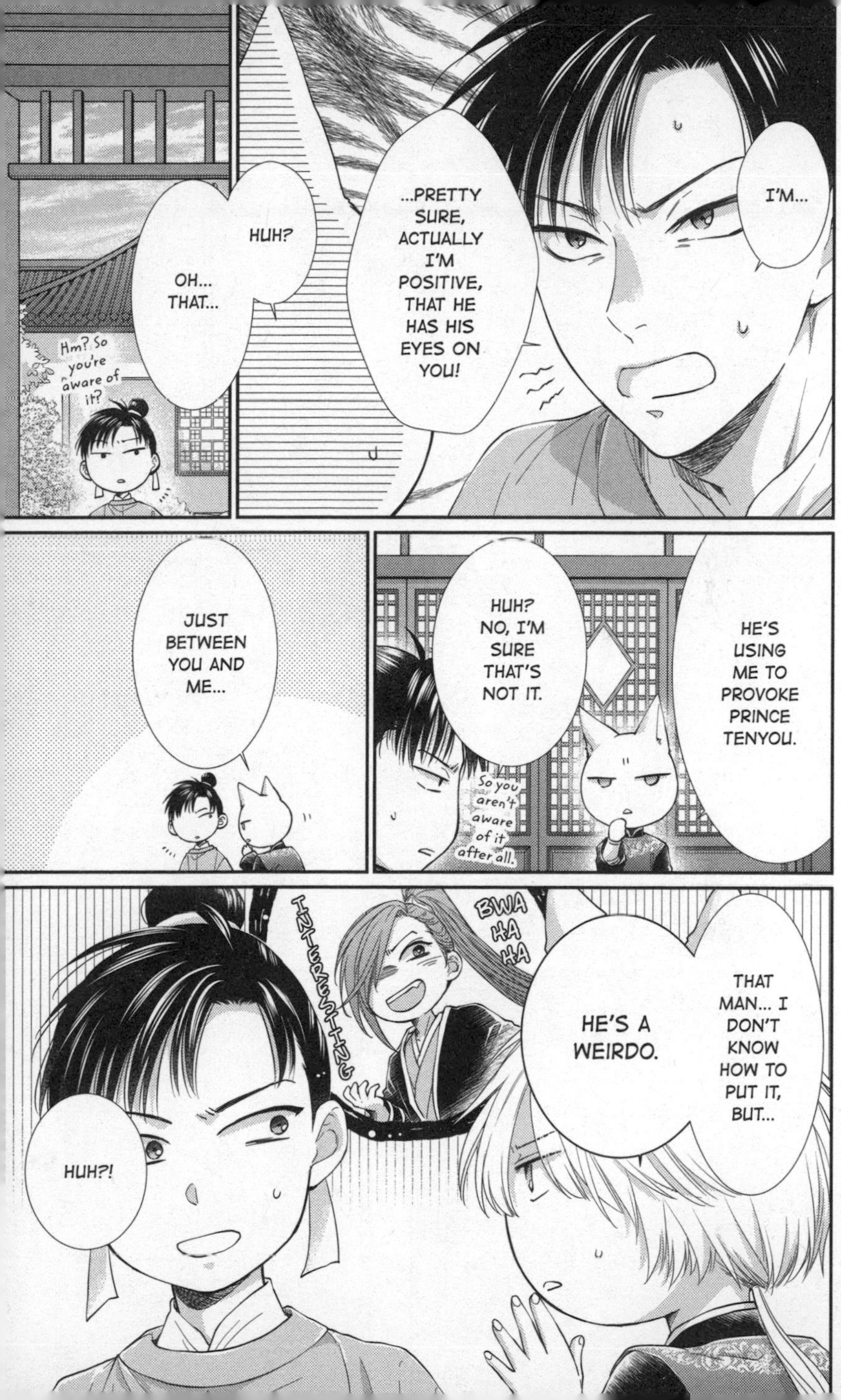
I'M...
...PRETTY SURE, ACTUALLY I'M POSITIVE, THAT HE HAS HIS EYES ON YOU!
HUH?
OH... THAT...
Hm? So you're aware of it?
HE'S USING ME TO PROVOKE PRINCE TENYOU.
HUH? NO, I'M SURE THAT'S NOT IT.
So you aren't aware of it after all.
JUST BETWEEN YOU AND ME...
THAT MAN... I DON'T KNOW HOW TO PUT IT, BUT...
HE'S A WEIRDO.
BWA HA HA
INTERESTING
HUH?!

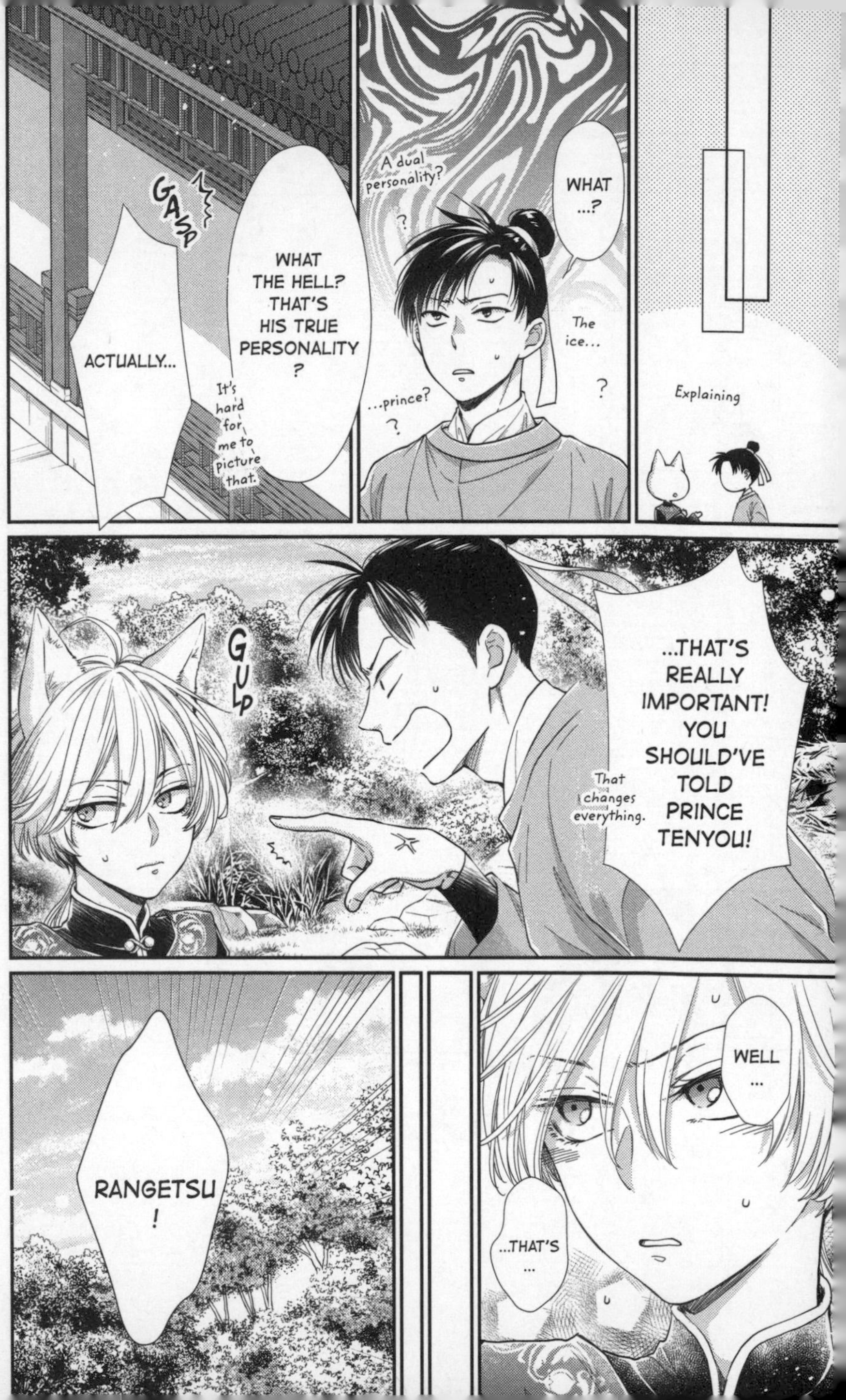

Explaining
WHAT ...?
A dual personality?
?
The ice...
?
...prince?
?
WHAT THE HELL? THAT'S HIS TRUE PERSONALITY ?
It's hard for me to picture that.
GASP
ACTUALLY...
...THAT'S REALLY IMPORTANT! YOU SHOULD'VE TOLD PRINCE TENYOU!
That changes everything.
GULP
WELL ...
...THAT'S ...
RANGETSU !

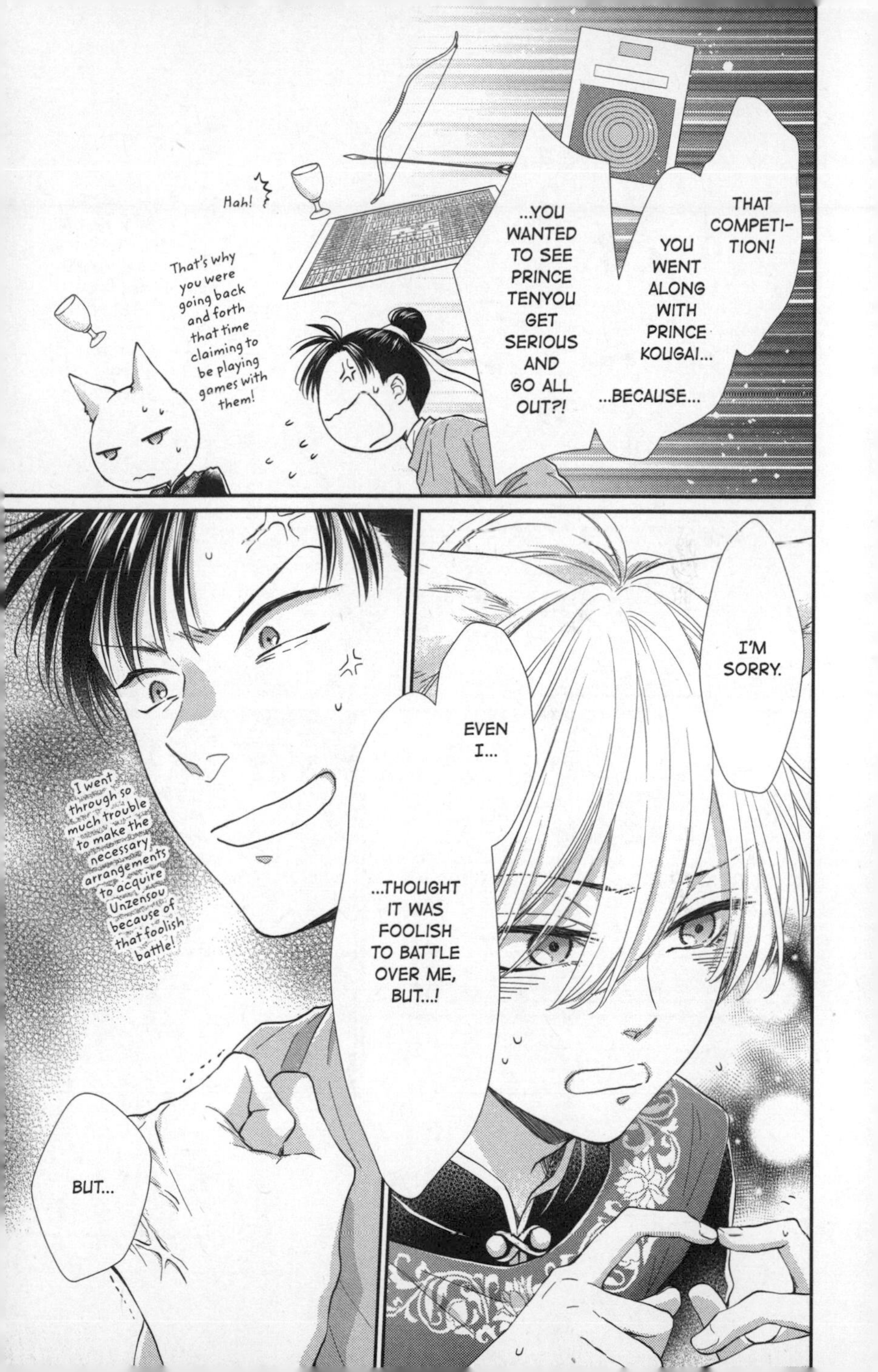
THAT COMPETITION!
YOU WENT ALONG WITH PRINCE KOUGAI... ...BECAUSE...
...YOU WANTED TO SEE PRINCE TENYOU GET SERIOUS AND GO ALL OUT?!
Hah!
That's why you were going back and forth that time claiming to be playing games with them!
I'M SORRY.
EVEN I...
...THOUGHT IT WAS FOOLISH TO BATTLE OVER ME, BUT...!
I went through so much trouble to make the necessary arrangements to acquire Unzensou because of that foolish battle!
BUT...

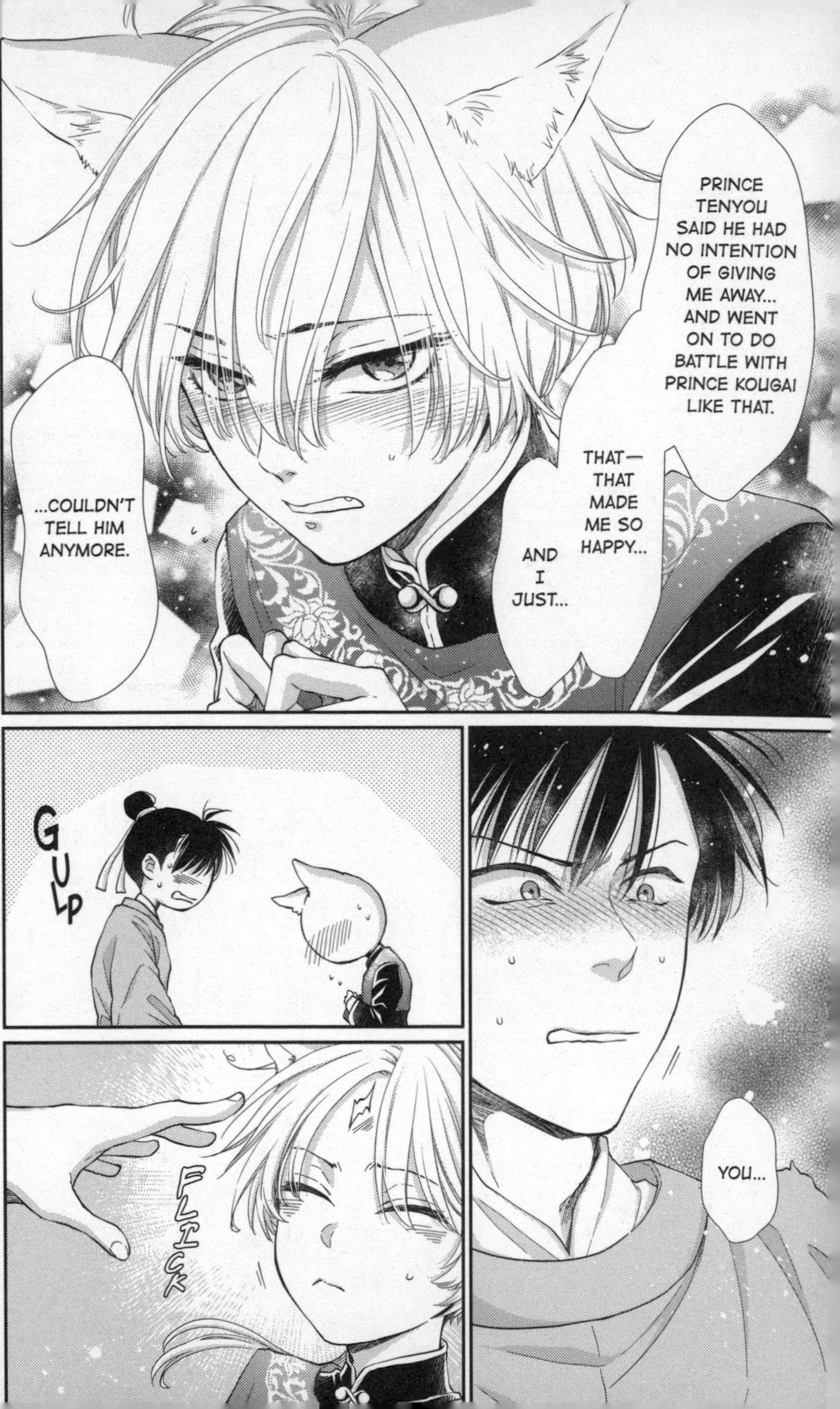
PRINCE TENYOU SAID HE HAD NO INTENTION OF GIVING ME AWAY... AND WENT ON TO DO BATTLE WITH PRINCE KOUGAI LIKE THAT.
THAT— THAT MADE ME SO HAPPY...
AND I JUST...
...COULDN'T TELL HIM ANYMORE.
YOU...
GULP
FLICK

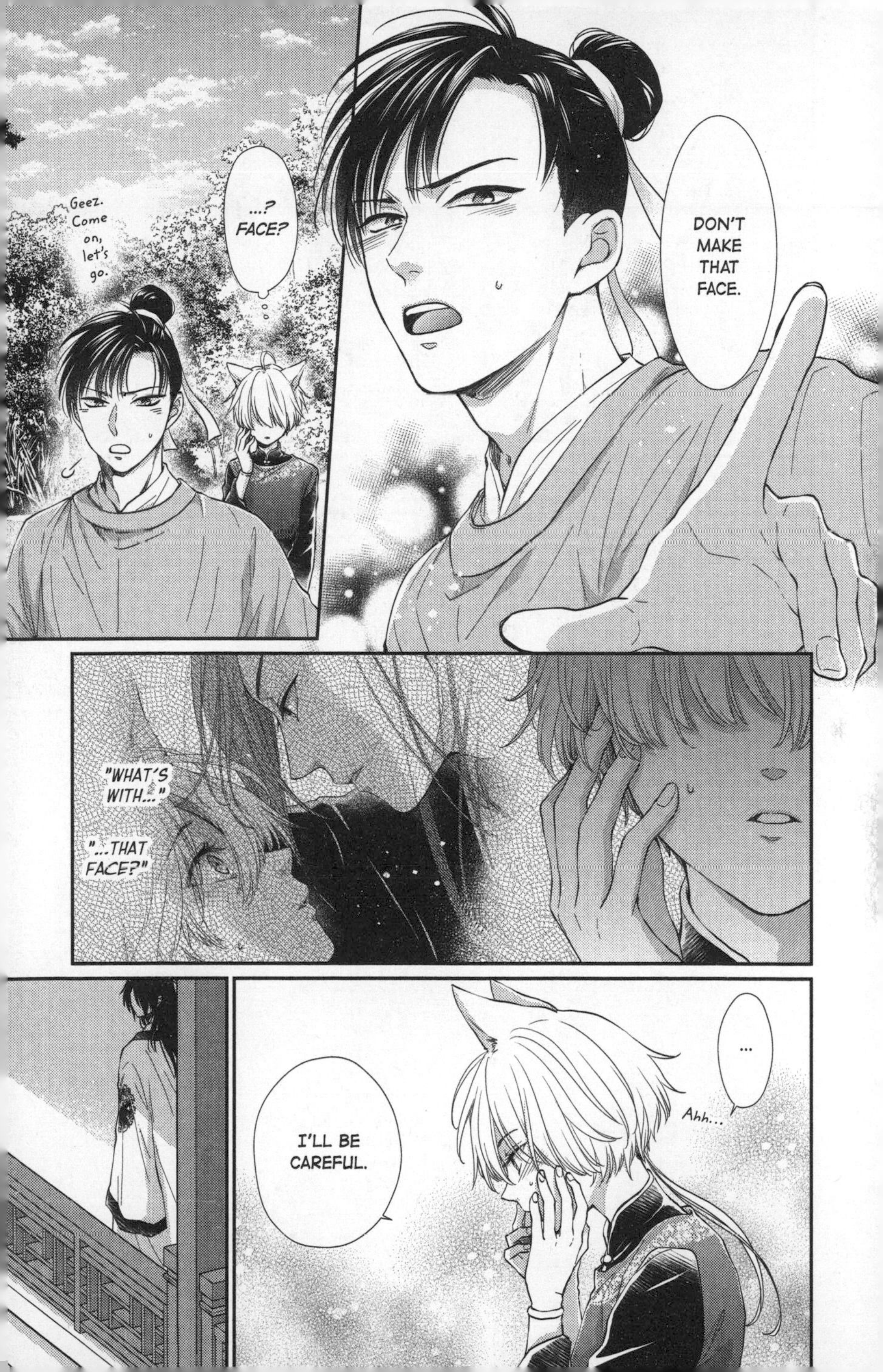
DON'T MAKE THAT FACE.
...? FACE?
Geez. Come on, let's go.
"WHAT'S WITH..."
"...THAT FACE?"
...
Ahh...
I'LL BE CAREFUL.

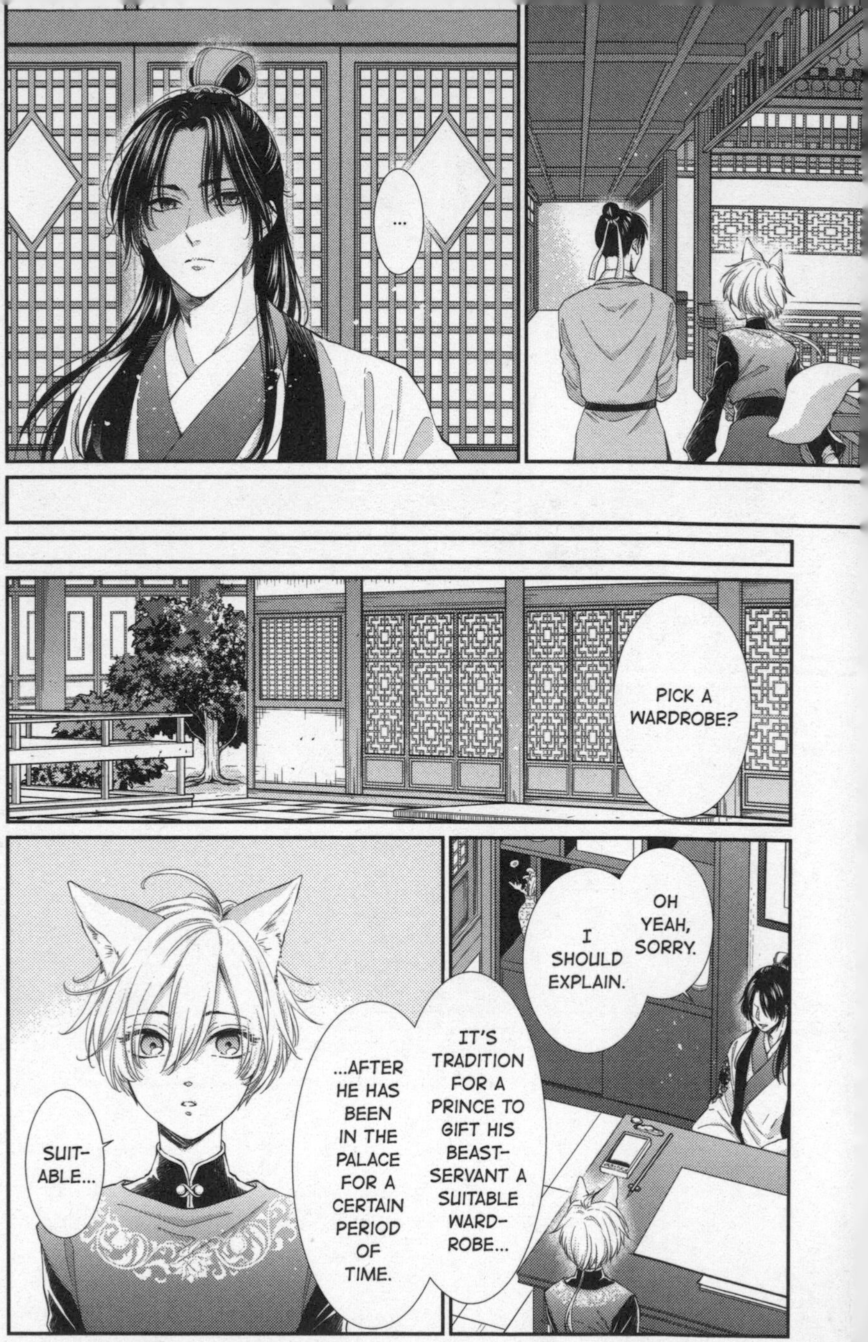
...
PICK A WARDROBE?
OH YEAH, SORRY.
I SHOULD EXPLAIN.
IT'S TRADITION FOR A PRINCE TO GIFT HIS BEAST-SERVANT A SUITABLE WARDROBE...
...AFTER HE HAS BEEN IN THE PALACE FOR A CERTAIN PERIOD OF TIME.
SUITABLE...

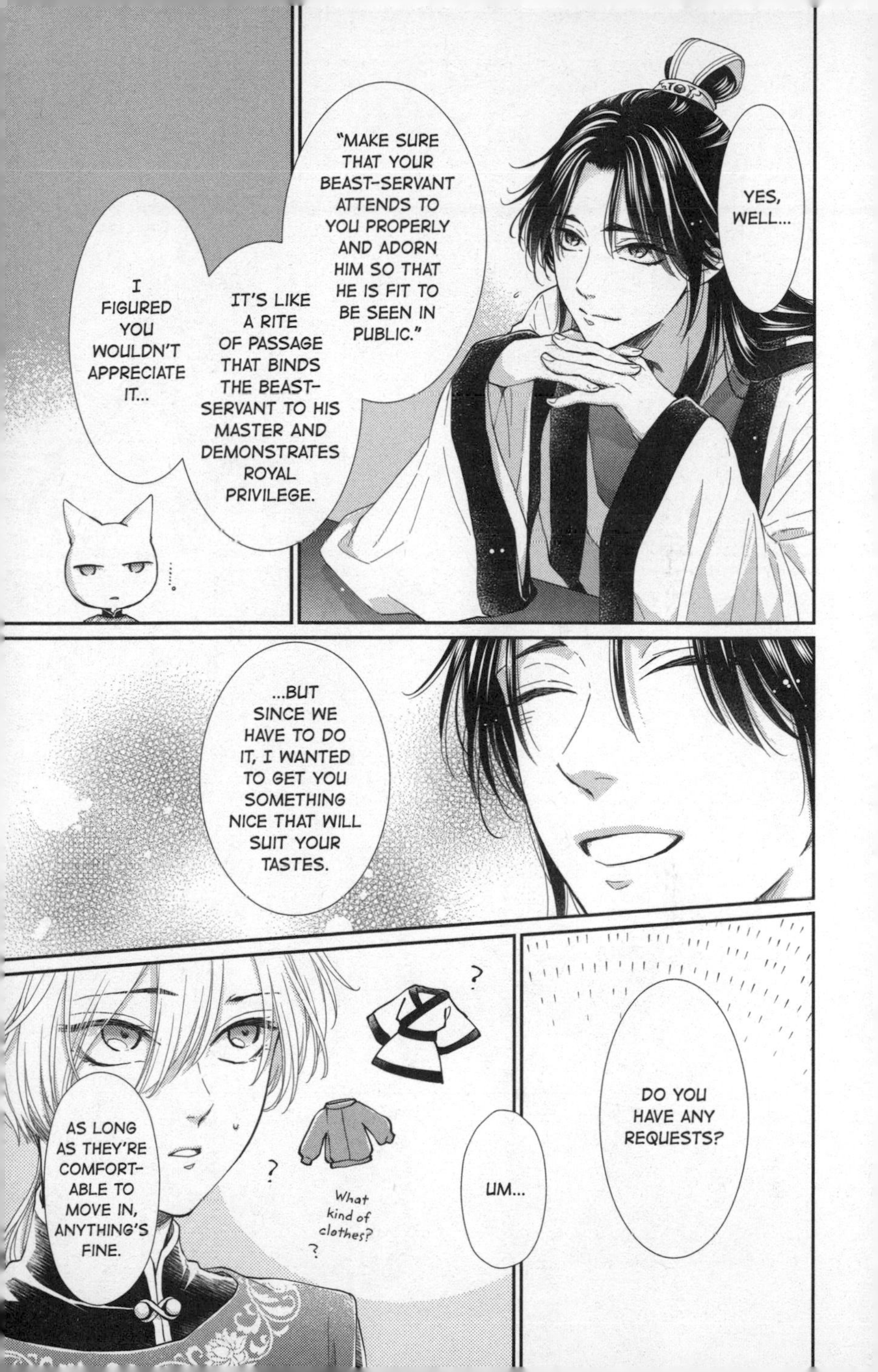
YES, WELL...
"MAKE SURE THAT YOUR BEAST-SERVANT ATTENDS TO YOU PROPERLY AND ADORN HIM SO THAT HE IS FIT TO BE SEEN IN PUBLIC."
IT'S LIKE A RITE OF PASSAGE THAT BINDS THE BEAST-SERVANT TO HIS MASTER AND DEMONSTRATES ROYAL PRIVILEGE.
I FIGURED YOU WOULDN'T APPRECIATE IT...
......
...BUT SINCE WE HAVE TO DO IT, I WANTED TO GET YOU SOMETHING NICE THAT WILL SUIT YOUR TASTES.
DO YOU HAVE ANY REQUESTS?
UM...
What kind of clothes?
AS LONG AS THEY'RE COMFORT-ABLE TO MOVE IN, ANYTHING'S FINE.

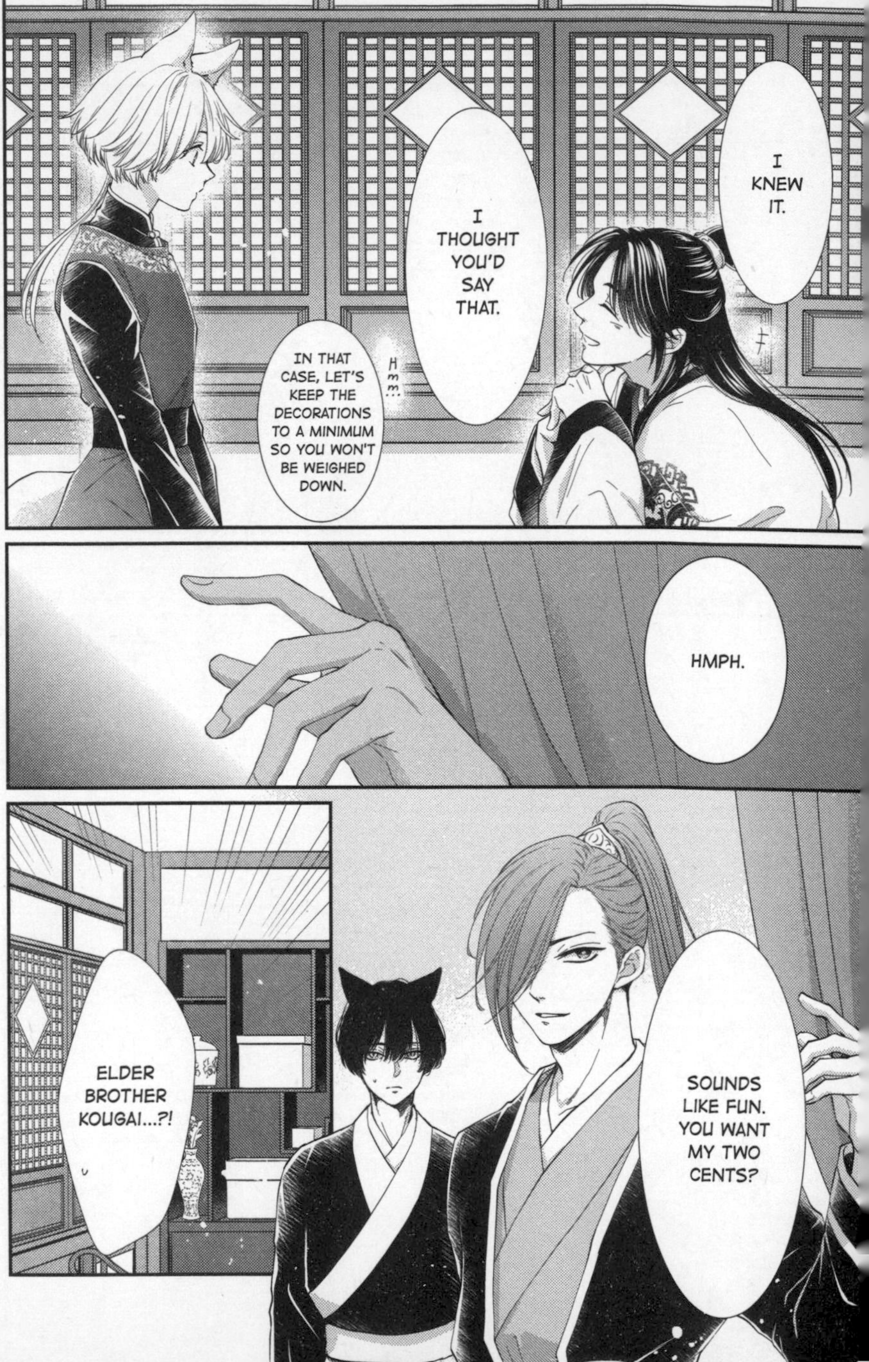
I KNEW IT.
I THOUGHT YOU'D SAY THAT.
Hmm...
IN THAT CASE, LET'S KEEP THE DECORATIONS TO A MINIMUM SO YOU WON'T BE WEIGHED DOWN.
HMPH.
SOUNDS LIKE FUN. YOU WANT MY TWO CENTS?
ELDER BROTHER KOUGAI...?!

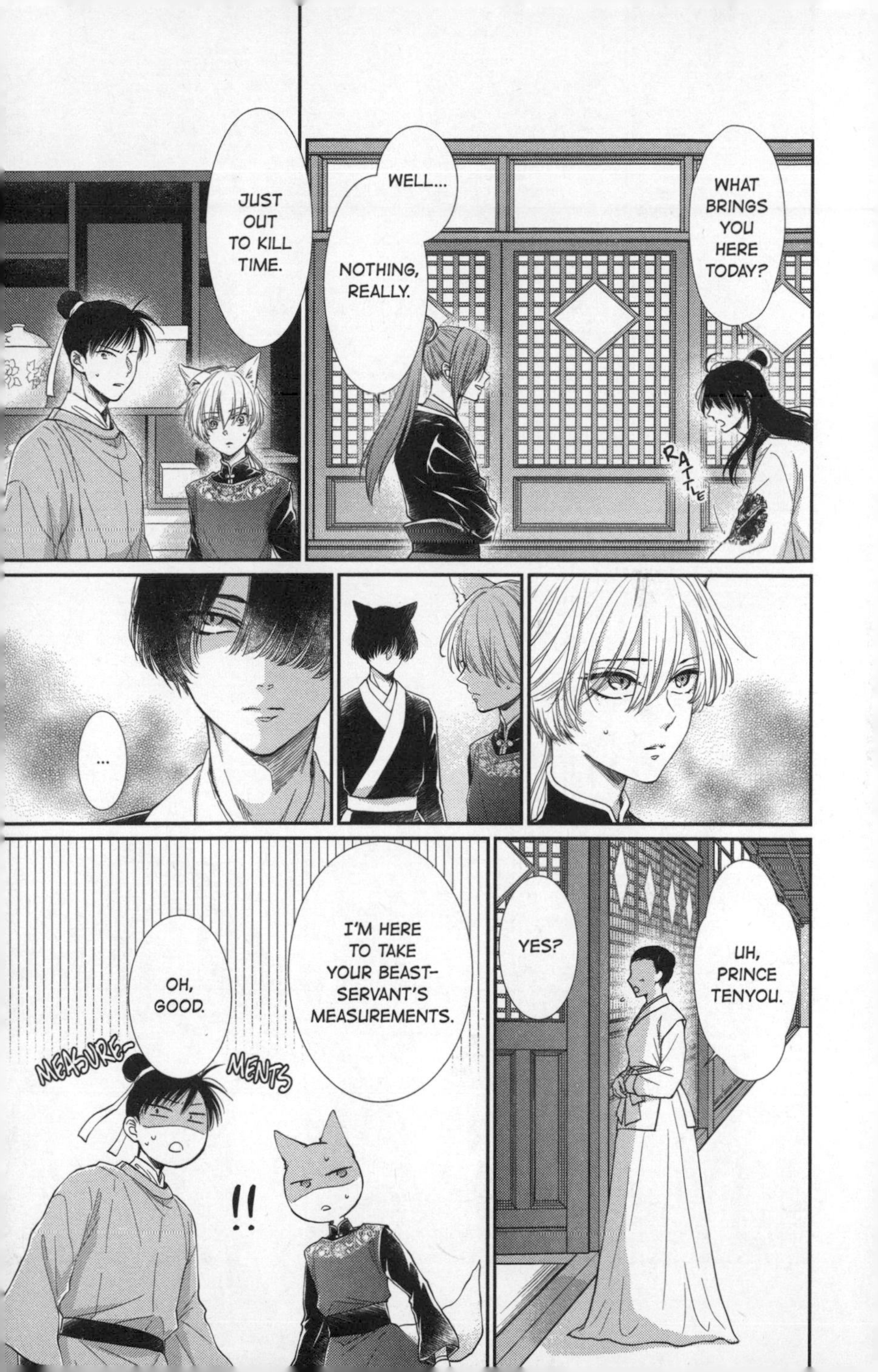
WHAT BRINGS YOU HERE TODAY?
RATTLE
WELL...
NOTHING, REALLY.
JUST OUT TO KILL TIME.
...
UH, PRINCE TENYOU.
YES?
I'M HERE TO TAKE YOUR BEAST-SERVANT'S MEASUREMENTS.
OH, GOOD.
MEASURE-MENTS
!!

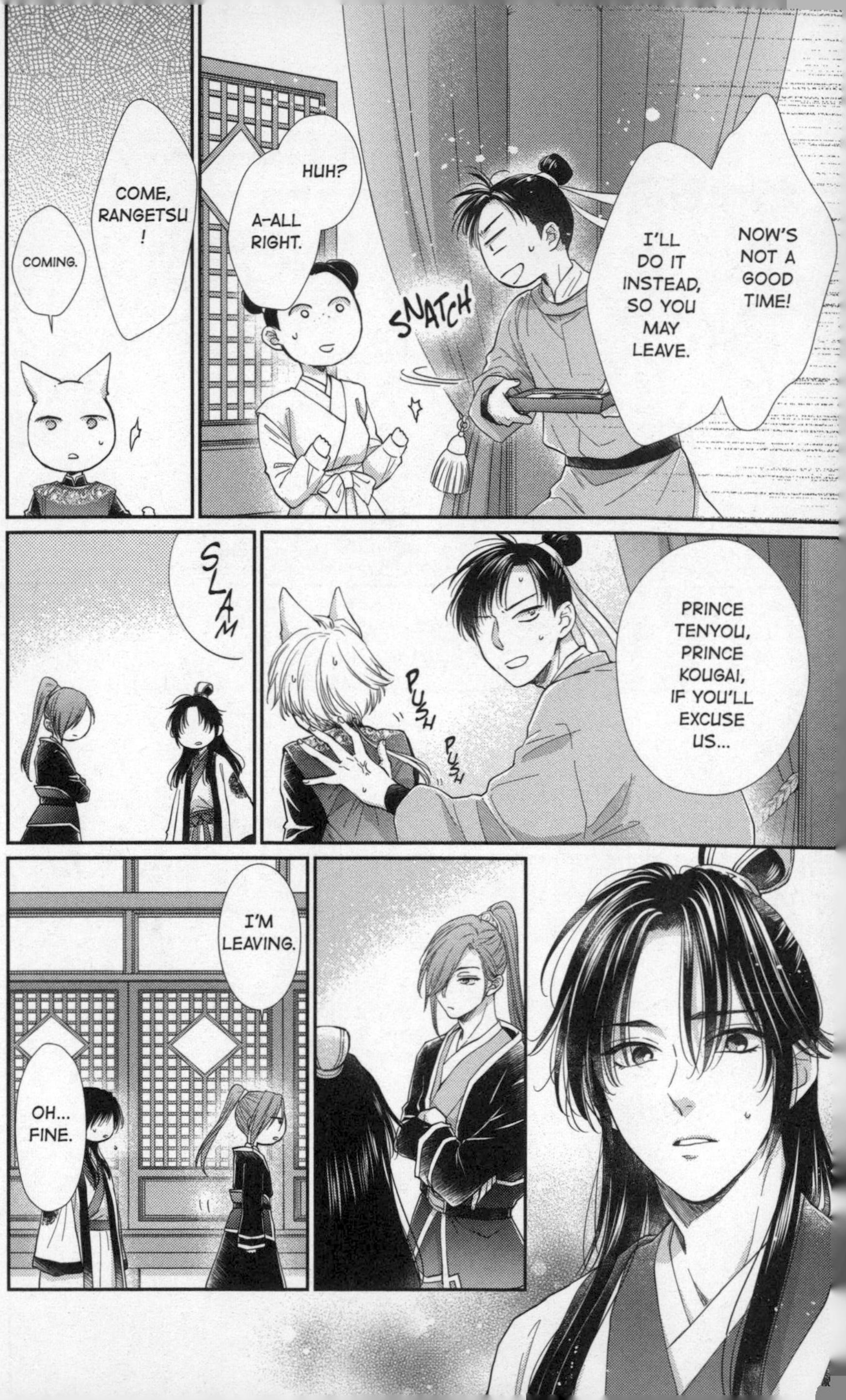
NOW'S NOT A GOOD TIME!
I'LL DO IT INSTEAD, SO YOU MAY LEAVE.
SNATCH
HUH?
A-ALL RIGHT.
COME, RANGETSU!
COMING.
PRINCE TENYOU, PRINCE KOUGAI, IF YOU'LL EXCUSE US...
PUSH
PUSH
SLAM
I'M LEAVING.
OH... FINE.

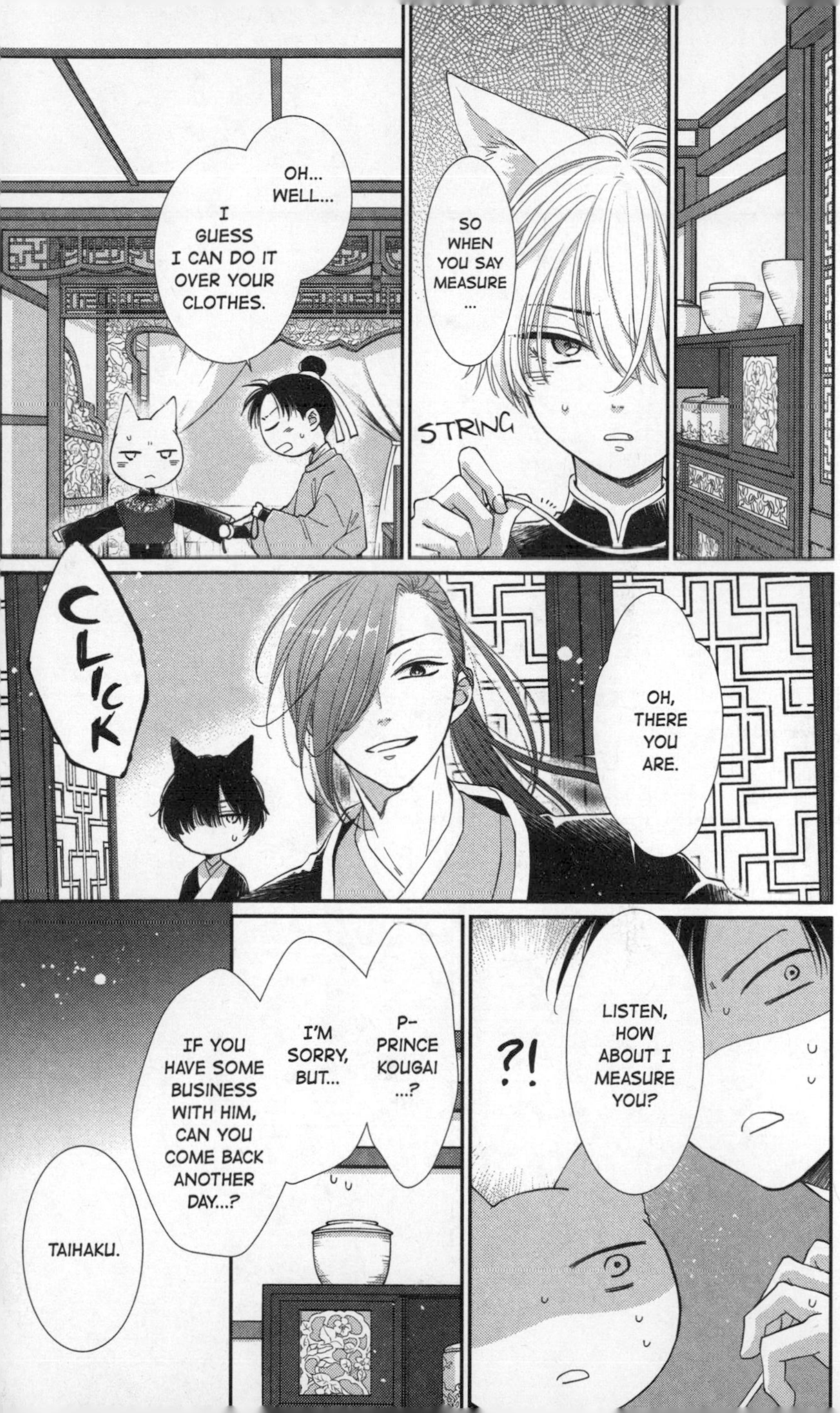
SO WHEN YOU SAY MEASURE ...
STRING
OH... WELL...
I GUESS I CAN DO IT OVER YOUR CLOTHES.
CLICK
OH, THERE YOU ARE.
LISTEN, HOW ABOUT I MEASURE YOU?
?!
P-PRINCE KOUGAI ...?
I'M SORRY, BUT...
IF YOU HAVE SOME BUSINESS WITH HIM, CAN YOU COME BACK ANOTHER DAY...?
TAIHAKU.

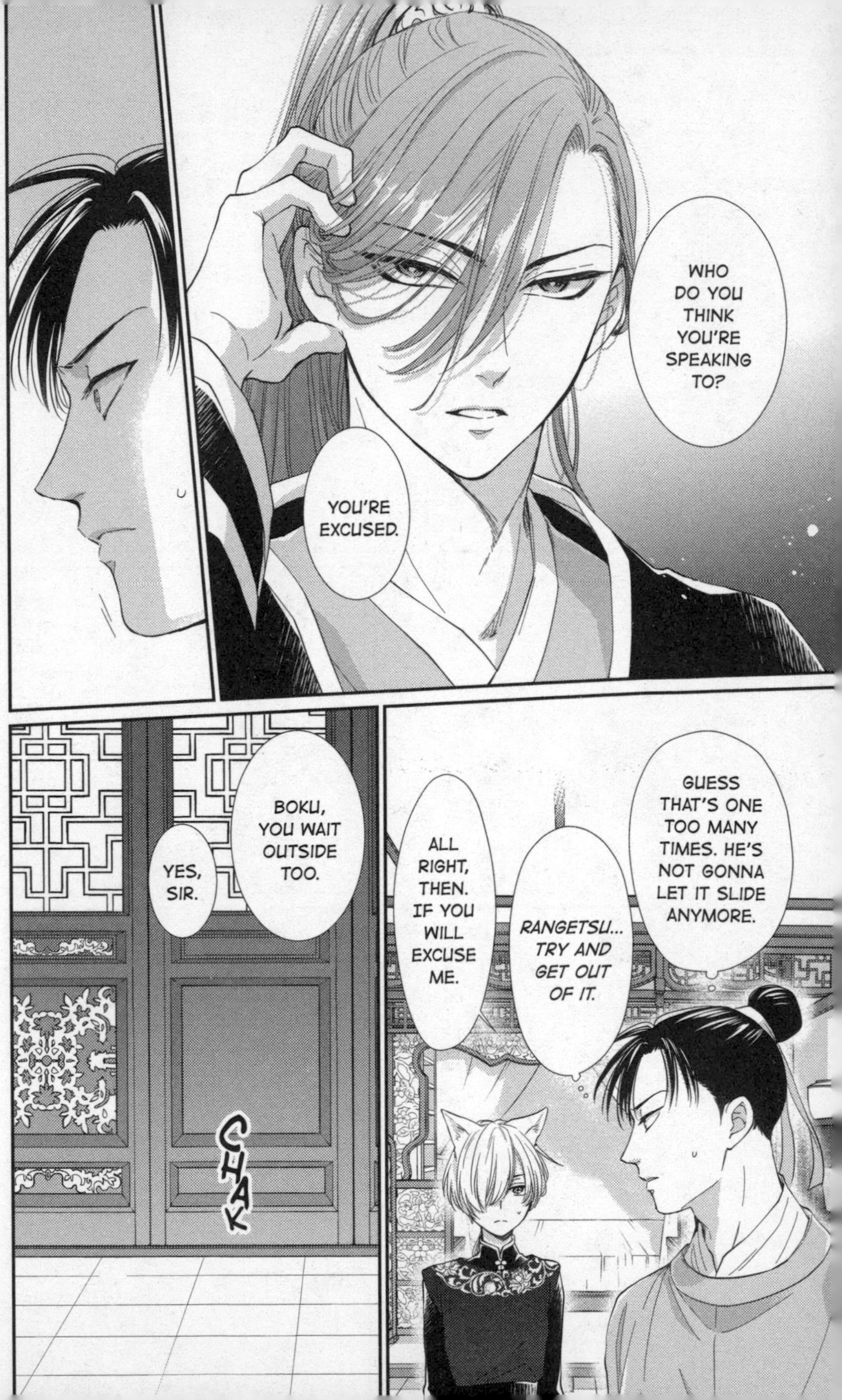
WHO DO YOU THINK YOU'RE SPEAKING TO?
YOU'RE EXCUSED.
GUESS THAT'S ONE TOO MANY TIMES. HE'S NOT GONNA LET IT SLIDE ANYMORE.
RANGETSU... TRY AND GET OUT OF IT.
ALL RIGHT, THEN. IF YOU WILL EXCUSE ME.
BOKU, YOU WAIT OUTSIDE TOO.
YES, SIR.
CHAK

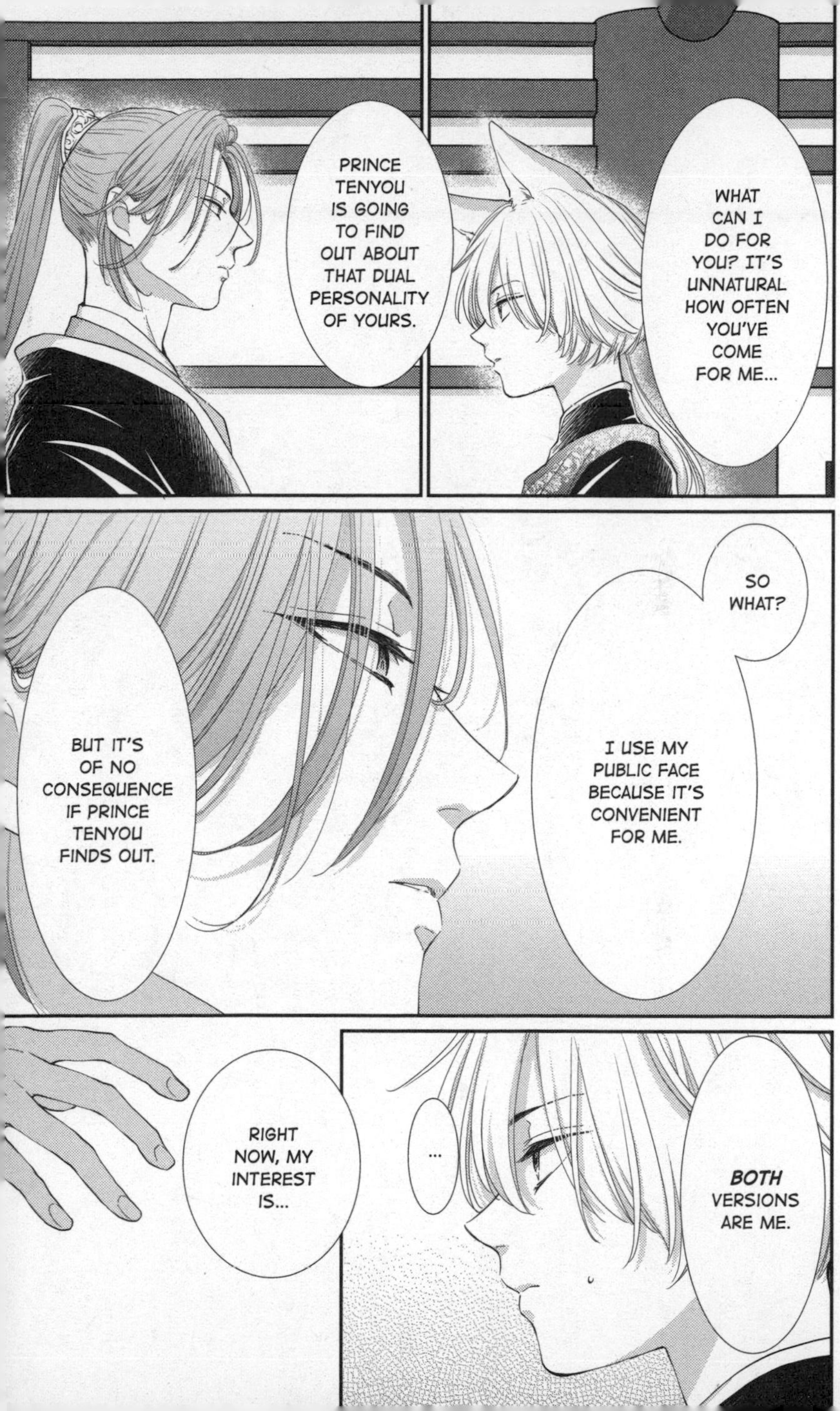
WHAT CAN I DO FOR YOU? IT'S UNNATURAL HOW OFTEN YOU'VE COME FOR ME...
PRINCE TENYOU IS GOING TO FIND OUT ABOUT THAT DUAL PERSONALITY OF YOURS.
SO WHAT?
I USE MY PUBLIC FACE BECAUSE IT'S CONVENIENT FOR ME.
BUT IT'S OF NO CONSEQUENCE IF PRINCE TENYOU FINDS OUT.
BOTH VERSIONS ARE ME.
...
RIGHT NOW, MY INTEREST IS...

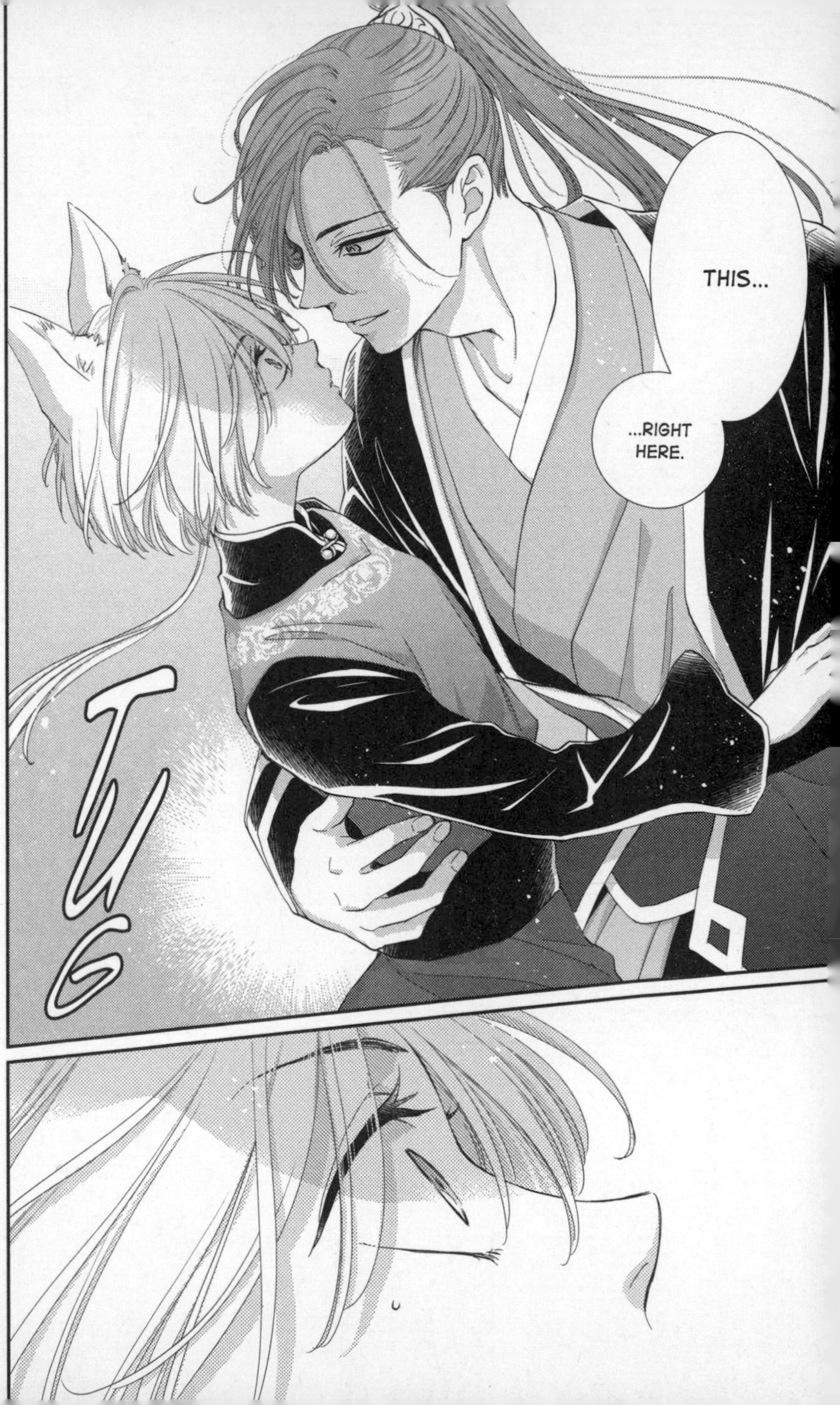
THIS...
...RIGHT HERE.
TUG

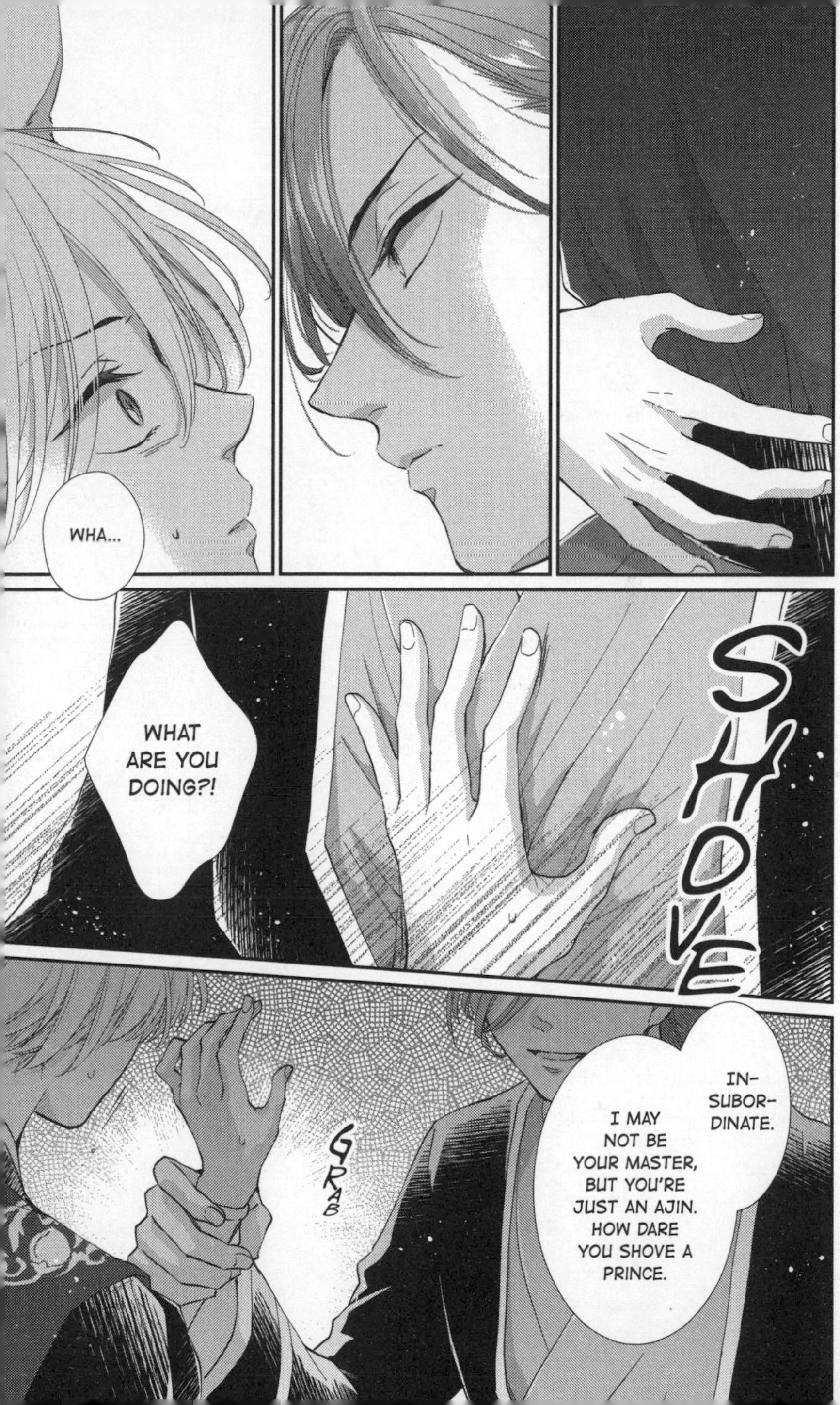
WHA...
SHOVE
WHAT ARE YOU DOING?!
IN-SUBOR-DINATE.
I MAY NOT BE YOUR MASTER, BUT YOU'RE JUST AN AJIN. HOW DARE YOU SHOVE A PRINCE.
GRAB

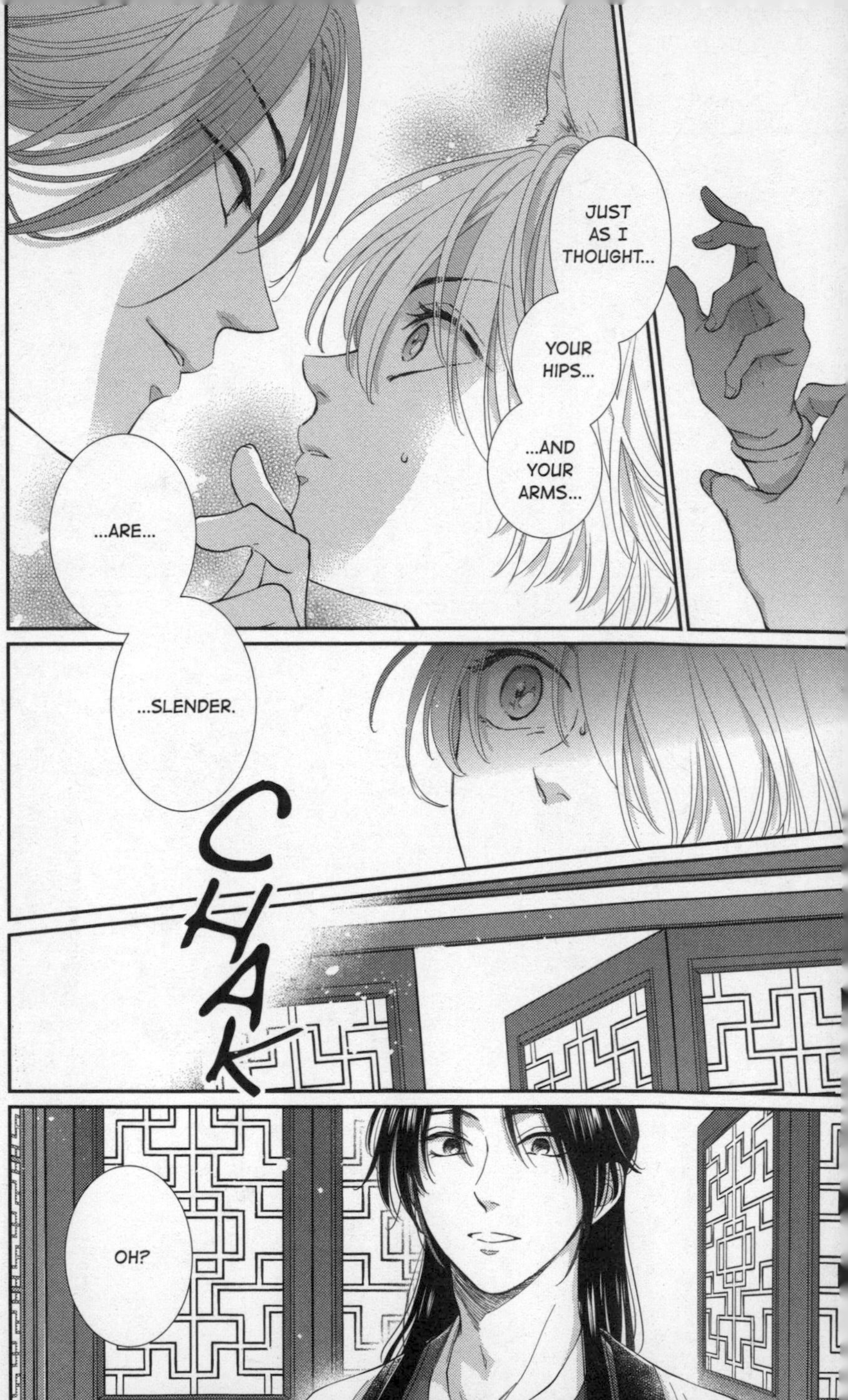
JUST AS I THOUGHT...
YOUR HIPS...
...AND YOUR ARMS...
...ARE...
...SLENDER.
CHAK
OH?

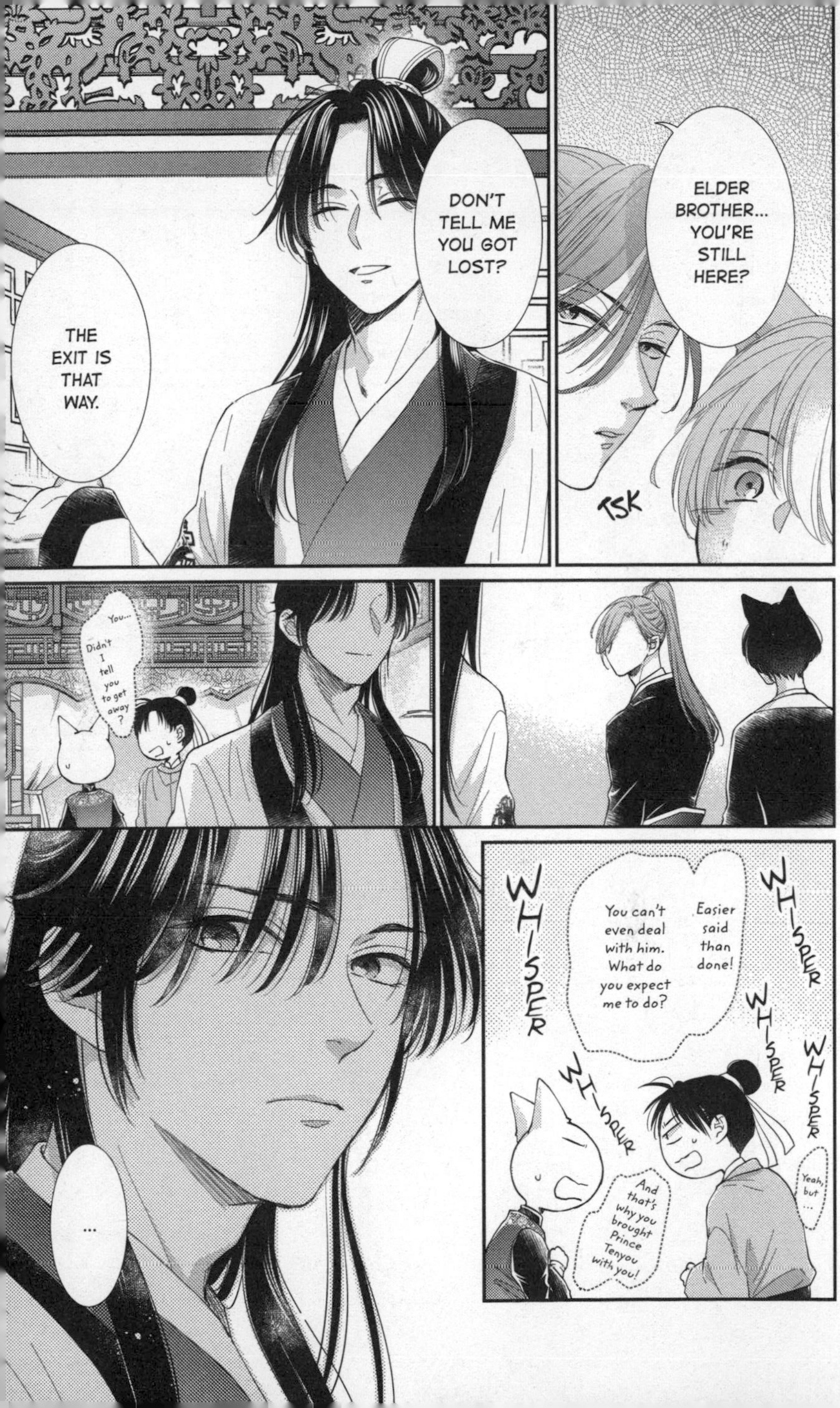
ELDER BROTHER... YOU'RE STILL HERE?
TSK
DON'T TELL ME YOU GOT LOST?
THE EXIT IS THAT WAY.
You... Didn't I tell you to get away?
WHISPER
Easier said than done!
You can't even deal with him. What do you expect me to do?
WHISPER
WHISPER
WHISPER
WHISPER
Yeah, but...
WHI-SPER
And that's why you brought Prince Tenyou with you!
...

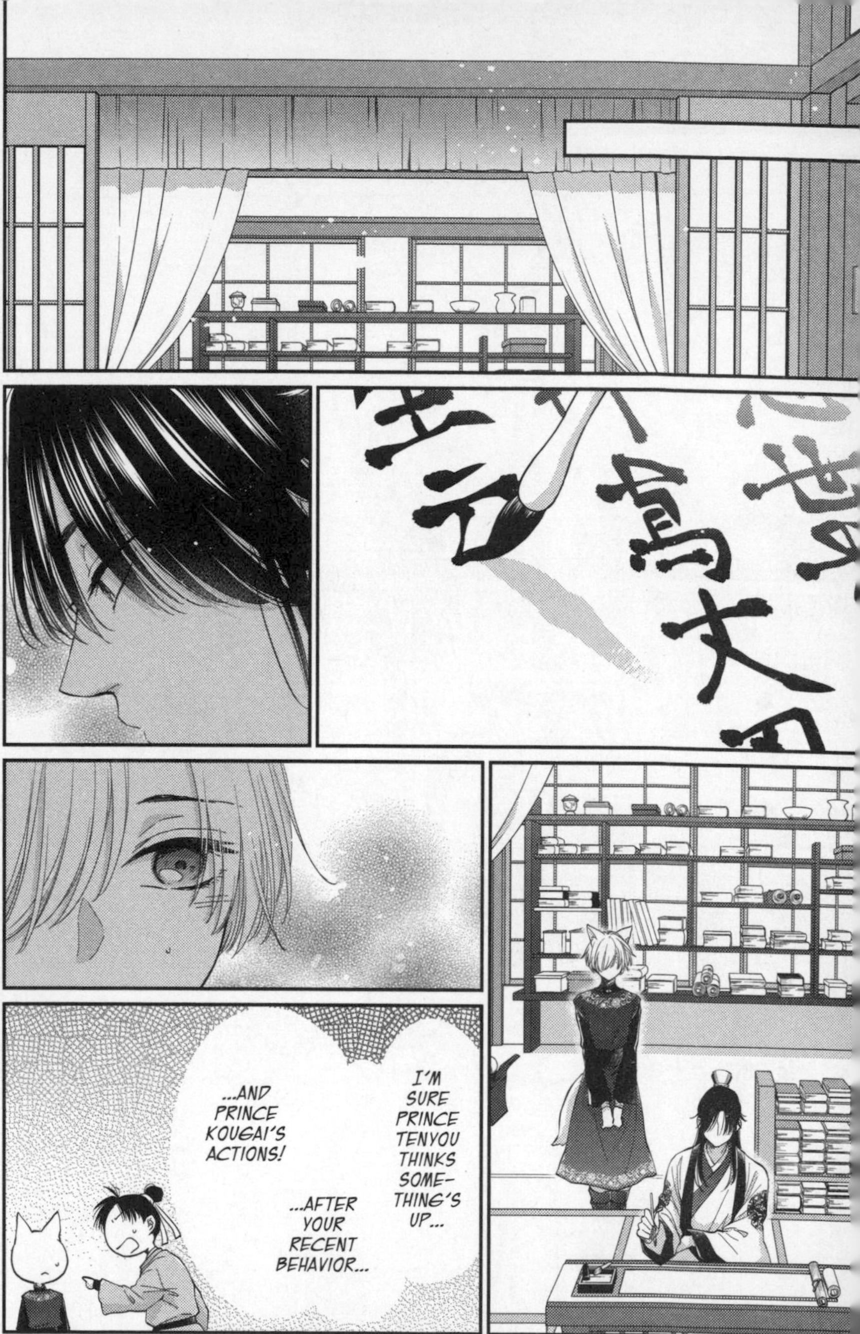
I'M SURE PRINCE TENYOU THINKS SOME-THING'S UP...
...AFTER YOUR RECENT BEHAVIOR...
...AND PRINCE KOUGAI'S ACTIONS!

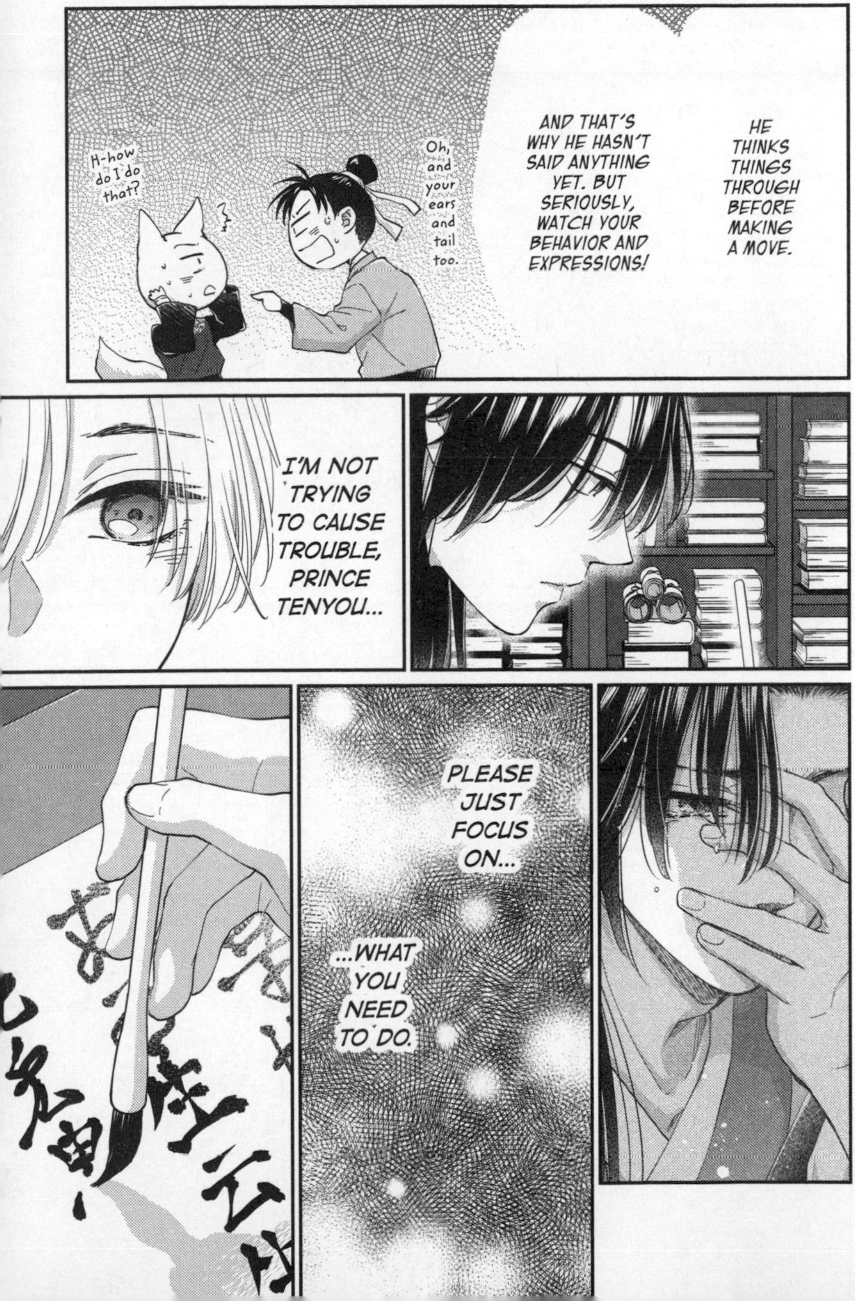
HE THINKS THINGS THROUGH BEFORE MAKING A MOVE.
AND THAT'S WHY HE HASN'T SAID ANYTHING YET. BUT SERIOUSLY, WATCH YOUR BEHAVIOR AND EXPRESSIONS!
Oh, and your ears and tail too.
H-how do I do that?
I'M NOT TRYING TO CAUSE TROUBLE, PRINCE TENYOU...
PLEASE JUST FOCUS ON...
...WHAT YOU NEED TO DO.

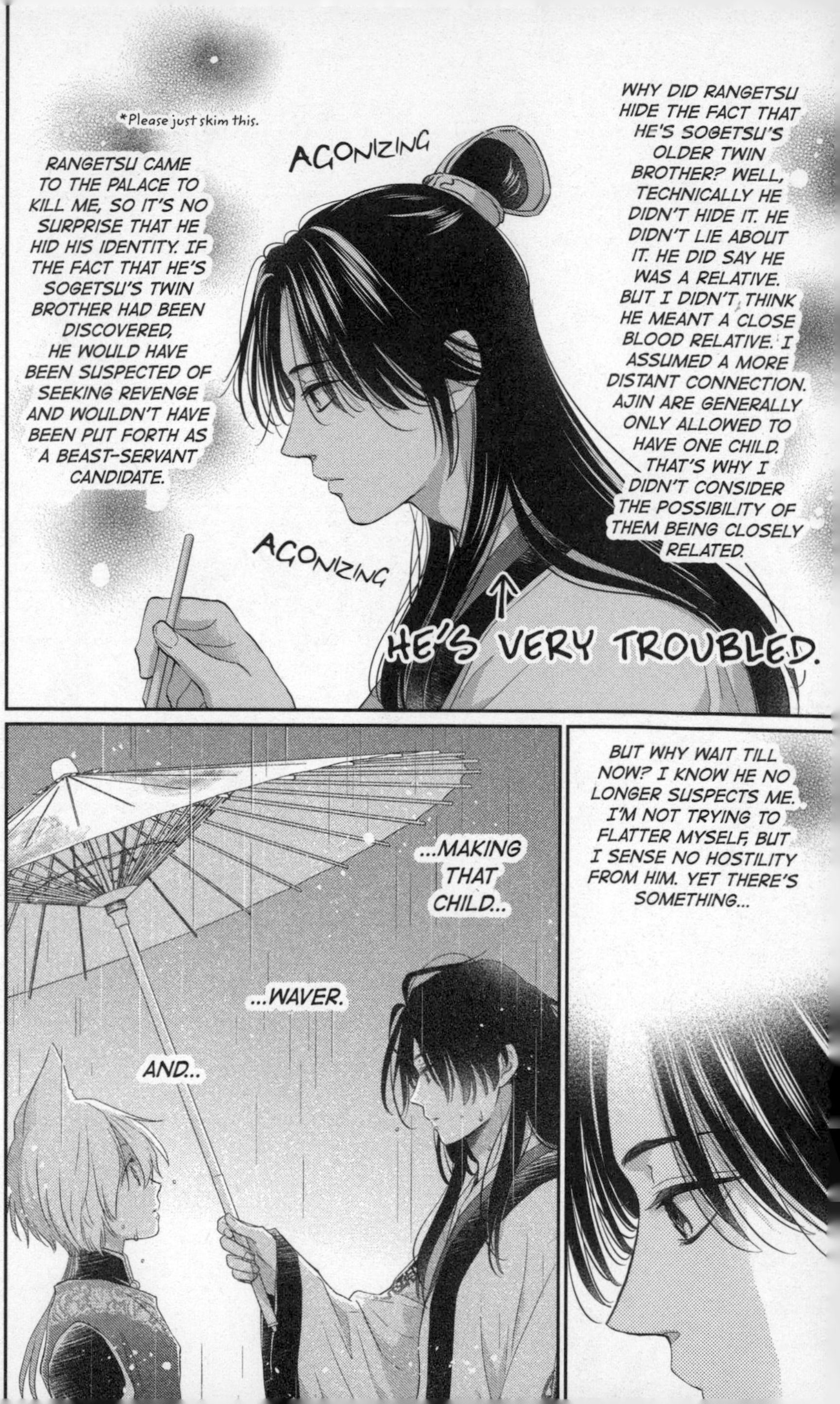
WHY DID RANGETSU HIDE THE FACT THAT HE'S SOGETSU'S OLDER TWIN BROTHER? WELL, TECHNICALLY HE DIDN'T HIDE IT. HE DIDN'T LIE ABOUT IT. HE DID SAY HE WAS A RELATIVE. BUT I DIDN'T THINK HE MEANT A CLOSE BLOOD RELATIVE. I ASSUMED A MORE DISTANT CONNECTION. AJIN ARE GENERALLY ONLY ALLOWED TO HAVE ONE CHILD. THAT'S WHY I DIDN'T CONSIDER THE POSSIBILITY OF THEM BEING CLOSELY RELATED.
AGONIZING
*Please just skim this.
RANGETSU CAME TO THE PALACE TO KILL ME, SO IT'S NO SURPRISE THAT HE HID HIS IDENTITY. IF THE FACT THAT HE'S SOGETSU'S TWIN BROTHER HAD BEEN DISCOVERED, HE WOULD HAVE BEEN SUSPECTED OF SEEKING REVENGE AND WOULDN'T HAVE BEEN PUT FORTH AS A BEAST-SERVANT CANDIDATE.
AGONIZING
HE'S VERY TROUBLED.
BUT WHY WAIT TILL NOW? I KNOW HE NO LONGER SUSPECTS ME. I'M NOT TRYING TO FLATTER MYSELF, BUT I SENSE NO HOSTILITY FROM HIM. YET THERE'S SOMETHING...
...MAKING THAT CHILD...
...WAVER.
AND...

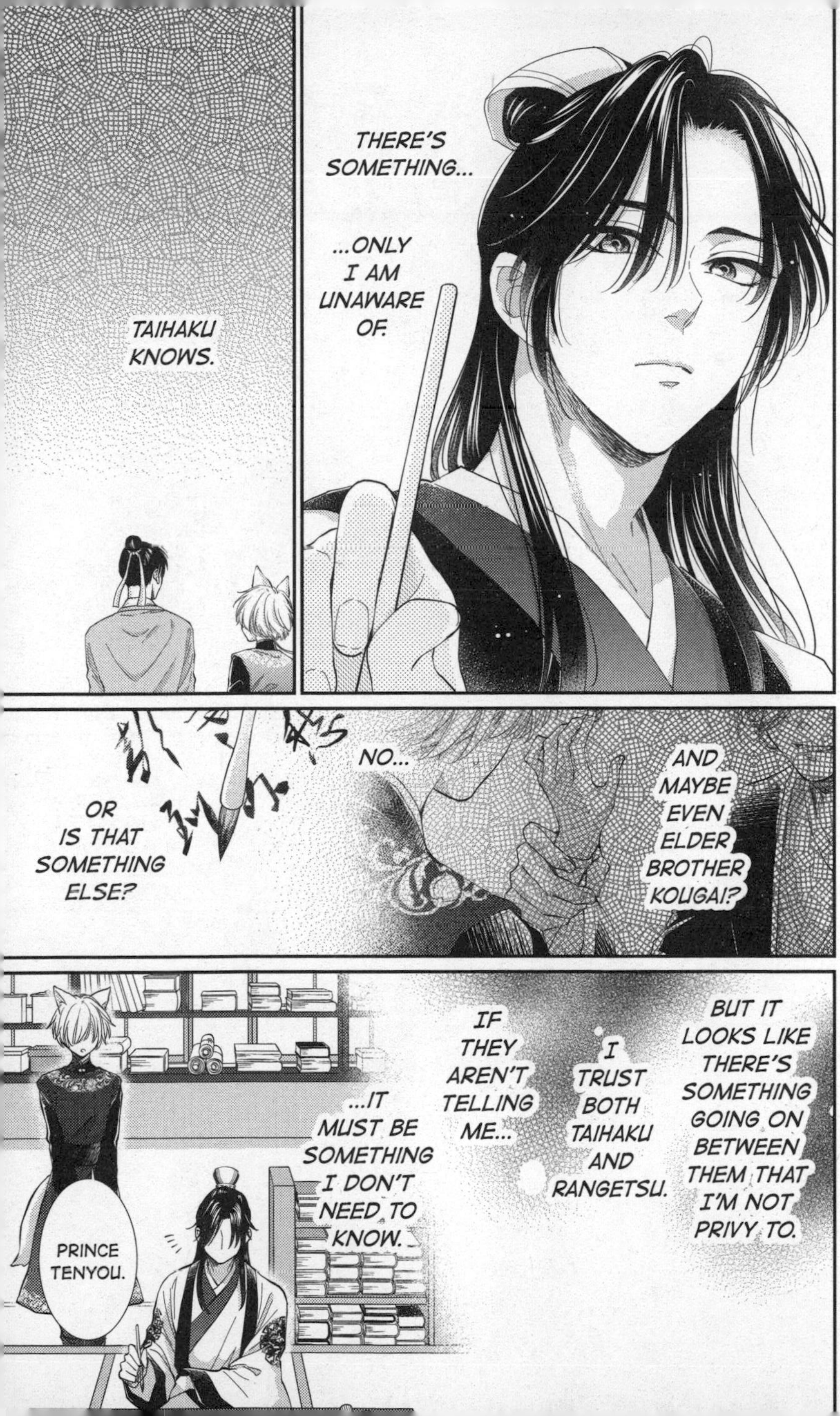
THERE'S SOMETHING...
...ONLY I AM UNAWARE OF.
TAIHAKU KNOWS.
AND MAYBE EVEN ELDER BROTHER KOUGAI?
NO...
OR IS THAT SOMETHING ELSE?
BUT IT LOOKS LIKE THERE'S SOMETHING GOING ON BETWEEN THEM THAT I'M NOT PRIVY TO.
I TRUST BOTH TAIHAKU AND RANGETSU.
IF THEY AREN'T TELLING ME...
...IT MUST BE SOMETHING I DON'T NEED TO KNOW.
PRINCE TENYOU.

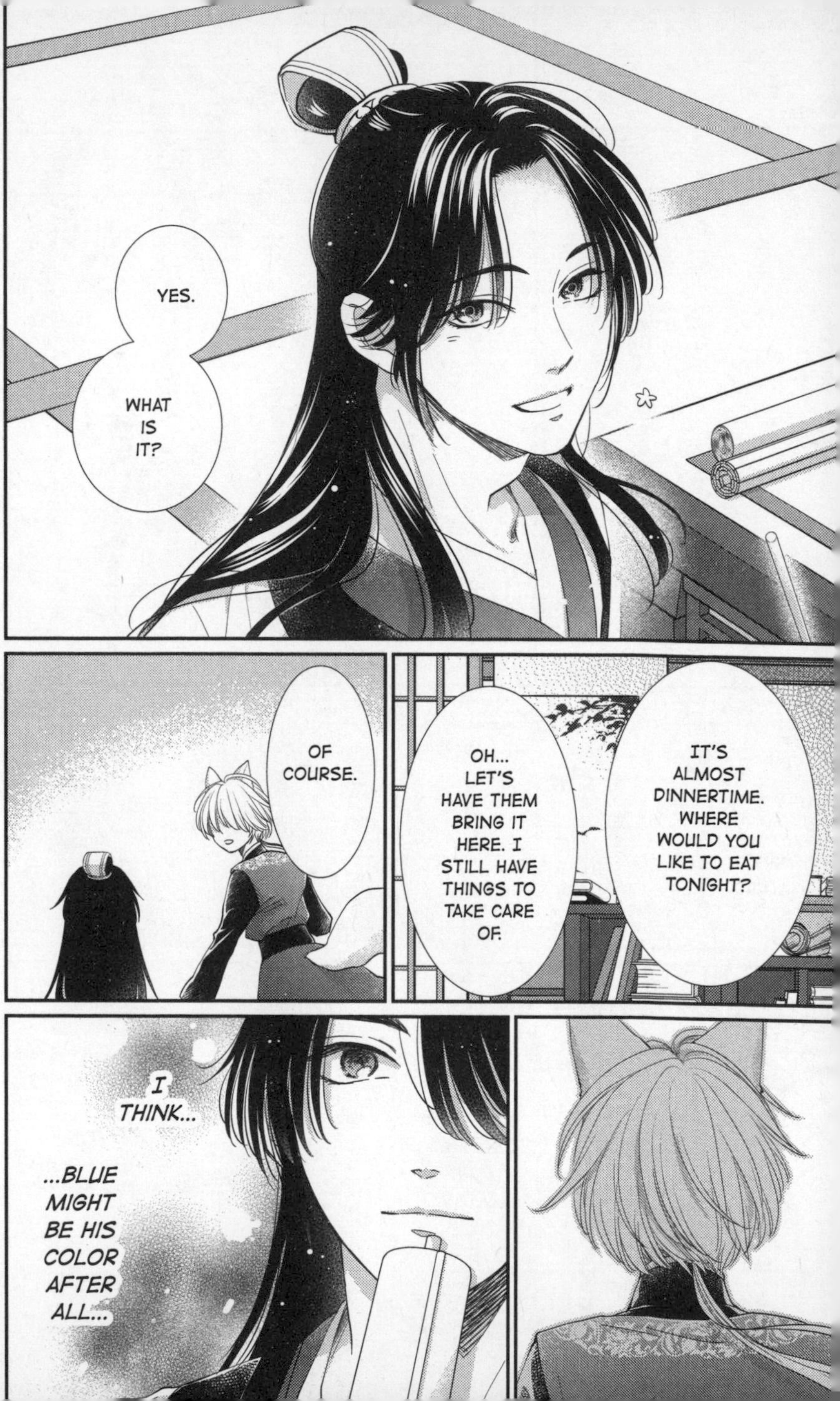
YES.
WHAT IS IT?
IT'S ALMOST DINNERTIME. WHERE WOULD YOU LIKE TO EAT TONIGHT?
OH... LET'S HAVE THEM BRING IT HERE. I STILL HAVE THINGS TO TAKE CARE OF.
OF COURSE.
I THINK...
...BLUE MIGHT BE HIS COLOR AFTER ALL...

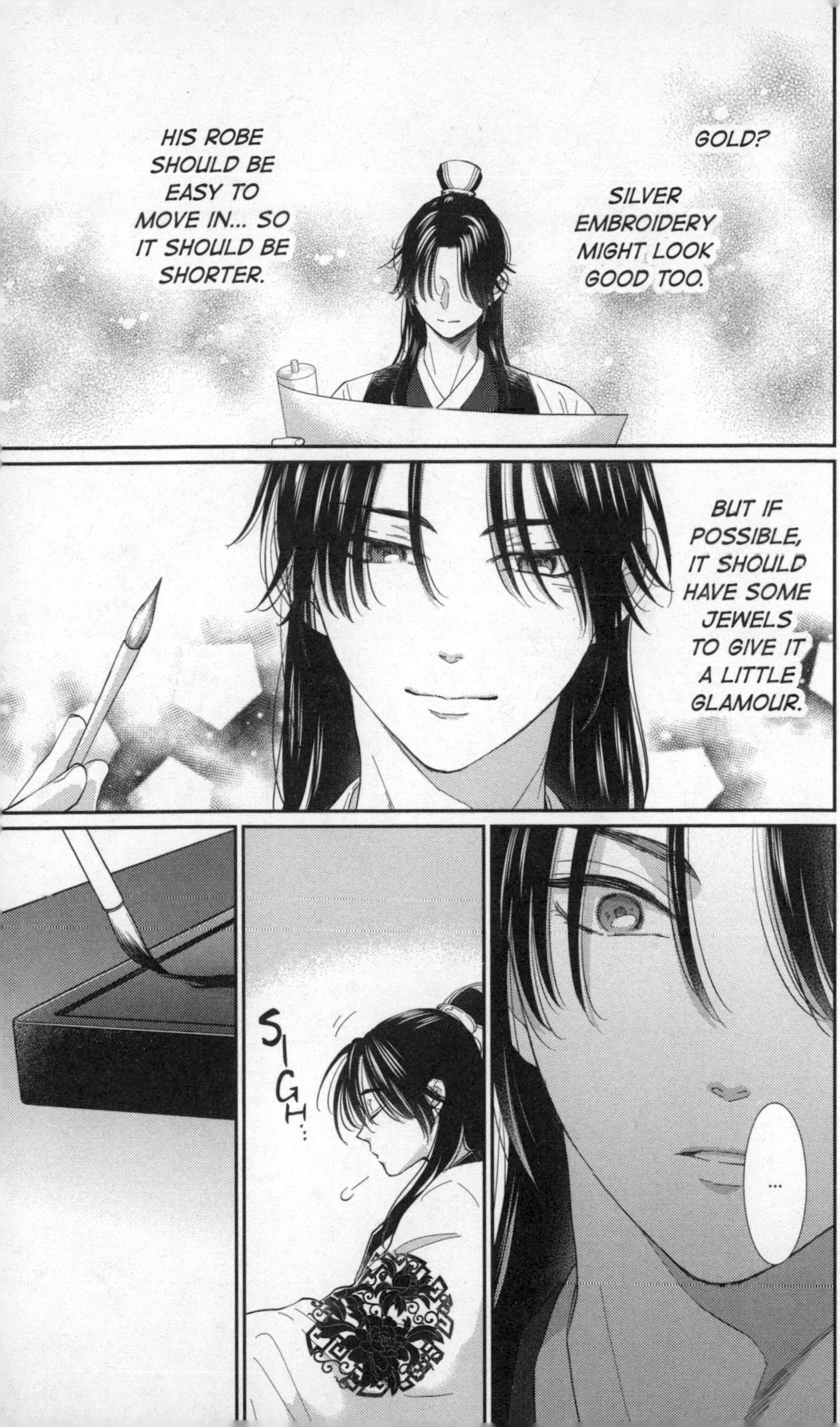
GOLD?
SILVER EMBROIDERY MIGHT LOOK GOOD TOO.
HIS ROBE SHOULD BE EASY TO MOVE IN... SO IT SHOULD BE SHORTER.
BUT IF POSSIBLE, IT SHOULD HAVE SOME JEWELS TO GIVE IT A LITTLE GLAMOUR.
...
SIGH...

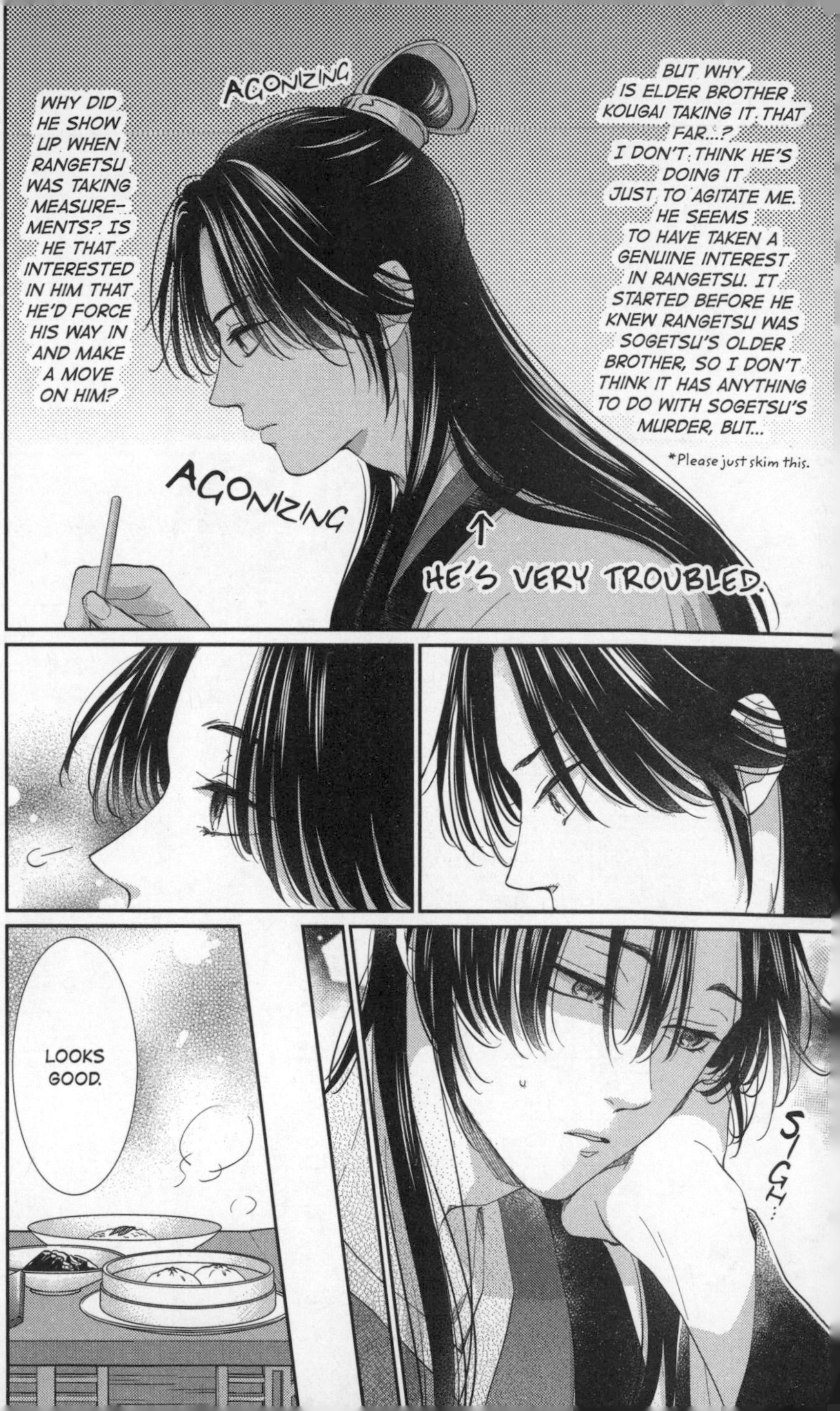
BUT WHY IS ELDER BROTHER KOUGAI TAKING IT THAT FAR...? I DON'T THINK HE'S DOING IT JUST TO AGITATE ME. HE SEEMS TO HAVE TAKEN A GENUINE INTEREST IN RANGETSU. IT STARTED BEFORE HE KNEW RANGETSU WAS SOGETSU'S OLDER BROTHER, SO I DON'T THINK IT HAS ANYTHING TO DO WITH SOGETSU'S MURDER, BUT...
AGONIZING
WHY DID HE SHOW UP WHEN RANGETSU WAS TAKING MEASURE-MENTS? IS HE THAT INTERESTED IN HIM THAT HE'D FORCE HIS WAY IN AND MAKE A MOVE ON HIM?
*Please just skim this.
AGONIZING
HE'S VERY TROUBLED.
SIGH...
LOOKS GOOD.

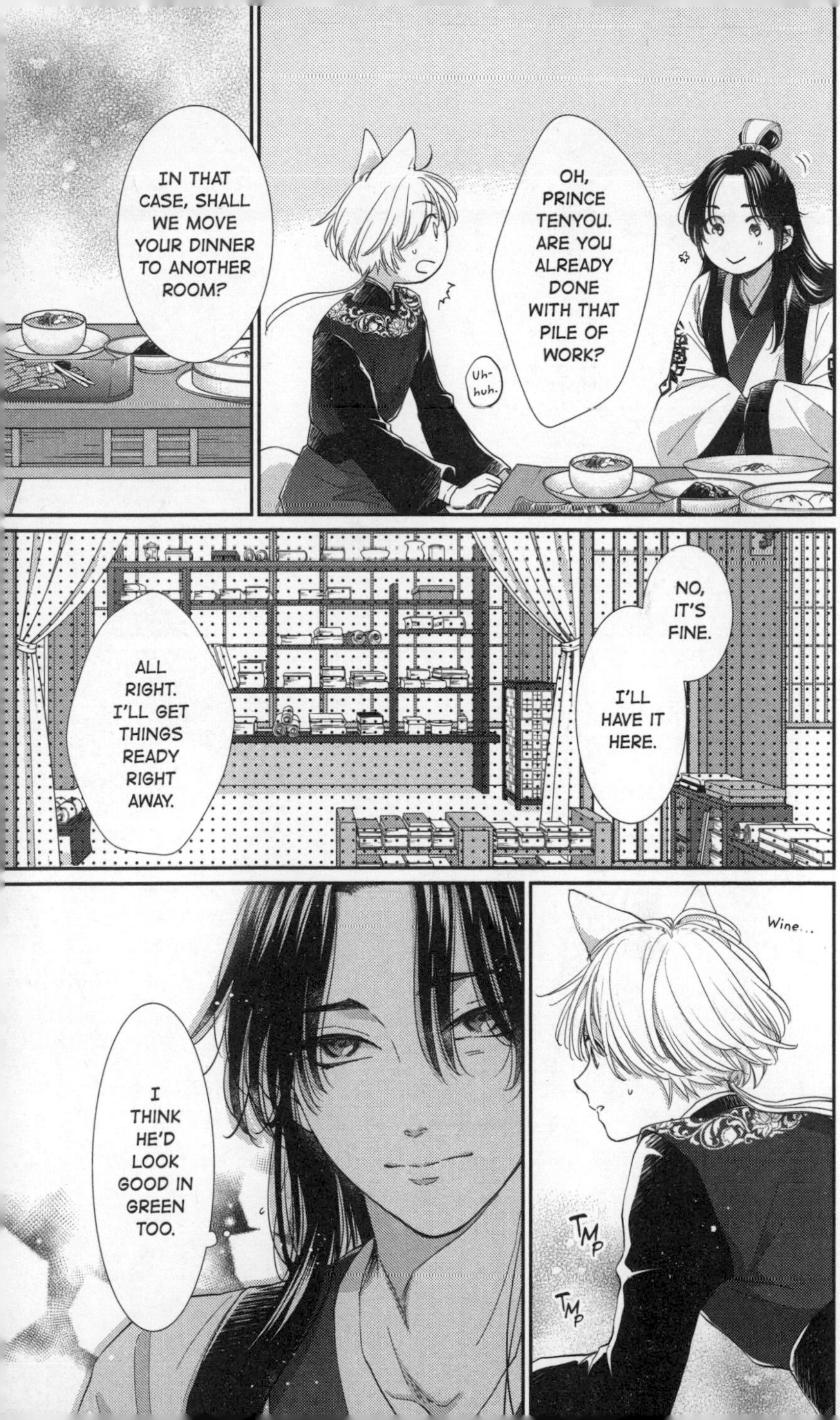
OH, PRINCE TENYOU. ARE YOU ALREADY DONE WITH THAT PILE OF WORK?
Uh-huh.
IN THAT CASE, SHALL WE MOVE YOUR DINNER TO ANOTHER ROOM?
NO, IT'S FINE.
I'LL HAVE IT HERE.
ALL RIGHT. I'LL GET THINGS READY RIGHT AWAY.
Wine...
TMP
TMP
I THINK HE'D LOOK GOOD IN GREEN TOO.

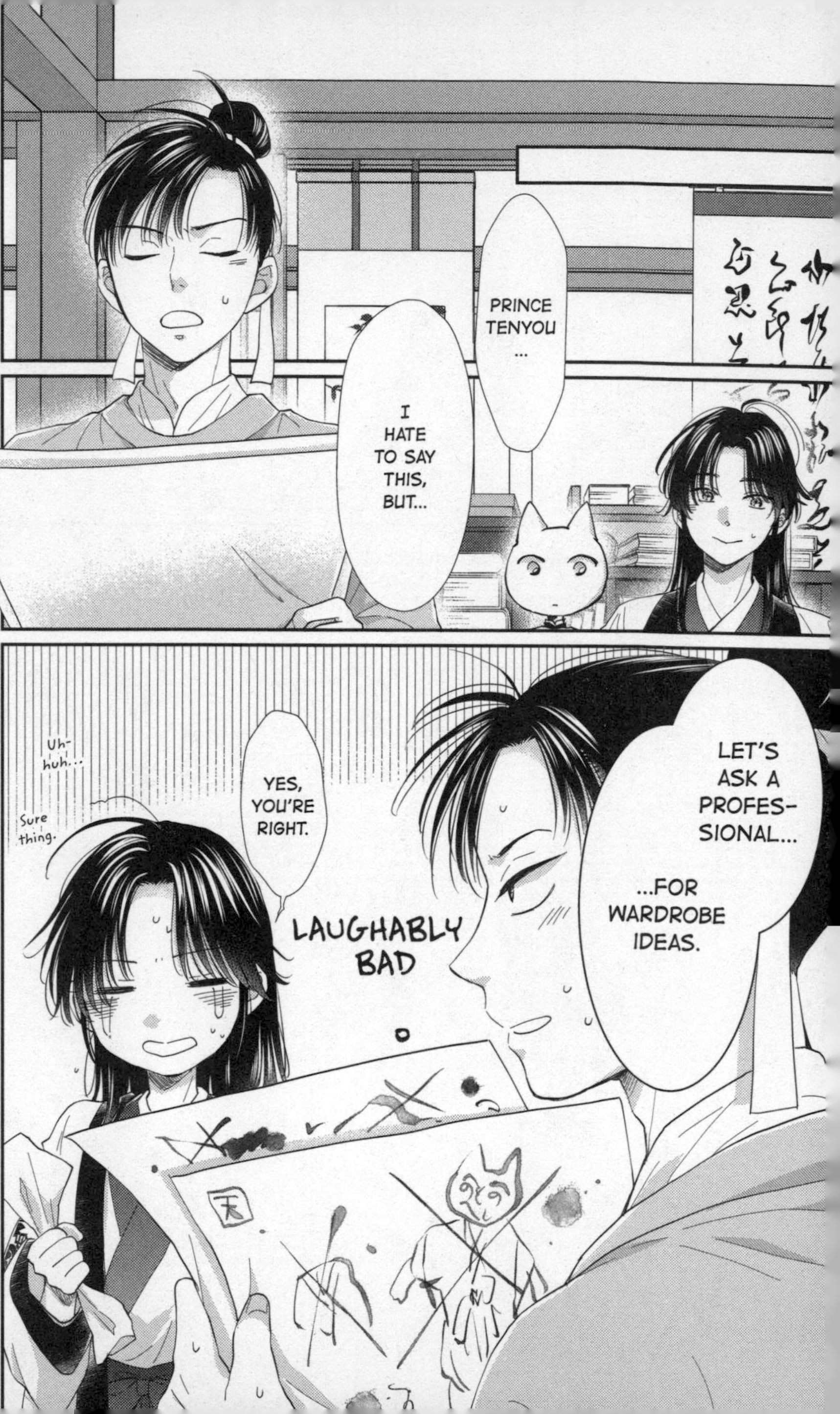
PRINCE TENYOU ...
I HATE TO SAY THIS, BUT...
LET'S ASK A PROFES-SIONAL...
...FOR WARDROBE IDEAS.
YES, YOU'RE RIGHT.
LAUGHABLY BAD
Uh-huh...
Sure thing.

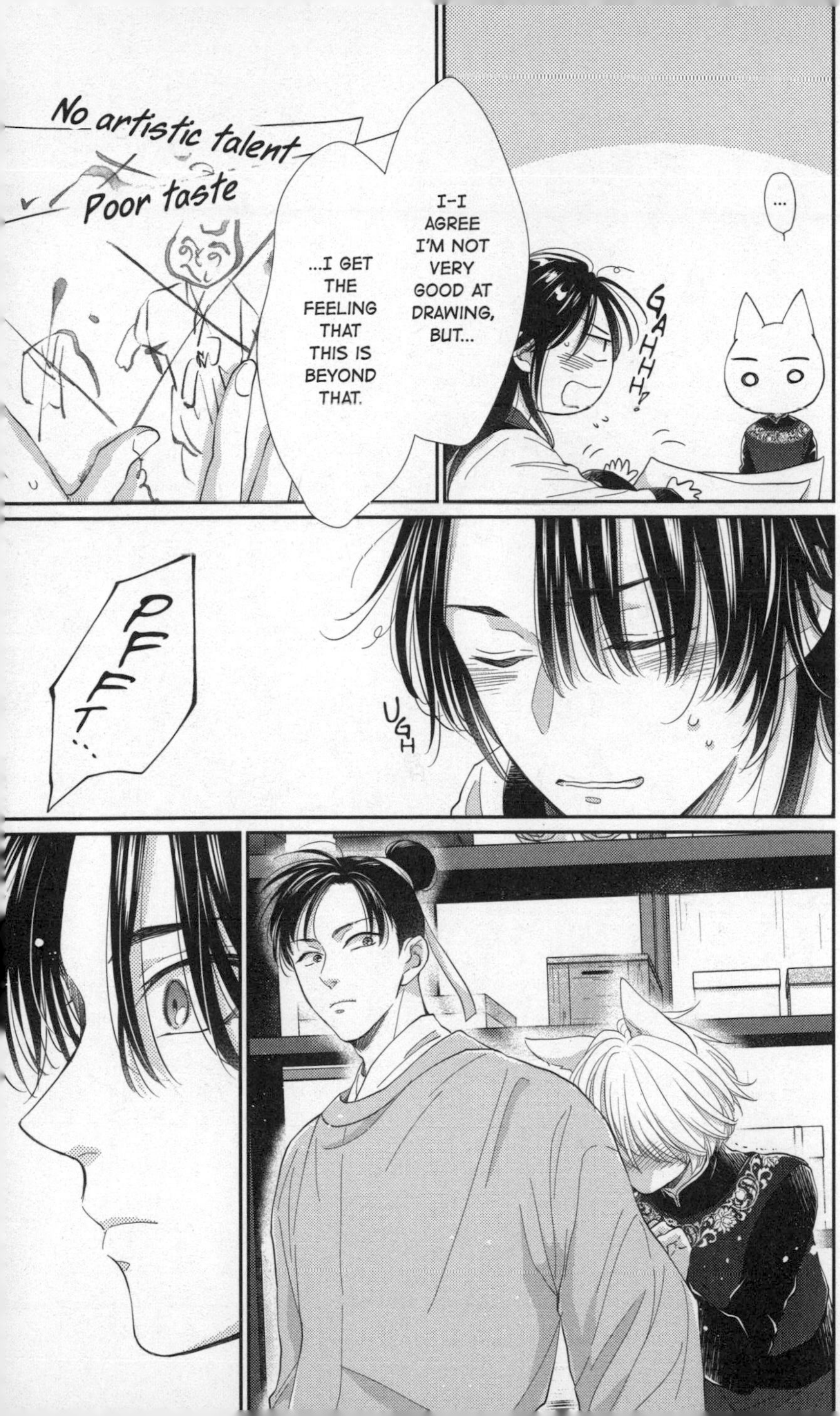
...
GAHHH!
I-I AGREE I'M NOT VERY GOOD AT DRAWING, BUT...
...I GET THE FEELING THAT THIS IS BEYOND THAT.
No artistic talent
Poor taste
UGH
PFFFT...

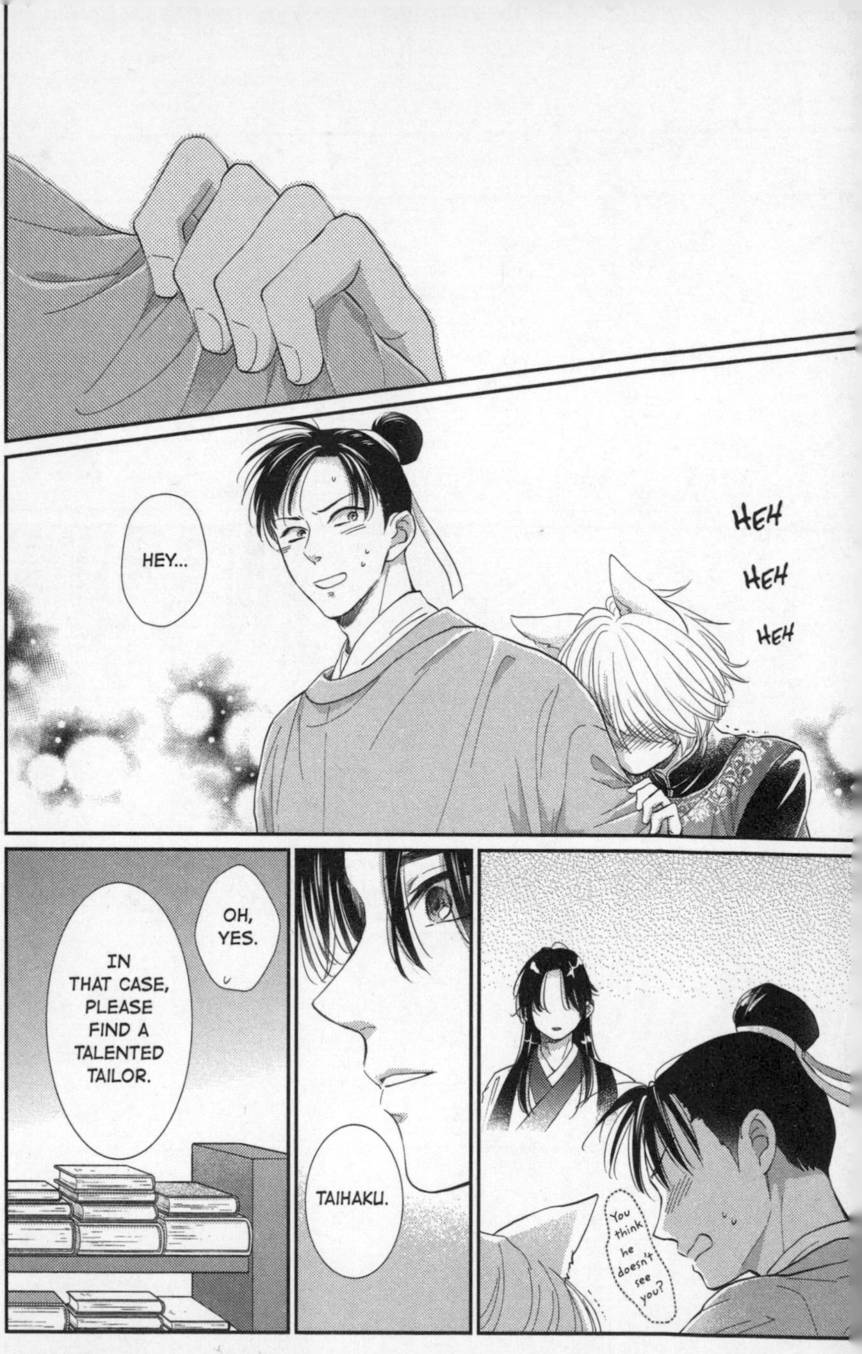
HEH
HEH
HEH
HEY...
You think he doesn't see you?
TAIHAKU.
OH, YES.
IN THAT CASE, PLEASE FIND A TALENTED TAILOR.

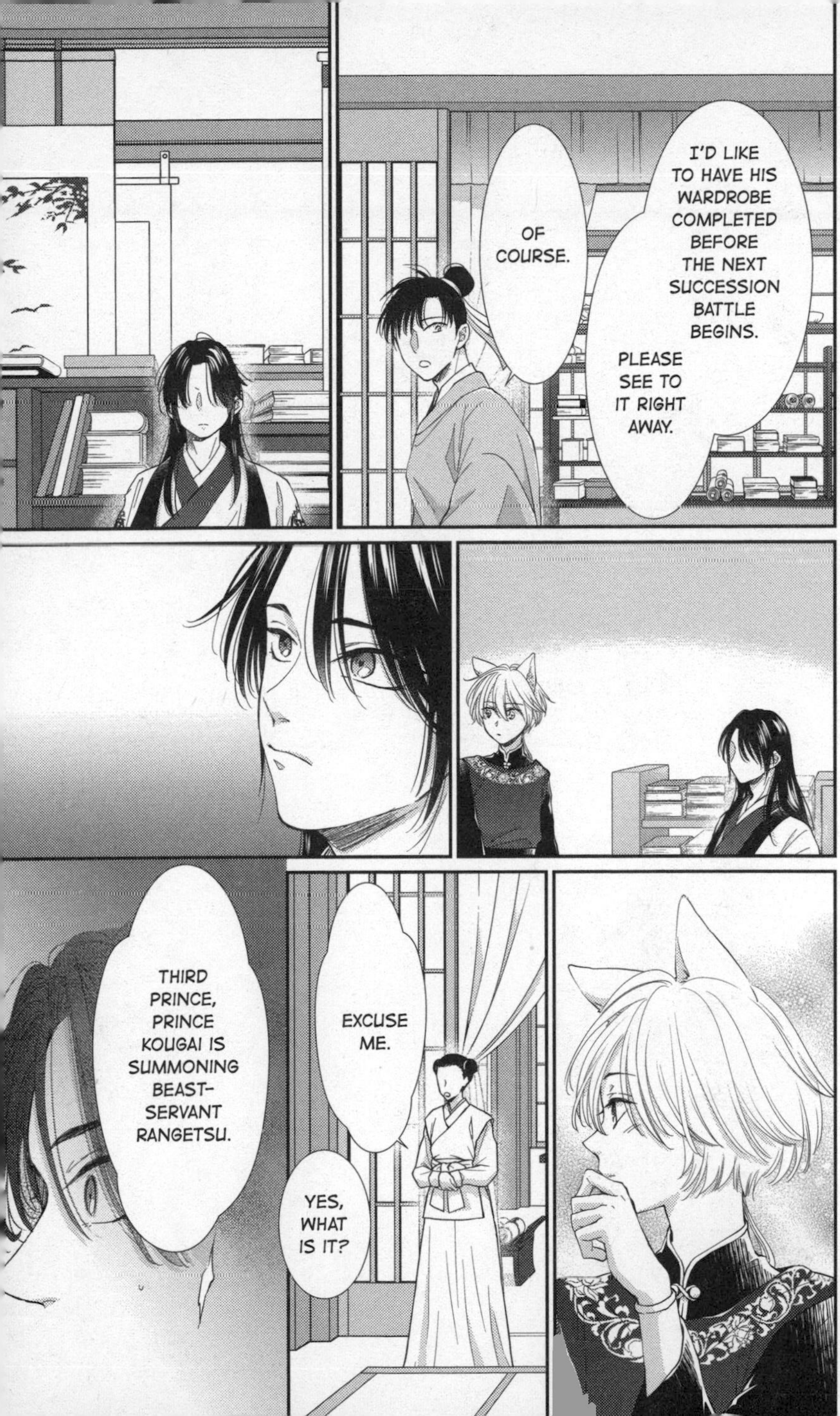
I'D LIKE TO HAVE HIS WARDROBE COMPLETED BEFORE THE NEXT SUCCESSION BATTLE BEGINS.
PLEASE SEE TO IT RIGHT AWAY.
OF COURSE.
EXCUSE ME.
YES, WHAT IS IT?
THIRD PRINCE, PRINCE KOUGAI IS SUMMONING BEAST-SERVANT RANGETSU.

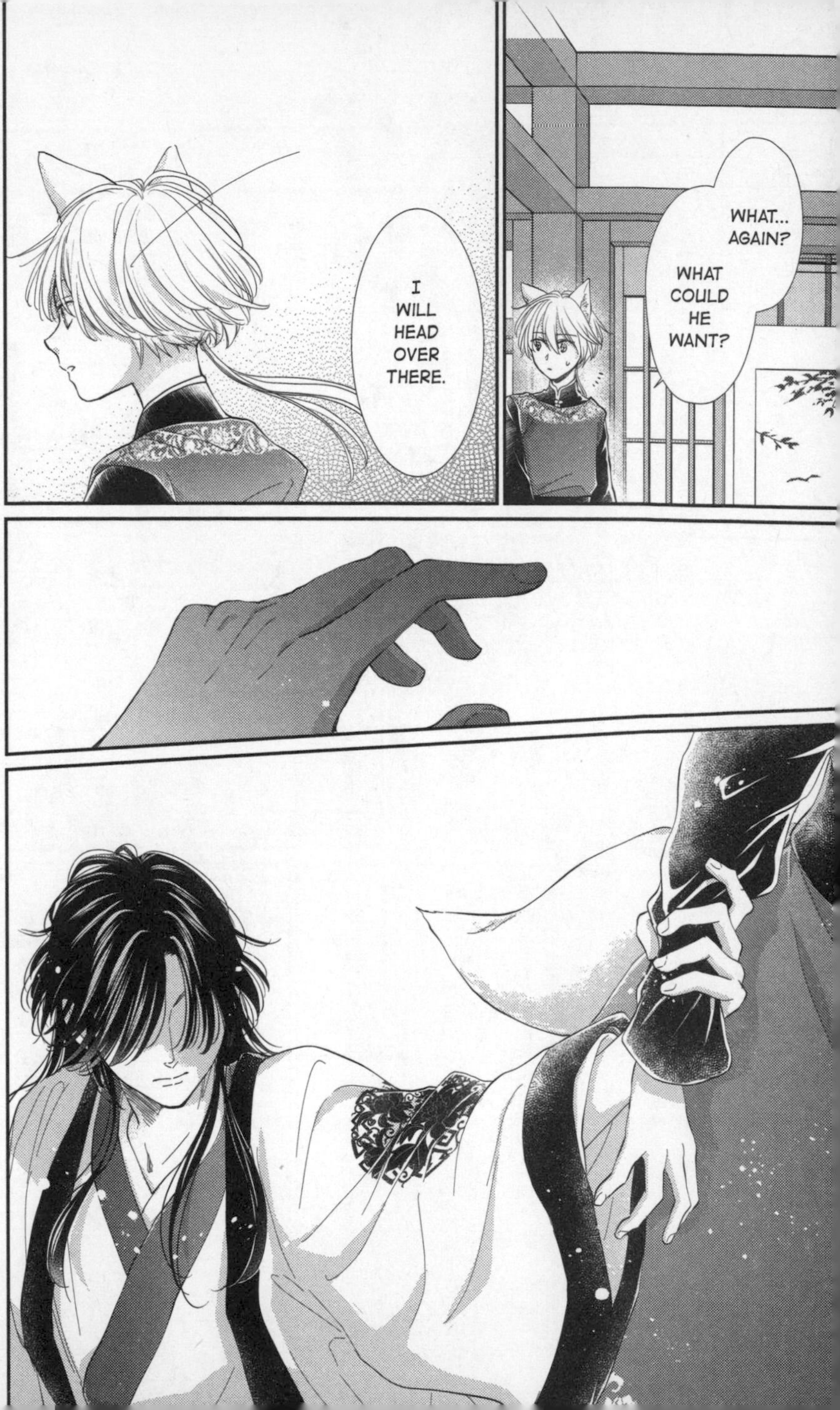
WHAT... AGAIN?
WHAT COULD HE WANT?
I WILL HEAD OVER THERE.

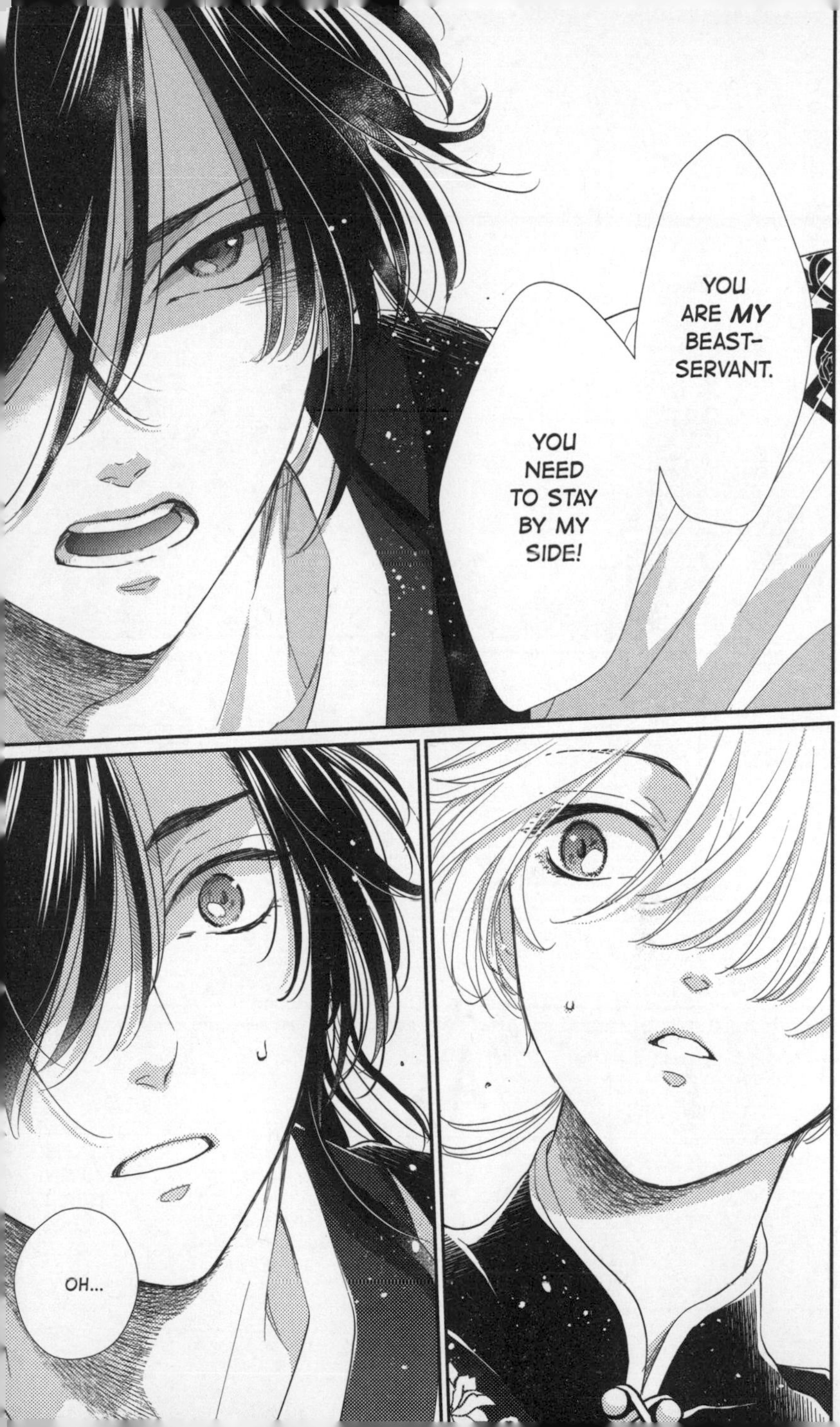
YOU ARE *MY* BEAST-SERVANT.
YOU NEED TO STAY BY MY SIDE!
OH...

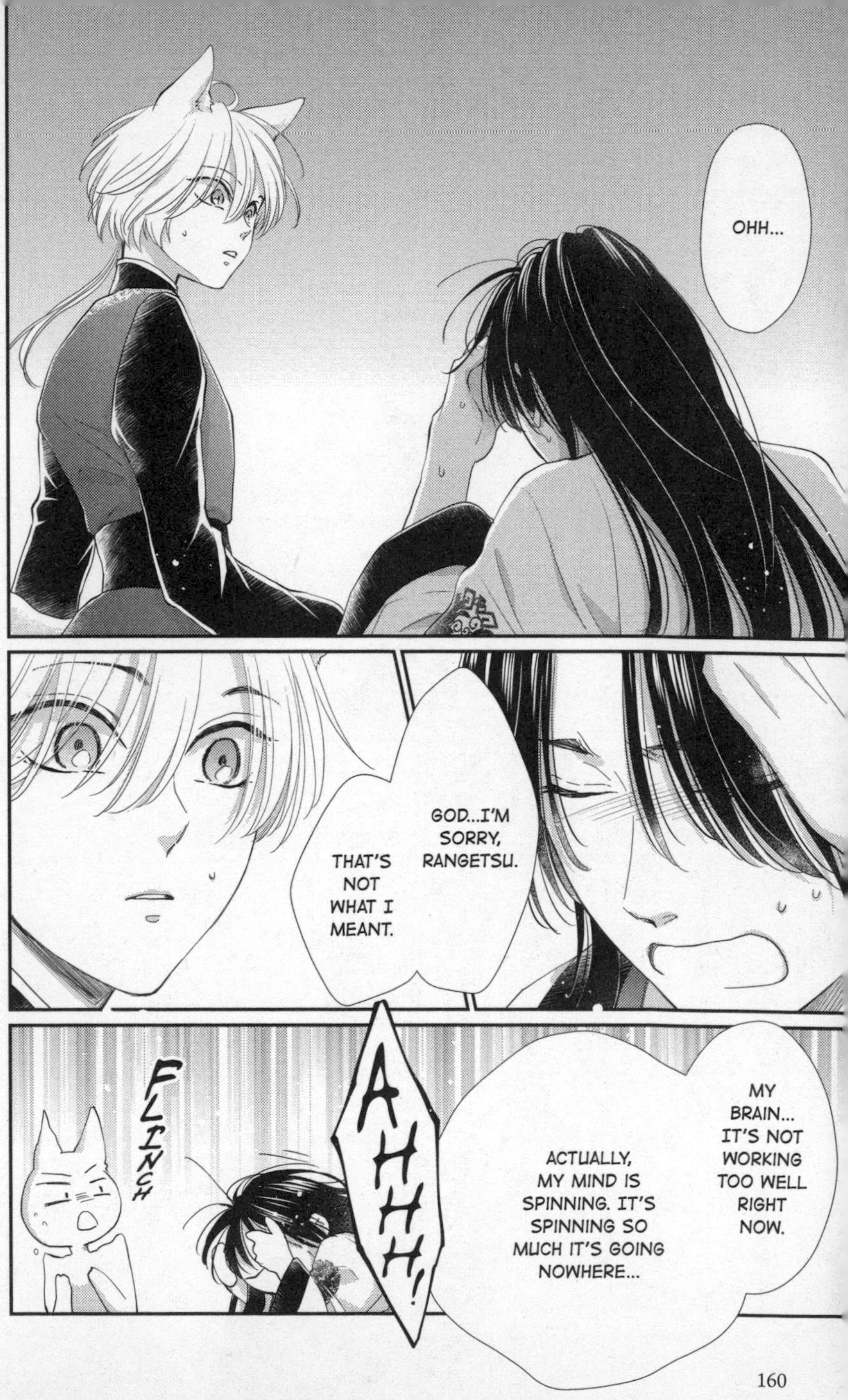
OHH...
GOD...I'M SORRY, RANGETSU.
THAT'S NOT WHAT I MEANT.
MY BRAIN... IT'S NOT WORKING TOO WELL RIGHT NOW.
ACTUALLY, MY MIND IS SPINNING. IT'S SPINNING SO MUCH IT'S GOING NOWHERE...
AHHH!
FLINCH

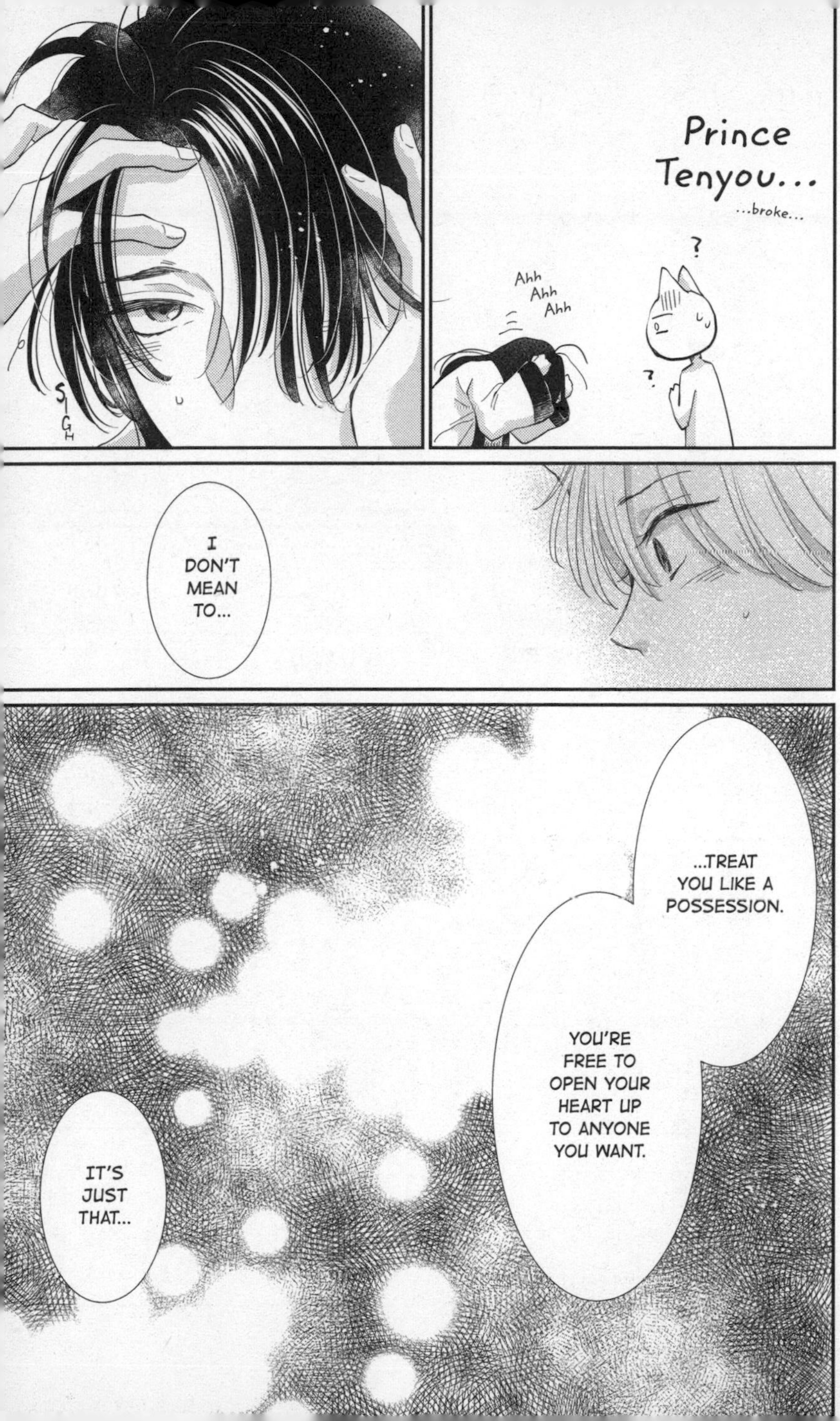
Prince Tenyou...
...broke...
?
Ahh Ahh Ahh
?
SIGH
I DON'T MEAN TO...
...TREAT YOU LIKE A POSSESSION.
YOU'RE FREE TO OPEN YOUR HEART UP TO ANYONE YOU WANT.
IT'S JUST THAT...

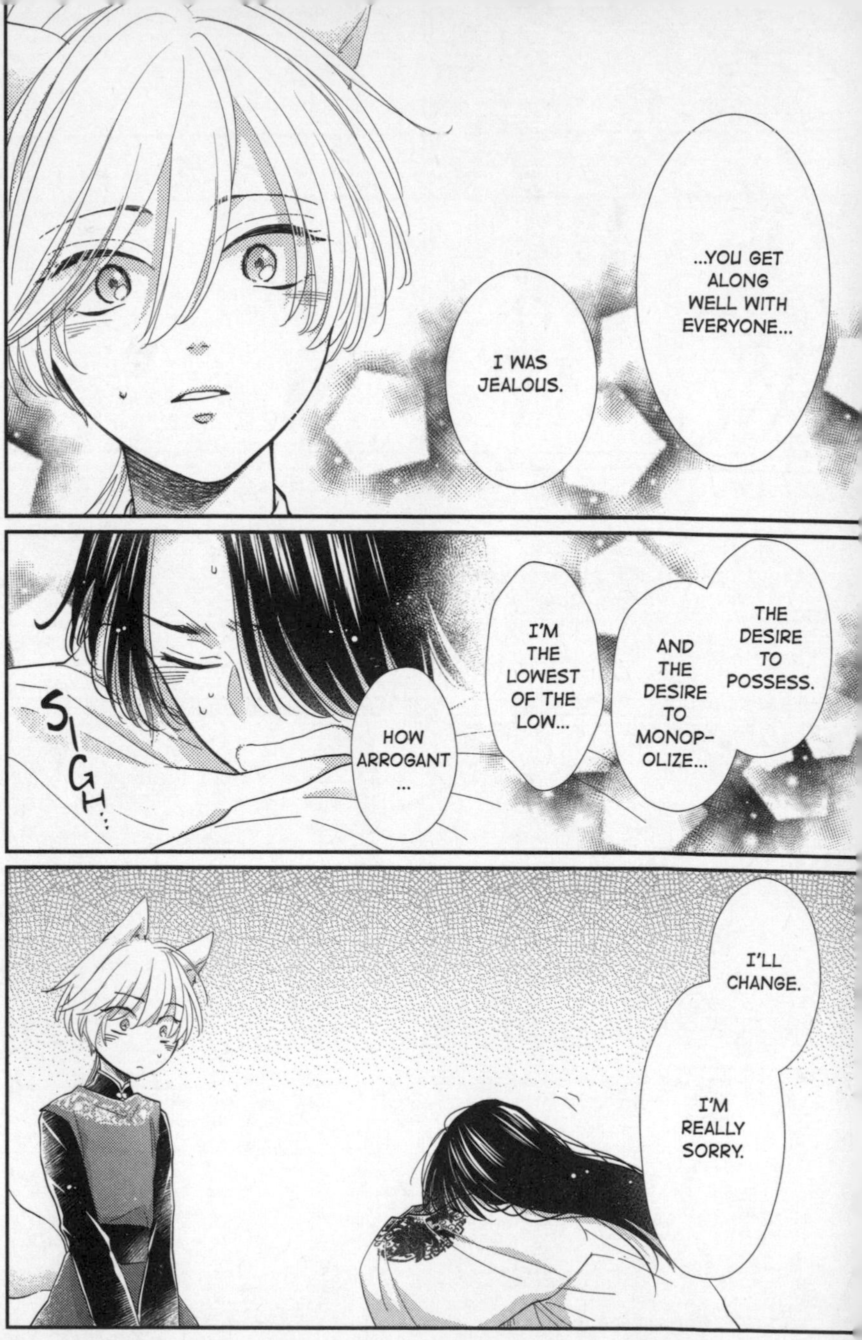
...YOU GET ALONG WELL WITH EVERYONE...
I WAS JEALOUS.
THE DESIRE TO POSSESS.
AND THE DESIRE TO MONOP-OLIZE...
I'M THE LOWEST OF THE LOW...
HOW ARROGANT ...
SIGH...
I'LL CHANGE.
I'M REALLY SORRY.

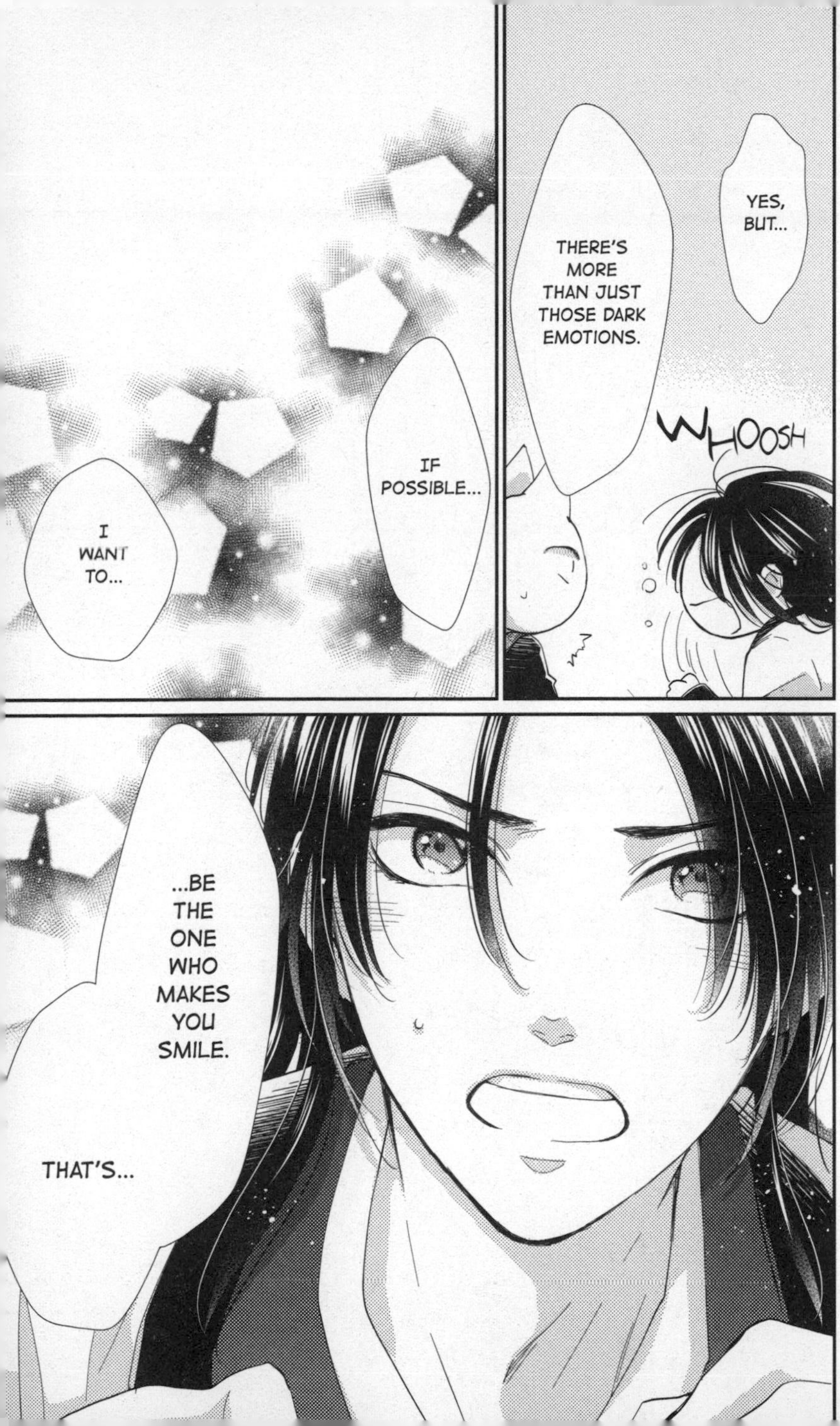
YES, BUT...
THERE'S MORE THAN JUST THOSE DARK EMOTIONS.
WHOOSH
IF POSSIBLE...
I WANT TO...
...BE THE ONE WHO MAKES YOU SMILE.
THAT'S...

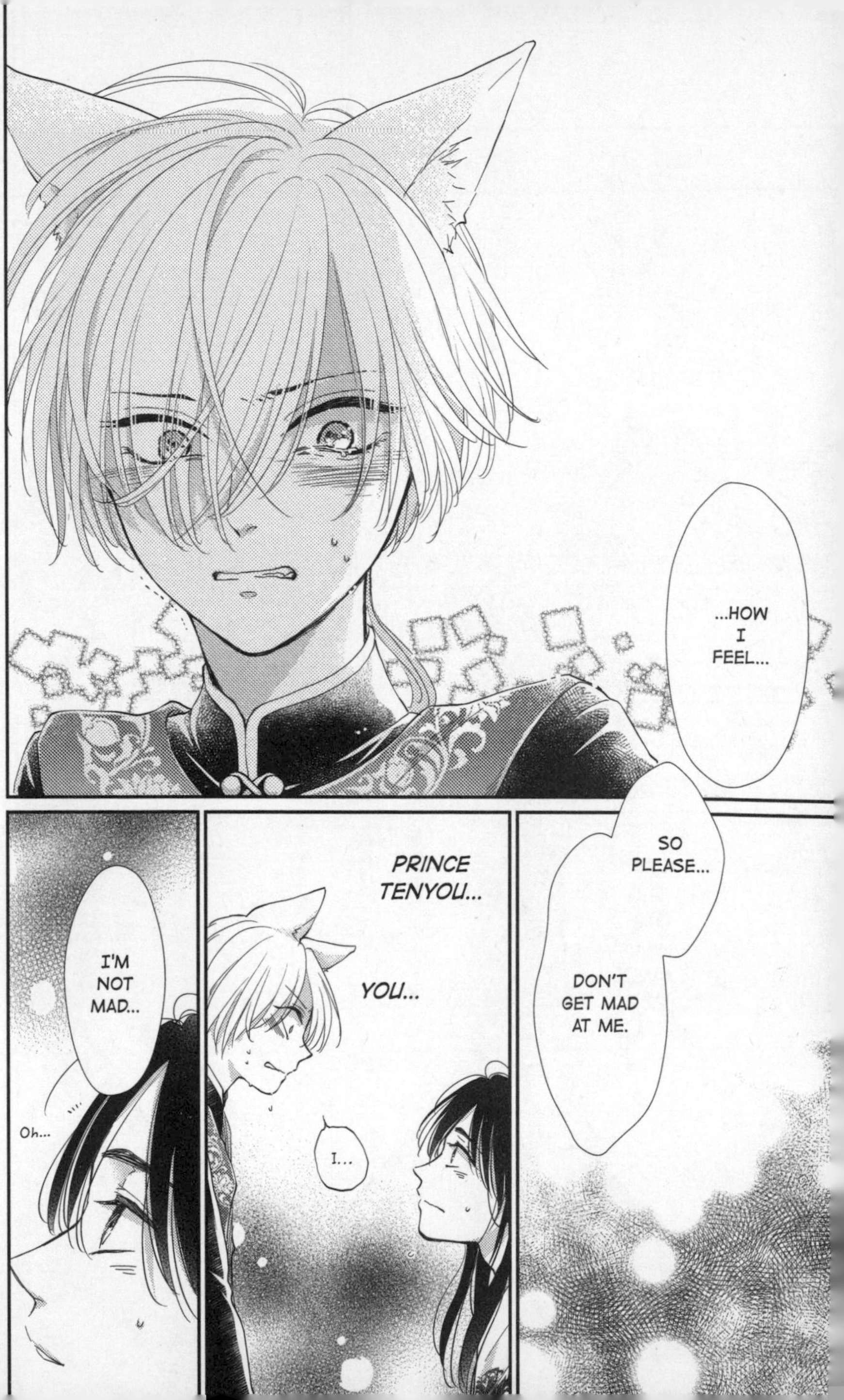
...HOW I FEEL...
SO PLEASE...
DON'T GET MAD AT ME.
PRINCE TENYOU...
YOU...
I...
I'M NOT MAD...
Oh...

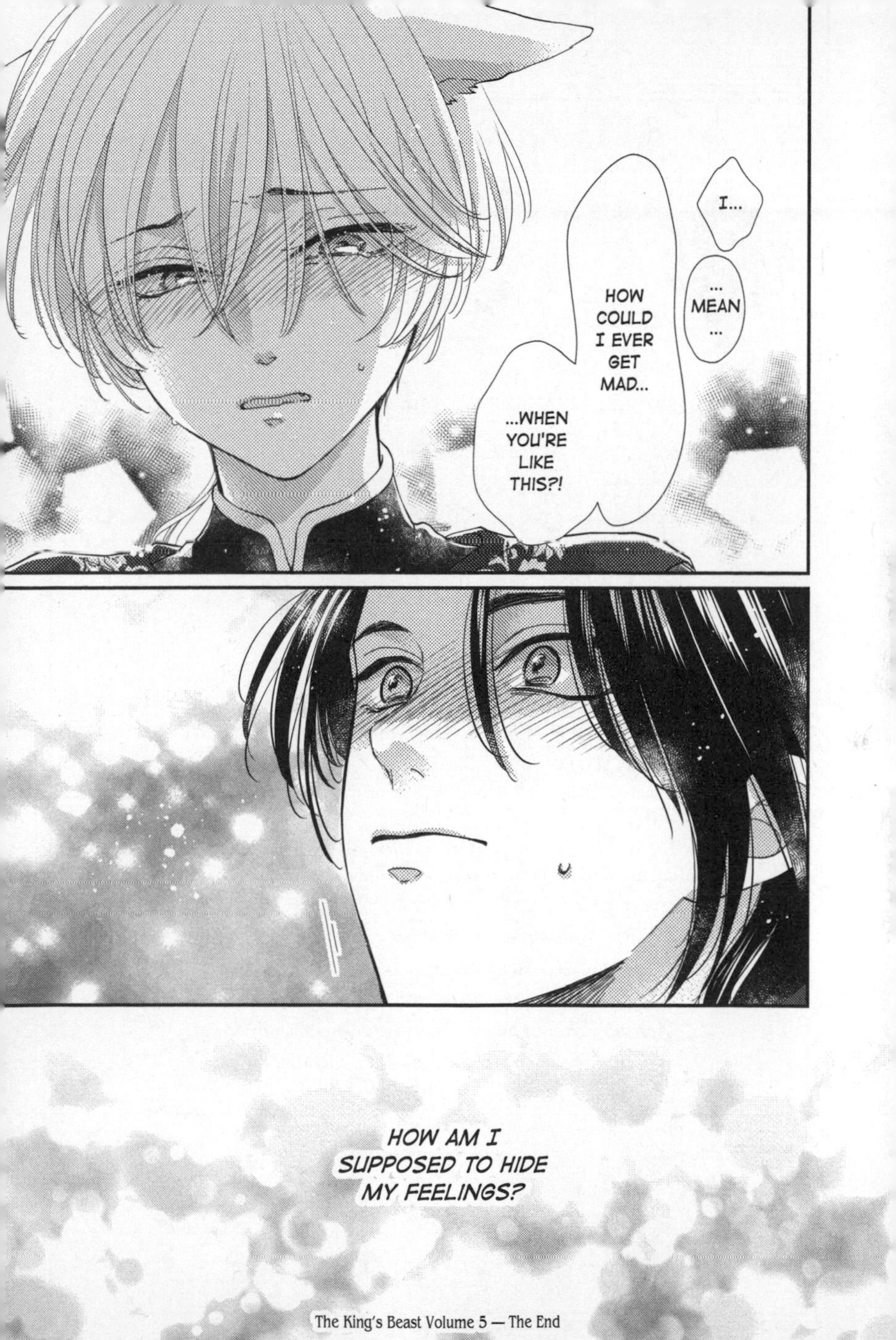
I...
...MEAN...
HOW COULD I EVER GET MAD...
...WHEN YOU'RE LIKE THIS?!
HOW AM I SUPPOSED TO HIDE MY FEELINGS?

The King's Beast Volume 5 — The End

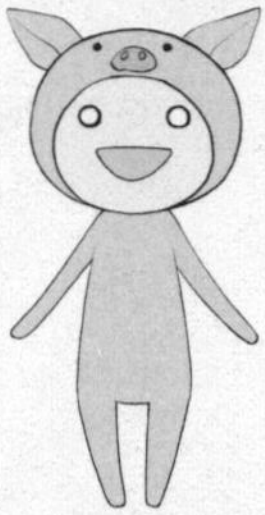

I always have a hard time deciding
what animal costume to draw here.

—*Rei Toma*

Rei Toma has been drawing since childhood, and she created her first complete manga for a graduation project in design school. When she drew the short story manga "Help Me, Dentist," it attracted a publisher's attention and she made her debut right away. After she found success as a manga artist, acclaim in other art fields started to follow as she did illustrations for novels and video game character designs. She is also the creator of *Dawn of the Arcana* and *The Water Dragon's Bride,* both available in English from VIZ Media.